Marcus Berkmann writes a weekly column for the *Independent* magazine and contributes regularly to *Private Eye*, the *Oldie* and the *Daily Mail*. He recently ended (voluntarily) an epic twenty-eight-year stint as the *Spectator*'s pop critic. His previous books include *Rain Men* (once voted the eleventh-best cricket book ever by a panel of experts and friends of his) and the *Sunday Times* Top Ten bestseller *A Shed of One's Own*.

SET PHASERS TO STUN

50 Years of
STAR TREK

Marcus Berkmann

Little, Brown

LITTLE, BROWN

First published in Great Britain in 2016 by Little, Brown

1 3 5 7 9 10 8 6 4 2

A CIP catalogue record for this book
is available from the British Library.

ISBN 978-1-4087-0683-1

Typeset in Dante by M Rules
Printed and bound in Great Britain by
Clays Ltd, St Ives plc

Papers used by Little, Brown are from well-managed forests
and other responsible sources.

MIX
Paper from
responsible sources
FSC
www.fsc.org   FSC® C104740

Little, Brown
An imprint of
Little, Brown Book Group
Carmelite House
50 Victoria Embankment
London EC4Y 0DZ

An Hachette UK Company
www.hachette.co.uk

www.littlebrown.co.uk

To Martha and James

CONTENTS

INTRODUCTION

On 8 September 1966 a new weekly drama series made its first appearance on American network television. 'Space, the final frontier,' the voiceover intoned, as a curiously shaped vessel whooshed past. 'These are the voyages of the starship *Enterprise*. Its five-year mission: to explore strange new worlds, to seek out new life and new civilizations, to boldly go where no man has gone before!' And the theme tune, even then sounding a little creaky and old-fashioned, roared in.

We can only imagine what it must have been like to watch this for the first time and think, 'Oh, this might be quite fun.' What is a 'trek' exactly? Is the guy in the mustard shirt the captain? And how about the one with the ears? Can't he get a better haircut than that?

Those first viewers, if they didn't flip channels to watch something else, will have discovered a world, or maybe universe, that had already been imagined in some detail. Transporters, shuttlecraft, phasers on stun, warp engines, dilithium crystals: they are all there right from the beginning. In other, equally important ways, though, the *Star Trek* universe resembles our own. The captain is a young man, good-looking, charismatic, clever, a strong leader. His second-in-command, the man with the ears, is even cleverer. The ship's doctor is a crusty old everyman, a sawbones. The engineer is Scottish. All the women wear terrifyingly short skirts. It's the 1960s, four hundred years on.

That first episode, 'The Man Trap', wasn't the best or most distinctive episode with which to start. It was the tenth to have been made, but it had a monster in it, and NBC wanted to start with a monster. Other science-fiction shows had monsters. Viewers liked monsters. Network executives liked monsters. Everyone knew where they were with them.

Science-fiction television was not an advanced form in 1966. *Lost in Space*, considered a kids' show in the UK (because essentially it was), was as SF as you could get on US primetime. 'Danger, Will Robinson!' said the robot. 'The pain! The pain!' said Dr Zachary Smith. And having landed on a new planet, which looked exactly like last week's planet, the extraordinarily dull Robinson family would immediately be threatened by the latest monster – or as we thought of him, the man in the monster suit.

(Irwin Allen, creator of this show, had a profitable line in SF concepts that never progressed, ever, by a single nanometre. *Voyage to the Bottom of the Sea* found what at the bottom of the sea? Monsters usually. In *Land of the Giants*, an Earth spaceship landed on a mysterious planet where everybody they encountered was twelve times larger than they were, but still spoke English in an American accent. The crew spent two years and fifty-one episodes avoiding giant beetles.)

Star Trek was designed to be better than this. With its sucker-thumbed shape-changing salt vampire, 'The Man Trap' was atypical, and you get the feeling that NBC never forgave or forgot. The three-year history of the series would be one of constant battles with an unsympathetic network, which never began to work out what it had within its grasp. NBC drifted out of the picture in 1969 when it cancelled the show, but *Star Trek* is still with us, fifty years later. To be celebrating its half-century, possibly with a glass of Romulan ale, seems bizarre. TV shows come and go, and the vast majority of them stay gone. But *Star Trek* has come and gone and come and gone, and it's here once again in the form of J. J. Abrams's rebooted film series. One day, I'm sure, it really will all be over, but we may all be dead by then.

I myself came to *Star Trek* both early and late. I saw the first episode to be shown on British television – 'The Man Trap' again – and was instantly entranced. This was in September 1969, and I was nine years old. I wasn't to know that, although I was an early adopter in the UK, the series had already run its course in the US and been cancelled. A new generation of British fans was being nurtured as their American equivalents were writing furious letters to the network and tuning tearfully into the syndicated reruns on local TV stations. But the effect, if delayed, was much the same. At my school it rapidly became clear that you were either a *Star Trek* fan or a *Doctor Who* fan – a Trekkie or a Whovian, as we might now say in moments of weakness. I was always a Trekkie. I watched *Doctor Who* with pleasure, and I still do, but such loyalties are imprinted young, and they neither fade nor falter.

A quick word on terms here. The word 'Trekkie' has long carried a slight tone of flippancy or even disparagement, possibly from the days when to be a signed-up fan of anything was to cash in all your remaining dignity chips and settle for a life of chronic uncoolness. To be a Trekkie was to contemplate buying *Star Trek* uniforms and wearing them in the privacy of your own home. I never went that far, although I did buy James Blish's novelisations and read and reread them while waiting for the episodes to be shown again. When I played *Star Trek* games with my friends, I always wanted to be Captain Kirk and was very disappointed if I ended up being Mr Sulu.[*]

---

[*] As was Mr Sulu.

Sometime in the 1970s, though, Trekkies became tired of people laughing at them and decided that henceforth they wished to be known as Trekkers. I always thought this was a bad move. The implication was that Trekkies were sad and lonely individuals with no lives, while Trekkers were more outgoing, culturally inclusive types with good jobs and attractive girl/boyfriends, but I'm not sure anyone was fooled. Indeed, it seemed to me that saying, 'I'm a Trekker, I'm not a Trekkie' was far more tragic and desperate than actually being a Trekker or a Trekkie. Who cares what anyone else thinks? It's a great series and I have never seen any problem in acknowledging my love of it. To come out of the Trekkie closet, you need to have been in it in the first place.

That said, this book isn't really aimed at the deranged *Trek* fan, whether Trekkie, Trekker or some other subgroup I haven't identified. There are already hundreds of books geared towards the specialist market, from detailed histories and photographic records, to fascinating monographs on the science or design of the show, to autobiographies of the participants and, in greatest profusion of all, spin-off novels, of which there are so many you wouldn't know where to start. What I haven't seen is a book aimed at the general reader, at the person who has grown up with *Star Trek* and watched it with enthusiasm, but has never felt the pressing need to wear a prosthetic Klingon forehead over their real head. This is that book.

So why *Star Trek* exactly? It's a question often asked by those who don't get the show, and answered, sometimes with difficulty, by those who do. Failure, in a TV show or anything, is often too easy to diagnose and deconstruct. Success can be slightly more elusive. But taking it from the start, I think there are three significant factors.

The first was the show's palpable seriousness. Gene Roddenberry, *Star Trek*'s mercurial creator, pitched his series to NBC as '*Wagon Train* to the stars', which promised simple, solid action-adventure with an outer-space setting. But he had a higher intent. *Star Trek* was conceived from the beginning as a vehicle for serious dramatic themes, artfully concealed behind standard action-adventure conventions. Roddenberry's first pilot for the show, 'The Cage', was thoughtful, talky and a little slow. NBC said no and asked for a bit more fighting. Roddenberry learned quickly to moderate his preachy tendencies and throw in a few space battles, but the show's underlying seriousness was never diluted. When he unveiled the second pilot at an SF convention in early September 1966, an audience of three thousand SF aficionados (including Isaac Asimov) applauded wildly, and asked to see more.

The second factor was the characters. As we shall see, the grand trinity of Kirk, Spock and McCoy took a pilot or two to come together, but once they did, their chemistry was so strong you felt they had been doing this for years. Season one of *Star Trek* finds its feet astonishingly quickly – you might say miraculously so. From nothing to 'The City on the Edge of Forever' in less than a year is some going. It was the strength of the characters, and the absolute suitability of the actors who played them, that made this possible.

Finally, and crucially, the show's optimism. Science fiction is a miserable old genre. Almost all of it is telling us how appalling the future is going to be. Its raw material is how appalling the present is: it then stretches and twists it and extrapolates from it, and the result can usually bring the most cheerful soul to the edge of breakdown. The great science-fiction films of the 1950s were almost all warnings of incipient catastrophe. The only previous American SF TV series of note, *The Twilight Zone* and *The Outer Limits*, were not so much pessimistic as nihilistic, if often playfully so. *Star Trek*, by contrast, really did boldly go where no man had gone before. It posited a future where, broadly, things worked. Our world had found peace, money had been abolished, poverty had disappeared, humanity had finally become civilised. Now we were venturing into deep space on a mission of peace and exploration, not to conquer but out of sheer curiosity. And every problem we encountered, we felt we had a chance of solving, mostly in less than fifty minutes of screen time. My God, even religion had been abandoned.

The late 1960s were turbulent times, and *Star Trek*'s optimism, if they noticed it at all, might well have suited the NBC executives' innate conservatism and cautiousness. Anything with a more obvious countercultural message would not have crept under their radar. Instead, *Star Trek* carried all sorts of unobvious countercultural messages, which its audience delighted in. Its bridge crew included a black woman in a position of responsibility. In season two a young Russian ensign was introduced with a slightly unexpected Beatles haircut. In the future, we understood, clever and well-intentioned people would prevail. Those of us growing up who happened to consider ourselves clever and well-intentioned found this very much to our taste.

And what I think has enabled *Star Trek* to keep going is that there has never been anything else quite like it. One or two other shows have briefly taken up the baton, but remarkably few have been directly inspired by this most apparently fertile of formats. Maybe Roddenberry's vision was so particular that other producers did not even try to duplicate it. Later *Star Trek* producers knew not to mess too much with it. Like a Borg cube, it appears to be resistant to all forms of attack.

This book, then, is a celebration of a very singular TV show, for all its many and varied incarnations. That's not to say that it's moist-eyed with uncritical adoration, for that which we love can also drive us mad with rage and disappointment. Is there in truth no beauty? as one episode title asks. For the world is hollow and I have touched the sky, says another. This was at a point in the series when the episode titles were more enjoyable than anything you might see in the actual show.

Story, of course, is everything. *Star Trek* had some of the best stories you could see on TV, but its own story is, in some ways, even better. Cancelled after three years, it stayed alive through the urgent advocacy of a smallish group of dedicated fans, who quite simply wanted more. The wholly unexpected, globe-straddling success of *Star Wars* gave it a second life in the cinema; the popularity of the films led to *Star Trek: The Next Generation*; and the popularity of that show gave us a dizzying variety of spin-offs. Finally, when that seam appeared to have been thoroughly worked out, J. J. Abrams went back to the original series and remade it with new young actors as a big, bold, primary-coloured action film. Not everyone, I understand, has maintained contact with the show through its long and tortuous history. For the sake of the general reader, then, I have given much more emphasis in the narrative to the show's more popular incarnations: the original *Star Trek* series (1966–9), *The Next Generation* (1987–94) and the films, both ancient and modern. That's not to say that *Deep Space Nine* (1993–9), *Voyager* (1995–2001) and *Enterprise* (2001–5) are inferior series, although some would say just that. (I would defend *Deep Space Nine* to the hilt. It took a while to find its way, but grew into a drama of epic scope and ambition.) But non-aficionados barely know them, and this is not the place to learn more than the basics.

By curious coincidence, I have been writing this chapter in the week that Leonard Nimoy died. Perhaps ridiculously, given that I came no closer to meeting him than to climbing Everest, I felt bereft at his passing, even though he had clearly lived long and prospered. What did surprise me, though, was that I wasn't alone in this. There was a sense, in that week, that someone genuinely significant had gone, and with him a slice of our childhoods – or, if we're going to be honest about this, our lives. On Facebook someone I know juxtaposed two stills from the original series. In the first, Kirk, Spock, Bones and Scotty are in the *Enterprise* meeting room discussing something of import. In the second, there's a long shot of the same table and only Kirk is sitting there. Their vision of the future, we now realise, was an awful long time ago.*

Hooray, then, for DVDs and streaming services, for hard disks and for a culture that has grown to value the ephemeral telly rubbish of the distant past.† While preparing for this book, I took the opportunity to introduce the original series in its remastered glory to my fourteen-year-old daughter, who had developed a taste for science fiction and fantasy that, in my own childhood, would not have been encouraged. She loved it, needless to say. My son, then eleven, was less impressed: it was all a bit too talky and needed more action. He hopes one day to get a job as an NBC executive.

* Nimoy sadly did not live to see his character name turned into a verb. The Bank of Canada's five-dollar note carries a portrait of the country's seventh Prime Minister, Sir Wilfrid Laurier, who died in 1919. If you draw Spock's hairstyle, sideburns and pointy ears on Sir Wilfrid, the resemblance is uncanny. Canadians marked the death of their esteemed Vulcan countryman by 'spocking' these notes in their thousands. A week later the Bank put out a press release asking them to desist. 'The Bank of Canada feels that writing and markings on bank notes are inappropriate as they are a symbol of our country and a source of national pride.' But it wasn't actually illegal, so no one took any notice. Nimoy's final tweet had ended with the letters 'LLAP': live long and prosper.

† Although not everyone has. When Sajid Javid was appointed culture secretary in April 2014, the Guardian's response was an article headlined 'The arts must embrace this Star Trek-loving philistine'.

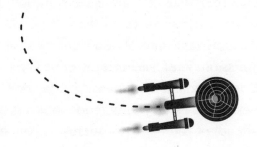

CHAPTER 1

WHERE NO MAN HAS GONE BEFORE

In the beginning was the word, and the word was 'fascinating'.

In the beginning, Gene Roddenberry was a Los Angeles policeman who wanted to write episodic drama for television. His wife Eileen preferred that he stay with the force – steady job, good prospects – but Gene made the jump, and by the late 1950s was writing for *Have Gun, Will Travel* and other shows. He was a jobbing writer, in a town full of them. If you wanted power and money, you needed to be producing a series, and preferably one you had also created, which meant an automatic fee for every episode. Roddenberry submitted some pilot scripts. 'Night Stick' was about a cop on the beat in Greenwich Village in New York; '333 Montgomery Street' was about a real-life criminal lawyer, played by DeForest Kelley; 'APO 923' was about three servicemen stationed on a Polynesian island during the Second World War. All three were filmed; none became a series.

But he persevered, and in 1963 one of Roddenberry's pilots led to a full series commission. *The Lieutenant* introduced the character of William T. Rice, second lieutenant, US Marine Corps, played by Gary Lockwood. He is young, good-looking, ambitious, a recent graduate of the Naval Academy at Annapolis, and newly assigned to Camp Pendleton in California. There was a real Camp Pendleton, on the coast between Los Angeles and San Diego, and in return for the right to film there and use their uniforms and equipment, Roddenberry's executive producer gave the Defense Department an informal veto over script content. This turned out to be a mistake.

The problem arose with a script called 'To Set It Right', in which a black marine, played by Don Marshall, joins Rice's platoon and immediately attacks a fellow soldier, Dennis Hopper, without provocation. Lieutenant Rice finds out that they knew each other at school. Hopper's character used to hang around with the local toughs, and they made the black kids' lives a misery. Now the pair of them are in the Marines, and they will have to learn to work together. They do so, develop mutual respect, bury the hatchet. Marshall's wife, by the way, was played by a young black actress called Nichelle Nichols.

The Department of Defense read the script. They didn't like it. There were no racial problems in the military, they said.

'We're going to do it anyway,' said Roddenberry. He did, and the Pentagon withdrew all support from the series. Camp Pendleton was now out of bounds. Jet fighters couldn't be filmed. Marines were no longer allowed to work as extras. These are our uniforms: go and make your own.

By the following February, *The Lieutenant* was no more, cancelled by NBC despite promising ratings. Roddenberry needed a new idea. He went to a ball game with a friend, fellow writer Christopher Knopf.

Roddenberry asked him if he wanted to hear an idea for another series.

Knopf said no, he was watching the game.

'I've got another series idea,' said Roddenberry. 'I'm going to place it at the end of the nineteenth century. There's a dirigible, see? And on this dirigible are all these people of mixed races, and they go from place to place each week, places no one has discovered yet.'*

This idea was quickly rejected by the studio for reasons of expense, if not for being completely ludicrous.

But how about putting the dirigible in space?

Roddenberry's agent, the deliciously named Alden Schwimmer, suggested he devise a science-fiction series. The time was right. The space race was up and running. John F. Kennedy had promised to put a man on the moon within a decade. And what was space if not the final frontier?

Thus was *Star Trek* born, or at least conceived. To begin with, Roddenberry worked on the format with Herbert F. Solow, the executive in charge of production at Desilu.† (Among other contributions, Solow suggested the captain's log voiceover.) Roddenberry then approached his friend Samuel A. Peeples, prolific TV writer and novelist, and an avid collector of SF magazines. 'I don't think Gene had ever written science fiction before,' Peeples told Joel Engel. 'He came to my house and looked at my collection several times.' Brains were being picked. Ideas were coalescing. Solow pitched the idea to NBC. The network agreed to finance a pilot script, but wished to be offered three well-developed script ideas, to get a view of what the show would be like. By July 1964, Roddenberry had his three outlines ready.

---

* This magnificent story, which I very nearly believe, is told in Joel Engel's biography of Gene Roddenberry, *The Myth and the Man behind Star Trek* (1994).

† A small, boutique Hollywood studio owned by, and named after, Lucille Ball and her ex-husband Desi Arnaz. Its main product at the time was *The Lucy Show*, then and for some years to come a mainstay of primetime TV light entertainment.

'The Women' had this synopsis: 'Duplicating a page from the "Old West": hanky-panky aboard [the *Enterprise*] with a cargo of women destined for a far-off colony.' In time this unpromising idea would turn into the episode 'Mudd's Women'.

'Landru's Paradise', which would eventually air as 'The Return of the Archons', was about a world in which the inhabitants are repressed by a giant computer with flashing lights. 'Archon is anything but a paradise. What can be seen on the street, the happy friendliness and tranquility, masks despair, dullness, almost a living death. There are no police, no crime, no jails, because the slightest infraction is stamped out ruthlessly by The Lawgivers.'

NBC chose the third idea, 'The Cage'. Captain Robert April of the USS *Yorktown* is captured by 'crablike creatures' on the planet Sirius IV, telepaths who wish to eavesdrop on his innermost thoughts and fantasies. April resists and demands his freedom, but his fellow captive, Vina, tells him to go with the flow. 'It's pleasant, isn't it? Everything looks real, feels real. The pleasure can be equally real.' Over subsequent drafts, the crablike creatures became Talosians, Robert April became Christopher Pike and the *Yorktown* became the *Enterprise*. Budgets were agreed and shooting was scheduled for late November and early December 1964.

By the standards *Star Trek* itself would set, 'The Cage' now looks creaky and half-formed. But given how quickly it was thrown together, it's already recognisably *Star Trek*. The *Enterprise*, designed by Walter 'Matt' Jefferies, resembled no spaceship previously seen on film or television. Unlike *Sputnik* or the *Mercury* spacecraft, it was designed to look good. There were no fiddly bits on the outside. All working parts were within the bulkhead. There was no need to go spacewalking to repair anything. Jefferies's ship was a thing of beauty.

And while Starfleet was not yet called Starfleet, its craft already had a distinctly naval feel. The *Enterprise* had decks rather than floors; it had forward and aft, port and starboard;

it was commanded by a captain, and had ensigns and yeomen. 'Aye, sir,' people would say, although Roddenberry decided early that no one would salute.

Yet Captain Pike was not a warrior, but an intense, rather thoughtful man, not unlike the man who played him. With thirty-odd films to his credit, including John Ford's *The Searchers*, Jeffrey Hunter was a bit of a catch for Roddenberry and his team. Only a few years before, he had played Jesus Christ in *King of Kings*. Captain of the *Enterprise* represented only a minor demotion.

Second in command was the otherwise unnamed Number One, who, in a bold departure from the norm, was played by a woman, a virtually unknown young actress called Majel Barrett. Virtually unknown, that is, to everyone but Gene Roddenberry, with whom she was having an affair. Roddenberry's marriage was now in its final stages, and Barrett would one day become his wife, but there's something wonderfully Old Hollywood about giving such a plum role to your main squeeze. Not everyone who needed to know actually knew of the relationship, and those who did know may not have got round to telling those who didn't. Number One was steely and undemonstrative, the rational counterpoint to the more emotional Captain Pike. In one form or other, everything important was there, right from the beginning.

According to Herbert Solow and Robert Justman,* DeForest Kelley was at the top of Roddenberry's list for the role of the crusty old ship's doctor. But Robert Butler, the experienced director of 'The Cage', had seen the older and even crustier John Hoyt in a Shakespeare festival, and recommended him for the role. Watching his performance now, you can only marvel that someone so advanced in years would wish to serve in deep space, so far from home and hearth. He looked

* *Inside Star Trek: The Real Story* by Herbert F. Solow and Robert H. Justman (1996).

ready for retirement, not adventure. One day, much younger audiences would have similar feelings watching *Star Trek VI: The Undiscovered Country*.

The crucial casting decision, though, was that of the *Enterprise*'s token alien. Dorothy 'D.C.' Fontana had worked as a secretary on *The Lieutenant*, and was Roddenberry's PA on the new series; in time she would become one of its most important writers. In early 1964, after reading the first *Star Trek* outline, she said, 'I have only one question. Who's going to play Mr Spock?'

Roddenberry said nothing and pulled an eight-by-ten glossy photo from his desk drawer. It was of a young actor named Leonard Nimoy. Fontana recognised him. She had already had six scripts of her own produced, and in the first of them, for a western series called *The Tall Man*, Nimoy had had a small role as a deputy sheriff. He had also been in *The Lieutenant*, playing a flamboyant Hollywood producer who wanted to make a movie about the Marine Corps. As Roddenberry told Gross and Altman,* 'I looked at him during those days and I thought that if I ever did this science-fiction series, I'd use him because of his Slavic face and his high cheekbones.' So he rang him up and asked him to come over.

Nimoy went in thinking he was auditioning. 'Once I was there I got the feeling that I was really being sold on the idea of doing the job,' he told Engel. 'Gene, I guess, had made up his mind and was showing me the various phases of pre-production – what was happening in the wardrobe department and the prop department, for example. We talked about the characters, and I was hired.'

Did they show him the pointy ears he would have to wear? My guess is not.†

---

* *Captain's Logs: The Complete Star Trek Voyages* by Edward Gross and Mark A. Altman (1993).

† If Nimoy had said no, Roddenberry's second choice for the role was Martin Landau.

Main guest star was Susan Oliver, who would play Vina, the girl trapped on the planet with Captain Pike, in a variety of costumes and make-up regimes. One of these was the green-skinned dancing girl that would adorn the end credit sequence for most of the first season. If there was a running theme to Roddenberry's years in charge of *Star Trek*, it was that the women, whether human or alien, would never be wearing quite enough clothes.

'The Cage' is more interesting now for what it promises and signifies than for anything within its rather drawn-out seventy-eight minutes' running time. Jeffrey Hunter's Captain Pike is good-looking, heroic and, one has to say, slightly dull. When the pilot was completed, the producers set up a screening for him. He didn't show up, but his wife did. She watched to the end, and gave her verdict. 'This is not the kind of show Jeff wants to do, and besides, it wouldn't be good for his career. Jeff Hunter is a movie star.' That was the end of him, then. Three years later he was injured in an explosion on a film set, suffered a concussion, came home, had a massive stroke, fell over, fractured his skull and died the following day, aged forty-two.*

The screening for NBC was rather more successful: Herb Solow says it was the best he ever put on for network executives. They loved the look of it, its ambition, its scope, its feel. They were not so sure about some of the actors, 'but that's what pilots are for,' said Solow, 'as research and development tools, to see what works and what doesn't.' NBC's head of programming couldn't have been more enthusiastic. 'I must tell you something, Herb. I've seen many science-fiction, outer-space films. I never believed the crew was a real crew. But you guys gave me the feeling of true belief. I loved it. Grant and I will be in touch.'

---

* Had he signed on for *Star Trek*, he might have lived to a comfortable old age. But *Star Trek* wouldn't have been *Star Trek* with Jeff Hunter. It might not have survived beyond its first season and surely would not have grown into what it is today. So we owe Mrs Hunter our gratitude, even if Jeff did not: they divorced in 1967.

They said no.

According to popular legend, NBC passed because they thought the show was 'too cerebral'. Roddenberry had sold them 'Wagon Train to the stars' and delivered something nearly as brainy as the Talosians themselves, with their vast, visibly throbbing cerebellums. (The three Talosians, though supposedly male, were played by three diminutive middle-aged women and voiced by male actors. The throbbing veins on their heads were connected to a squeeze bulb that associate producer Bob Justman was holding just out of shot.)

In reality, there were other problems. According to Solow and Justman, NBC was worried about the 'eroticism' of the pilot. They also knew, or had discovered, that Roddenbery had cast his girlfriend as the second-in-command.

Moreover, the network's sales arm, which had disliked the idea of the series from the start, was instinctively hostile to the character of Mr Spock. They worried that advertisers and owners of affiliate stations, especially in the Bible Belt, might regard him as 'demonic'. It would be unfortunate if NBC's bright new autumn launch were thought to have been personally endorsed by Beelzebub.

But Star Trek still had its supporters in NBC, and they rallied in its favour. After much internal discussion, the network took the unusual step of commissioning a second pilot. There were just a handful of conditions:

- More action/adventure next time, please.
- Lose the girlfriend.
- Lose the guy with the ears.
- Absolutely no more erotic dancing by barely clothed green-skinned Orion slave girls.

Numbers one and four were easy to achieve, and Solow told Roddenberry that Majel Barrett had to go too. 'Gene seemed

Canadian and born in March 1931.* *Star Trek* would be his first TV series lead, and Roddenberry altered the captain's personality to suit him. Jeffrey Hunter's Pike had been more tortured and introspective: Horatio Hornblower 'tempered by a touch of doubting Hamlet', in Bob Justman's words. Kirk was more outgoing, less fretful. This captain was much more likely to get the girl, having spent much more time chasing the girl.

As a result, the balance between the characters shifted into patterns with which we would soon become intimately familiar. Now promoted to first officer, Spock took on the rational, unemotional baggage of Majel Barrett's Number One. Nimoy instantly appreciated Shatner's acting style. 'Bill's Captain Kirk was a swashbuckling Errol Flynn type of hero,' he wrote in one of his autobiographies.† 'He played the role with a great deal of energy and élan, and wasn't afraid to take chances.' Not for the last time, we would see the incalculable benefit of hiring theatrical actors to play science fiction. Film actors tend to internalise their emotions, and strip everything back to the tiniest nuance. Theatricals can't help being bigger and bolder, but still play everything with absolute conviction. Shatner possessed charisma and talent that weren't in Jeff Hunter's locker.

Peeples's script takes us to the edge of our galaxy and beyond. The radiation belts around Earth had recently been discovered, and Peeples's premise was that there might be something similar surrounding the galaxy. I remember thinking, 'No there isn't,' but still being captivated as the *Enterprise* battles its way through the energy barrier. They only just make it, but two guest stars on the bridge are zapped by what at first sight look like a substantial number of volts. Lieutenant Commander Gary Mitchell, played by Gary Lockwood (star of *The Lieutenant*), is an old chum of Kirk's from the Academy and,

---

* Nimoy was the younger by four days.

† *I Am Spock* (1995).

by the guess of it, third or fourth in command on the *Enterprise*. Dr Elizabeth Dehner, played by Sally Kellerman, is a psychologist who has recently joined the ship to study the effects on the crew of deep-space travel. Both have high ESP scores, and now Gary Mitchell has weird silver eyes and swiftly growing telepathic and telekinetic powers. The stronger he becomes, the madder, until he and Dr Dehner, who also acquires silver eyes, start to reimagine themselves as deities. 'You should have killed me while you could, James,' says Mitchell. 'Command and compassion are a fool's mixture.'

Absolute power, in other words, corrupts absolutely. Kirk's dilemma is that he must kill his friend before his friend kills him and everyone else. The science fiction element is well taken care of with all the extrasensory baloney. That said, the episode ends with an extended bare-knuckle fist-fight on a planet's surface between Kirk and Mitchell. Roddenberry believed it was this that sold the series to NBC.

In series terms, Lieutenant Commander Mitchell, Dr Dehner and the unfortunate Lieutenant Kelso (strangled by a floating metal cord) were merely ships passing in the night. There was another one-episode doctor, Dr Mark Piper, played by another gnarled old B-movie stalwart, Paul Fix, who gave us nothing that John Hoyt hadn't given us in 'The Cage'. But two more durable crew members were also introduced in this episode. George Takei was Physicist Sulu, who would soon abjure the sciences for decades of doughty helmsmanship. And James Doohan, Irish by blood and Canadian by birth and upbringing, came in as Lieutenant Commander Montgomery Scott. Doohan was known in the industry for his facility with accents, and at the audition he read for the part in several different voices. Roddenberry had not decided what nationality the character should be, and asked Doohan what he thought. 'Well, if he's going to be an engineer aboard a ship, then he ought to be a Scotsman,' said Doohan in a broad Aberdonian burr, and was hired on the spot.

In his highly entertaining autobiography,* George Takei remembers his first sighting of Leonard Nimoy in full Vulcan make-up.

> The most arresting thing about his appearance was his aston-ishing ears. They looked normal in all aspects but one. They curved to a point that rose sharply upwards like the ears of an alert cat. As bizarre as they may have looked, however, they were actually quite pleasing. There was grace and a sculptural balance to them. They looked oddly genuine ...
>
> What a sensational entrance, I thought. To step onto the set for the first time and be completely and compellingly in character. And what a fantastic character!

'Where No Man Has Gone Before' would eventually be aired third in the series. It remains a bracing shower of odd-ness. Spock smiles again while losing to his captain at chess. The costumes look rather wintry for the heat of the studio and the sun of California. Scotty is wearing some sort of beige blouson that's at least a size too large. Kirk gives weird-sounding instructions, such as 'Neutralise warp, Mr Mitchell,' and 'Address intercraft.'

'Deflectors full intensity!' shouts Mr Spock.

'Helmsman! Lateral power!' yells Kirk.

When Kirk and Mitchell are bashing three shades of hell out of each other on the planet's surface, Mitchell creates a grave for his old friend, complete with headstone, and on it the legend 'James R. Kirk'. Later chroniclers, trying to make sense of this anomaly, have come up with every kind of excuse for the incorrect middle initial. Maybe it was a parallel universe, or an in-joke of Gary Mitchell's. In fact, at this stage of the show's development, Kirk's middle initial was R. By the time

* *To the Stars* (1994).

the series proper came to be made, it had been transformed, as if by magic, into the now familiar T (for Tiberius).*

Once again NBC executives trooped in to a screening, and on 6 March 1966 they officially gave Roddenberry the thumbs up for thirteen episodes. The first would be broadcast in September. The five-year mission had begun.

---

* After six episodes were in the can, Bob Justman suddenly remembered the gravestone with 'James R. Kirk' on it and thought, 'Whoops.'

CHAPTER 2

GENE AND GENE

A week is a long time in politics, a year is a long time in television, and fifty years quite some time in publishing. Almost everyone who ever had anything to do with *Star Trek* ended up writing a book about it. But Gene Roddenberry didn't. (He is co-credited on Stephen E. Whitfield's behind-the-scenes 1968 book *The Making of Star Trek*, but according to the Memory Alpha website, 'his contributions were minimal'.) I have often wondered about this. Such a dedicated myth-maker as Roddenberry would surely have wished to record the definitive version, although it's possible that he was too busy trying to make TV shows to worry about that. Most of the last twenty years of his life were dedicated to getting *Star Trek* back into production in one form or another. There may not have been time for anything else.

Fortunately, we have the views of others, many others, to fill in the gaps. Herb Solow's first impression of Roddenberry was of a 'tall unkempt person' who had 'recently learned how to dress himself but hadn't yet quite gotten the knack'. Leonard Nimoy remembers 'a pleasant man, very tall and gangly and loose-limbed – sort of floppy, you could say, but not sloppy, and obviously very bright'.

As the show went into production, says Solow, Roddenberry 'became overly protective of his new baby'. When the smallest thing went wrong, Roddenberry would cast around for scapegoats. Everything that wasn't Desilu's fault was NBC's. 'I cautioned Gene that having good reason at times was no excuse to continually cast blame, especially when dealing with people who had a lot to do with the future of the series and his ultimate survival. He didn't listen. He didn't want to.'

Solow goes on, more in sorrow than in anger. 'A new side of Gene slowly appeared: ownership of ideas. If a good story or series point came from anyone . . . Gene Roddenberry appropriated it. This subtle "these are all my ideas" syndrome would eventually affect Gene's relationships with many who worked on *Star Trek*: writers, composers, actors, agents, story editors, art directors, producers and me.' Bob Justman coined a name for him: the Great Bird of the Galaxy. Solow coined another: the Great Blotter of the Galaxy.

Or as T. S. Eliot put it, 'Immature poets imitate; mature poets steal; bad poets deface what they take, and good poets make it into something better, or at least something different.' *Star Trek* isn't poetry, and television drama is never just the work of one man, however controlling and keen to take all the credit he might be. My feeling is that if you are putting together a science-fiction series, the likes of which no one has ever seen before, and the people around you have good ideas, you would be a fool not to nab them. Roddenberry's most far-reaching creative act, I believe, was to put everything in place that would make *Star Trek* great. In the show's earliest days, he saw himself as the only person (other than possibly Dorothy Fontana) who truly understood what *Star Trek* was about and the way it was supposed to be. And so, when scripts came in, many of them commissioned from some of the leading SF writers of the day, he rewrote them personally, pretty much line by line.

This was unusual, even for the time, and caused much ill-feeling. John D. F. Black had been hired by Roddenberry as associate producer and story editor, and it was his job to liaise with the writers. A young man of great probity and integrity, Black treated his writers with huge respect and believed they should be allowed to rewrite their own work. But Roddenberry didn't have time for that. In Joel Engel's words, he 'intended to construct a cohesive universe, but since the raw materials he worked with were other people's scripts, he was left to mould their creations into shapes that coincided with his own vision ... Does it work? Does it make sense? Those were the criteria by which scripts and ideas were judged before becoming elements in the world of *Star Trek*.'

The writers, of course, were furious. If you have ever wondered why people like Harlan Ellison ('The City on the Edge of Forever') and Richard Matheson ('The Enemy Within') only wrote one episode of *Star Trek*, it's because the scripts as produced sometimes bore only a fleeting resemblance to the scripts they had written. Ellison, in particular, was so angry he submitted his original script for a Writers Guild award, and won it. But the rewrite, first by Gene L. Coon, then by Fontana and finally by Roddenberry, won a Hugo award and is widely considered the best episode of any *Star Trek* series. So who is right?

Most of the principals – Fontana, Justman, Solow and

the cast – side with Roddenberry on this, and I think with reason. One of the marvels of early *Star Trek* is how quickly it became what it was going to be. After the first half-dozen episodes there are remarkably few false notes: the universe is defined, the characters are clear, everything is the way it should be. Roddenberry didn't have all the ideas himself, although he would later take credit for as many as he could get away with. But his head was where all those ideas were stored. The confidence and cohesion of those early episodes would give the series room to grow and develop in its own way.

The first episode to be produced was 'The Corbomite Maneuver' (1.10),* in which the *Enterprise* encounters a strange glowing cube in deep, unexplored space. A sparky young navigator, Lieutenant Bailey, has an idea. 'We've got phaser weapons. I vote that we blast it.'

'I'll keep that in mind, Mr Bailey ... when this becomes a democracy,' says Kirk, who has his shirt off because he has just been undergoing an entirely unnecessary physical examination.

The cube, though, is merely a probe for an absolutely enormous spherical spaceship, a sort of vast interstellar golfball, commanded by a scary-looking, deep-voiced bald item called Balok. The *Enterprise* has shown hostile intent, says Balok, so he is going to blast it into smithereens.

'We therefore grant you ten Earth-time periods known as minutes to make preparations,' he says, careful not to glance at his watch.

Spock says that if this were a game of chess, they have just been checkmated.

Which gives Kirk an idea. 'Not chess, Mr Spock. Poker.' He

---

* The numbering system is shorthand for transmission order. 'The Corbomite Maneuver' was the tenth show of the first season to be broadcast. But we'll discuss the episodes in the order they were made.

tells Balok that the *Enterprise* is fitted with a substance called corbomite, which is so deadly that if the ship is attacked, it will react with equal force against the attacker. Balok has a think. Maybe he won't destroy the *Enterprise* today after all. The *Enterprise* breaks away from his tractor beam, and in so doing severely damages Balok's ship, which has now been revealed as something rather smaller and more modest than the mile-wide sphere. Kirk and Co beam over to offer their help, and Balok turns out to be a tiny child-alien thing, who was just testing them out to ascertain their true motives. He's the only person on board, although he does have some cushions and a drinks cabinet. The scary-looking bald gentleman was a puppet. But this real Balok is lonely.

'I miss company, conversation. Even an alien would be welcome. Perhaps one of your men for some period of time. An exchange of information, cultures.' Lieutenant Bailey volunteers to stay aboard with him, and we will never hear of either character again. By the next episode, Kirk, Spock and Bones have forgotten all about them. For all we know, Bailey is still stuck on this tiny craft with a tiny dome-headed alien (played by a real-life seven-year-old), wondering when he is going to be picked up. He will have heard all Balok's stories by now, for sure.

'The Corbomite Maneuver' was written by Jerry Sohl, but Memory Alpha lists three further drafts and two more sets of revisions after he finished with it. Although its premise is remarkably simple, it's really all about character and dialogue.

'Beats me what makes it go,' says Scott about the cube.

'I'll buy speculation,' says Kirk.

'I'd sell it if I had any,' says Scott. 'How a solid cube can sense us, block us, move when we move – it beats me. That's my report.'

Over in sickbay, we encounter our third Chief Medical Officer in three episodes, Dr Leonard 'Bones' McCoy, played by

DeForest Kelley. In his early forties, Kelley had worked steadily in Hollywood for many years, having become typecast as the sneering bad guy in scores of westerns. Nimoy called him 'a very calm, gentle soul, a true Southern gentleman' and noted 'that special twinkle in his eye' from his very first scene. The warmth in his character, however, is offset by an irritation that is never far from the surface.

'What am I, a doctor or a . . . moon-shuttle conductor?' he says in this episode.*

Also on debut is Nichelle Nichols as communications officer Lieutenant Uhura. (She was born Grace, but hated the name, and so asked her mother for a new one when she was eighteen and embarking upon a singing career.) In 'Corbomite' she gets to say 'Hailing frequencies open, sir' for the first time. Then, with minor variations, she gets to say it for the second, third, fourth, fifth, sixth and seventh times. Allan Asherman† notes that when Kirk convenes a meeting of senior officers, Uhura doesn't say anything or contribute in any way. But she is wearing a very short skirt, which in 1966 was the main thing.

(Yeoman Janice Rand, another new character, has even less to do, although she does bring the captain his coffee. In a scene filmed but mercifully not used, she goes into the captain's quarters, gets a clean uniform out of the wardrobe and lays it on the bed.)

There are several clues that this is a very early production. Kirk refers to 'the United Earth Ship *Enterprise*', which he won't do again. The black collars on the costumes are new, but they are higher and looser than they will subsequently appear, and Sulu's has a visible shoulder zip. If you are really paying attention, you might hear Uhura's chair squeak rather loudly

---

* He was known to everyone as 'De' but he was actually born Jackson DeForest Kelley. By coincidence, another prominent Hollywood star was born Humphrey DeForest Bogart.

† *The Star Trek Companion* by Allen Asherman (Titan Books, third edition 1993).

during the third act. In subsequent shows, stage noises will be carefully edited out.

The pivotal moment in the episode, though, comes when the ship first encounters the cube. It is meant to cause great consternation among the bridge crew, rising to panic in the case of Lieutenant Bailey. But what was Spock to do? He only had one word to say: 'Fascinating.'

'When I first rehearsed it,' Leonard Nimoy told Joel Engel, 'I said it in the same heat-of-excitement tone as everyone else. Joe [Sargent, the director] told me, "Be different. Do it cooler. Do it with curiosity. Be detached." So I said it as he suggested and we shot it that way. It gave me a whole handle that then became the spine of the character.'

First to be made, 'The Corbomite Maneuver' aired tenth because its complex special effects shots took more time to put together than anyone had expected. The shot of the puppet Balok would later come to adorn the end of the final credits sequence, with his eyes peeping menacingly over the legend 'Herbert F. Solow, Executive in Charge of Production'. Bob Justman did this as a joke.

We shall skate serenely past 'Mudd's Women' (1.6), the next script to be produced. No episode in the series, other than possibly its sequel 'I, Mudd' (2.8), has dated more painfully than this execrable sex comedy, which demonstrated for generations as yet unborn that Roddenberry had no talent for comedy and rather too much interest in sex. (Leonard Nimoy later pointed out that 'The Cage' was essentially a collection of sexual fantasies with the sex taken out.)

Richard Matheson's 'The Enemy Within' (1.5) was more like it, as you might expect from the writer of *The Incredible Shrinking Man* and *I Am Legend*, as well as 'Nightmare at 20,000 Feet', the *Twilight Zone* segment with Shatner and the gremlin. In this one, a transporter malfunction splits Captain Kirk into two: good Kirk and evil Kirk. Good Kirk is a gentle soul who finds it hard to make any decision at all. Evil Kirk wears eyeliner, sweats a lot and tries to have his way with Yeoman Janice Rand. On the planet below temperatures are rapidly falling, and Sulu and the landing party are freezing to death, but the transporter can't be used and as yet there's no hangar bay or shuttlecraft. (In case you were wondering, which I'll admit I always was.) For reasons we won't go into here, they test the transporter on an exotic alien creature, a dog with an enormous unicorn-style horn sticking out of the top of its head. The animal does not survive.

'He's dead, Jim,' says Bones.

Matheson himself didn't like the landing-party-on-the-cold-planet B-story, which was added in a later draft. But it does no harm. Sulu gets some of the best lines he will ever get, and for the first time we see people warming up by firing a phaser at a boulder, which then glows with heat. Back on the ship, Spock encounters evil Kirk in engineering. The script asked him to knock him out with a chop to the back of the head, but Nimoy didn't like that, so he improvised the Vulcan neck pinch for director Leo Penn.[*] As Nimoy was first to acknowledge, it was Shatner who sold it, by passing out so theatrically. Thus another vital bit of *Star Trek* business came into being.[†]

It may have been evil Gene, however, who wrote the last scene of the show, in which Spock says to Yeoman Rand, 'The impostor had some very interesting qualities, wouldn't you say, Yeoman?' In her autobiography Grace Lee Whitney, who played Rand, wrote, 'I can't imagine any more cruel and insensitive comment a man (or Vulcan) could make to a woman who has just been through a sexual assault! But then, some men really do think that women want to be raped.'[‡]

---

[*] Father of actor and director Sean.

[†] Spock's commitment to non-violence could be said to start here. His appeal to the late 1960s counterculture could probably be dated from the same moment.

[‡] *The Longest Trek: My Tour of the Galaxy* by Grace Lee Whitney (1998).

Fortunately, good Gene came in to work that day as well. There's a lovely moment when good Kirk is about to take evil Kirk into the transporter for the pair of them to be reconnected. Only Spock and McCoy are present.

'If this doesn't work . . . ' says good Kirk.

'Understood, Captain,' says Spock.

Already these friendships are strong enough that nothing more need be said. This was only the fifth episode they had made.

The transporter was an ingenious solution to a knotty problem. The *Enterprise* was not a ship that landed on planets, partly because that would have compromised the look of the thing, but mainly because landing it every week would take up too much story time and cost a mint in special effects. So Gene Roddenberry suggested they just 'dematerialise' in the transporter room, and then 'rematerialise' down there on the planet. It takes seconds and costs little, and there's something wonderfully exotic about the idea of having all your molecules transformed into pure energy, 'beamed' somewhere and then reconstituted at the other end. Whatever Dr McCoy might say.

Physicists have since observed that the transporter is the only technology in *Star Trek* that is genuinely impossible. Warp drive is not out of the question, and after *Star Trek*, the chances are that it will actually be called a 'warp drive'. Communicators we already have, of course, in the form of mobile phones, although I'd love mine to go CLICK-CLICK-CLICK whenever I flicked back the wire-mesh cover it sadly doesn't have. Sensors are already part of everyday life, and Dr McCoy's biobeds, which automatically read the patient's life signs and display them on a screen above, were developed after consultations with NASA. But the transporter is just so much hooey, even though it looks and sounds wonderful. The effect was achieved, incidentally, by dropping backlit grains of aluminium powder in front of a black backdrop.

And just as Sherlock Holmes never actually said, 'Elementary, my dear Watson,' in any of the stories by Sir Arthur Conan Doyle, so James T. Kirk never says, 'Beam me up, Scotty.' He says something similar half a dozen times, but never those words in that order. Even so, James Doohan chose the phrase for the title of his autobiography.

'The Man Trap' (1.1) was originally called 'The Unreal McCoy', which is so much better a title you can only scratch your head and wonder why they changed it. The sixth episode to be shot, it went out first because it had a monster and also because it was partly set on a planet. NBC loved the 'strange new worlds' part of the premise and they weren't so keen on shows set on the ship (which they often were to save money, because NBC's budget was so parsimonious). Kirk, Bones and crewman Darnell beam down to planet M-113 to check up on the only two inhabitants there, Professor Robert Crater and his wife Nancy, replenish their supplies and undertake routine medical examinations. Notice anything about that sentence? First, there's nothing ever 'routine' about anything in *Star Trek*. Second, no one in the world is called Crater, except irritable old scientists in science-fiction series. And third, crewman Darnell – young, innocent, doomed – has no purpose in the scenario other than to die horribly. Unusually, he gets both dialogue and a name, but neither can save him. Just to be sure, Kirk sends down two more crewmen, Sturgeon and Green. They die horribly too. Remarkably, not one of these three is wearing a red shirt. That's for later.

Nancy is a shapeshifting salt vampire, the last of her kind. Soon she is on the *Enterprise* emptying all available salt cellars and leaving circular sucker marks on all the people she kills. It's a good, solid episode, although later in the series Kirk would surely have found a way of saving the creature's life.

Respect for all life-forms, however repulsive, would become one of the show's defining themes. But no: Bones blasts it with a phaser. The creature's true appearance, revealed in death, has a terrible, inexpressible sadness that stays with you a while. Its huge sucker-mouth was made with an old gas mask.

Again, though, the sexual politics have not dated well. Everyone killed is male, lured to his death by a seductive temptress, although to Uhura, the creature appears as a hunky black crewman who whispers sweet nothings in Swahili to her. Yeoman Janice Rand has to fight off unwelcome male attention yet again, and crewmen go 'Phwoar!' when she walks past. It's amazing that no one is asked to take dictation.*

'The Naked Time' (1.4) was John D. F. Black's only solo screenplay during his tenure as script editor, and a memorable one. The *Enterprise* crew become infected by a virus that causes them to behave like drunks, without the staggering or the vomiting in taxis. Sulu takes his shirt off and becomes a demon swordsman. (Asked if he could fence, George Takei said 'Yes!' and raced off to get lessons.)† Nurse Christine Chapel – Majel Barrett with blonde hair – professes her undying love for Spock. And the First Officer himself has a famous solo scene in the briefing room, weeping and gnashing his teeth, as he is overpowered by waves of unleashed emotion. It wasn't in the original script: Nimoy asked Black for a last-minute rewrite and did it in a single take because there wasn't time in the schedule to do a second. 'My mother ... I could never tell her I loved her,' he tells Kirk. It's here that we realise that Spock is not someone without emotions, but

---

* Translated from the original Swahili, the hunky crewman's sweet nothings run as follows: 'How are you, friend? I think of you, beautiful lady. You should never know loneliness.'

† His fencing instructor, picked at random from a phone book, was the man who had choreographed Errol Flynn and Basil Rathbone's swordfights in *The Adventures of Robin Hood*.

someone who works hard to repress his emotions: far more dramatically interesting.

Scotty has to jump-start the engines in eight minutes or they will all die.

'I can't change the laws of physics,' he says. 'I've got to have thirty minutes.'

This is the first episode in which Bones develops a cure in the nick of time after staring for a while at lots of brightly coloured liquids in test tubes.

Dorothy Fontana's 'Charlie X' (1.2) introduced another human being with superhuman powers, barely five minutes after the last one. Young Charlie Evans, played by Robert Walker Jr with method intensity, was rescued by an alien race as a baby and given exceptional powers to help him survive. The crew realise too slowly that he is impossible to handle: an omnipotent toddler who can kill at will and does so more than once. After falling in love with Yeoman Janice Rand – the poor woman has no sort of life at all – Charlie provides one of the series' most terrifying single moments when he takes away a girl's face.* Fortunately the aliens turn up, apologise profusely and take him away. Charlie's final speech is pitiful and remarkably powerful:

'Oh, please, don't let them take me. I can't even touch them! Janice, they can't feel. Not like you! They don't love! Please, I want to stay!'

And he fades out with that last sentence echoing and echoing and echoing.

Fontana's script was one of the few that Roddenberry did not rewrite root and branch. One scene that could have happily been cut was the one in which Spock played the lyre and Uhura sang along, interminably. There are distinctly flirtatious undercurrents between the two characters, which would not

---

* It scared the hell out of me at age nine, and still does at age fifty-four.

be explored until J. J. Abrams made them a couple in his 2009 film reboot.

'Balance of Terror' (1.9) introduces the Romulans. No one has ever seen a Romulan before now, but they are known to be a warlike race, and a neutral zone has been in place between Federation space and the Romulan Empire since the last war between the two ended a century ago. Now the Romulans are back, blasting away at some of our outposts on this side of the neutral zone. Can Paul Schneider have realised, when he wrote this episode, how much fun would be gleaned over the years from this set-up?

Oddly enough, no one in the episode deigns to mention that Romulus was also one of the two brothers who founded the city of Rome, according to ancient myth. Further coincidence will see the Romulan commander's second-in-command addressed as 'Centurion' and another officer have the uncompromisingly Roman name of Decius. Who would have guessed it? In fact, this is the first manifestation of one of Roddenberry's wackier ideas, his parallel worlds theory. This suggested that there were many planets in our galaxy that had developed culturally in similar ways to our own Earth, which would allow stories to be told in Earthlike locations and save a few quid. In the episode 'Miri', this concept is taken to its illogical extreme when the *Enterprise* discovers a planet exactly like Earth, down to the shape of its continents, in 'the distant reaches of our galaxy'. Not only is this never explained – the captain just says, 'It seems impossible, but there it is' – but it's never referred to again, presumably for reasons of silliness. As the show developed, the 'parallel worlds theory' would be quietly shelved.*

---

* On the SF-dominated website io9.com, Diana Biller lists 'The 12 Plot Ideas That Every Single Classic TV Show Did To Death'. Number 6 is 'The Alien Society That Sure Looks a Lot Like the Romans'.

As it is, Uhura manages to intercept a Romulan transmission, so we see that they look remarkably like Vulcans. This enrages this week's guest navigator Lieutenant Stiles, who lost family in the Earth–Romulan war. What, a hundred years ago? That's like refusing to eat sauerkraut because your great-grandfather was killed on the Somme. Stiles's sole purpose here is to believe that our dear, beloved Spock is a Romulan spy. Kirk isn't having any of that.

'Leave any bigotry in your quarters,' he says. 'There's no room for it on the bridge.'

The episode develops into an intriguing cat-and-mouse game between Kirk and the Romulan commander, played by Mark Lenard. The Romulan ship has a cloaking device that renders it invisible to the *Enterprise*'s sensors but also vulnerable, as it can't fire its weapons when cloaked. Although we're clearly rooting for the *Enterprise*, we see that the Romulan is an honourable man, an old soldier who sees no need to make war for the sake of it, and knows that he is being politically manipulated. He and Kirk develop a mutual respect.

'I regret that we meet in this way,' says the Romulan. 'You and I are of a kind. In a different reality, I could have called you friend.'

Schneider based his story on the 1957 film *The Enemy Below*, in which an American destroyer tries to track down a German U-boat. (Other writers have noted resemblances to 1958's *Run Silent, Run Deep*.) Mark Lenard would have another run with the pointy ears as Spock's father Sarek the following year. (Most of the Romulan crew wore helmets to save the expense of making pointy ears for them too.) There's also one of the best B-stories of all, with Kirk very nearly presiding over the marriage of two crewmates.

'Since the days of the first wooden vessels,' he announces, 'all ship masters have had one happy privilege: that of uniting two people in the bonds of matrimony.'

The wedding is interrupted by the first Romulan attack, and by the end, the prospective groom has been killed.

'It never makes any sense,' Kirk tells the grieving non-bride. 'We both have to know that there was a reason.' But we know that he is not convinced.

This is my first five-star episode of the run. There aren't many, and there shouldn't be. Only the best of the very best qualify. (And you're allowed to disagree: everyone always does. There's a full list of my subjective and occasionally unreasonable star ratings at the end of the book.)

'What Are Little Girls Made Of?' (1.7) was the first script for *Star Trek* by Robert Bloch, who wrote *Psycho*. Dr Roger Korby is another eccentric solitary scientist who has been missing for years, and the *Enterprise* tracks him down on planet Exo III, living underground in a maze of tunnels with some androids. It's all a little unpromising, but Kirk beams down anyway with Nurse Christine Chapel, who was Roger's girlfriend years ago and still holds a candle for him. Probably best not to hold the candle too close to him, though, in case he melts, for we discover that he too is an android, and a more than averagely deranged one at that. I remember being genuinely shocked, even horrified, by the reveal when I first saw it in 1969, and enjoying it every bit as much whenever the show was repeated, as it frequently was. Now you can see it coming from a mile off. Ted Cassidy, who played Lurch in *The Addams Family*, and was never a looker, turns up here as Ruk, a 7ft 2in android with a grey pallor and the strength of several men. He is responsible for the series' first two genuine redshirt deaths, throwing the first of them down a conveniently placed bottomless well. Actually I was impressed by this at the age of nine as well. 'AAAAAAAAAAaaaaaaaaaaaaaaaaaaaaaaarrrrrrrggggghhhhh!' screams the redshirt as he falls. He may be falling still.

Dr Korby is meant to have turned himself into an android because he was freezing to death, and yet it's so comfortable in the caves now that the female androids dolly around in the skimpiest dresses seen this side of Risa the pleasure planet. More bizarre still, though, is the stalactite Kirk uses as a weapon when running away from Ruk. Once you have noticed its uncanny resemblance to the male sexual organ (complete with testicular appendages), you cannot unnotice it, or indeed concentrate on anything else.

'What Are Little Girls Made Of?' featured a duplicate evil Kirk, barely a couple of weeks after the last one. Roddenberry was already repeating himself. By now he had delegated almost all of his other production duties to Bob Justman and spent long hours redrafting scripts. The shoot for this episode overran by two days, mainly because Roddenberry was still rewriting as they were shooting.

'Dagger of the Mind' (1.9) took its title from *Macbeth*, Act II, Scene I: 'A dagger of the mind, a false creation, proceeding from the heat-oppressed brain'. Yet another mad scientist, this one in charge of a penal colony, has an amazing new machine that empties people's brains of all the bad things in there. Unfortunately it takes out all the good things as well. There's a barnstorming performance by Morgan Woodward as one of the victims, who manages to get on the *Enterprise* by hiding in a gigantic cardboard box. But he's now a wild, sweating loon. How to make contact with the few marbles he has left? Spock says that there is this old technique he knows, but 'it's a hidden, personal thing to the Vulcan people, part of our private lives'. Thus the first Vulcan mind-meld is carried out, at some length, because obviously it's the first time any of us have seen this, including Kirk and McCoy. In the future, for the sake of narrative compression, Spock will mind-meld with a carrot at a moment's notice, but here he hums and hahs and stretches it out for as long as humanly, or vulcanly, possible.

Roddenberry himself was stretched out, and close to

snapping. (Justman says that stamina was never his strong point. The first act of one of his rewritten scripts would be fantastic. The second act, not bad. The third act, weak. The fourth act, atrocious.) New eyes were needed. Enter Gene L. Coon, the other Gene, the forgotten Gene, and in the opinion of some, the true gene-genius behind *Star Trek*.

CHAPTER 3

STEADY AS SHE GOES, MR SULU

The English pop star and sage Neil Tennant, of the Pet Shop Boys, has spoken more than once of a pop group's 'imperial phase', that brief period in a career when one can do no wrong. During this time wondrous songs will be written and sell in massive quantities; the world will delight in you; everyone will want a piece of you. It won't last. A year, eighteen months, and that's your lot. The Beatles had four to five years, but they were the Beatles. Even their imperial phase had to end, and did so with a crunch, with the cinema release of *Yellow Submarine*.

Star Trek's imperial phase, I believe, began with the arrival of Gene L. Coon halfway through season one, and ended with his departure halfway through season two.

Coon was another old pro. Three years younger than Roddenberry, and another Second World War veteran, he had written for *Bonanza*, *Dragnet*, *Zorro*, *Have Gun Will Travel*, *Wagon Train* (not to the stars) and *The Wild Wild West*, for which he had also worked as producer. Known as an ideas man and as one of the fastest writers in town, Coon was able at a push to rewrite a script overnight, and to write an entirely new script over a weekend. In photographs he looks like a card-sharp who hasn't slept in several weeks, although to Bob Justman he looked more like 'the cold, cruel banker who forecloses on the widow's mortgage'. Justman's first response was instant dislike. 'Then, when I first saw what he could write, I practically fell in love with the guy . . . He'd just sit down, smoking and smiling, while he came up with these absolutely mind-bending ideas and the teleplays to flesh them out. He was just perfect for *Star Trek*, exactly what we needed.'*

Coon dreamed up the Klingons and the Prime Directive, wrote 'The Devil in the Dark' (of which more in a moment) and infused the show with a humour it had previously lacked. It was on Coon's watch that the three-way banter between Kirk, Spock and McCoy began to fly. As Shatner reports, it was Coon who decided that Kirk and Spock should try and drive a 1920s car in 'A Piece of the Action', and it was Coon who came up with Kirk's truly pitiful explanation for Spock's appearance in 'The City on the Edge of Forever'.

'My friend is obviously . . . Chinese,' Kirk tells a policeman. 'I see you've noticed the ears. They're actually easy to explain.'

'Perhaps the unfortunate accident I had as a child . . . ' says Spock.

'Yes, the unfortunate accident he had as a child,' says Kirk. 'He caught his head in a mechanical . . . er . . . rice-picker. But fortunately there was an American . . . um . . . missionary living close by who was actually a . . . er . . . skilled plastic surgeon in civilian life . . . '

* As told to William Shatner and Chris Kreski, *Star Trek Memories* (HarperCollins, 1993).

Although the *Star Trek* characters were conceived and created by Roddenberry, Shatner says it was Gene Coon who
really brought them to life.

In 'Miri' (1.8), Kirk, Spock, McCoy and Yeoman Janice
Rand, with her amazing lattice-like hairdo, beam down to
an Earthlike planet and discover a civilisation of children,
all three hundred years old but ageing rather slowly. As soon
as they reach adolescence the local plague will get them and
they will die horribly. As 'grups' (grown-ups), our landing
party immediately show symptoms of the virus. They cannot
go back to the ship, but Bones has a portable laboratory trans-
ported down so that he can find a cure. So it's a race against
time, but also an allegory on the generation gap, the first of a
few that *Star Trek* will attempt in its three years of production.
(This was the era of Vietnam, of rock 'n' roll, of psychedelic
drugs, of people wearing flowers in their hair. The *Star Treks*
that directly refer to these events are those that have dated
the most painfully.) 'Miri' was the first episode for which
Coon was credited as producer, with Roddenberry promoted
to executive producer. It was also one of four episodes that the
BBC refused to show for twenty years. An official statement
read thus:

'After very careful consideration a top-level decision was
made not to screen the episodes "The Empath", "Whom Gods
Destroy", "Plato's Stepchildren" and "Miri", because they all
dealt most unpleasantly with the already unpleasant subjects
of madness, torture, sadism and disease.'

According to Memory Alpha, when the corporation first
showed 'Miri' in 1970, several viewers wrote in to complain.
BBC executives sat down and watched the rest of the series and
decided that those four episodes were not acceptable. The ban
wasn't lifted until 1991.

'The Conscience of the King' (1.13) is the Shakespearean
one, a hotchpotch of ideas and plot points and scraps of

dialogue from *Hamlet* and *Macbeth*. The *Enterprise* is diverted to Planet Q to see some travelling players perform the Scottish play. Another old friend of Kirk's – they are scattered throughout the quadrant – thinks he has recognised the leader of the players, Anton Karidian, as Kodos the Executioner, a notorious multi-murderer long believed to be dead. The old-friend-of-Kirk's turns his face to reveal that one half of it has been replaced by a shiny mouse mat. Kodos did that, all those years ago. Only a handful of survivors would recognise the villain. Kirk is one. Friend-of-Kirk's is another, and he is soon murdered. A third is Lieutenant Riley, an annoying young officer previously seen in 'The Naked Time'. To solve the mystery, Kirk offers the theatre company a lift to their next port of call, and tries to work out whether Karidian is indeed Kodos, and why everyone who might recognise him keeps being murdered. The complicating factor in all this is Karidian's daughter Lenore, played by Barbara Anderson in a different diaphanous outfit for every scene. There's a toe-curling chat-up scene between Kirk and Lenore on the observation deck, with the lights turned down low because it's supposedly night on board.

'And this ship,' says Lenore, who was named after a fabric conditioner. 'All this power. Surging and throbbing, yet under control. Are you like that, Captain?'

I think we all know the answer to that.

The resolution, when it arrives, is even less likely than anything else in the episode, and yet again, someone apparently sane proves to be gibberingly mad. Whatever other technological advances may have been made in the twenty-third century, there seem to be a lot of lunatics running around the place.

'The Galileo Seven' (1.16) is not a fan favourite, but it has long been one of mine. Spock leads a survey team of seven in the *Galileo*, a shuttlecraft that crash-lands on the usual planet full of enormous boulders. Scotty and Bones are with him, and one or two other crewmen who aren't long for this world. The planet is lost in a haze of radiation or fluffy clouds that block communications and sensors. And huge proto-humanoids stalk the surface, throwing spears at our friends while Scotty tries to repair the damaged shuttle. The race against time here is that urgent medical supplies are needed on Planet Faraway, and a stuffed-shirt commissioner is stomping around the bridge insisting that Kirk abandon his crewmates on the planet and get going. Spock, meanwhile, is driving the rest of the *Galileo* seven round the bend with his remorseless logic. It's his first command and he is making a pig's ear of it. This is why many fans don't like the episode. Spock, they say, is un-Spocklike. It's one thing to be logical, but another to be a callous fool, as he sometimes is here. But you could also see the episode as a character piece, a crucial stage in Spock's development, both as a person and as a Starfleet officer. And the ending, in which Spock eschews all logic and acts on a crazy hunch, is magnificent.

'Mr Spock,' says one of the crewmen as they contemplate certain death, 'you said a while ago that there were always alternatives.'

'Did I?' says Spock. 'I may have been mistaken.'

'Well, at least I lived long enough to hear that,' says Bones.

One of the *Galileo* seven is one Yeoman Mears, who has little to do other than hold a tricorder and not get killed. The role had been earmarked for Yeoman Rand, but the character had been written out of the series after 'The Conscience of the King', in which she had only one brief scene. The official version was that the role of yeoman might cramp Captain Kirk's style, and limit the potential for other romantic entanglements. In reality Grace Lee Whitney had been struggling with substance abuse and had lost Roddenberry's confidence. It was a precipitous fall from grace: the three characters featured in early promotional pictures for the series had been Kirk, Spock and Yeoman Janice Rand. Who would pour the captain's coffee now? Who would lay his clean uniform out on his bed?*

Changes were afoot behind the scenes as well. Rewrite man John D. F. Black made his escape after thirteen episodes: he and his secretary opened a bottle of champagne to celebrate no longer having to work for Gene Roddenberry. He was replaced by Steven Carabatsos, imported from that bastion of hard SF, *Peyton Place*. Carabatsos went straight to work on 'Court Martial' (1.20), the first of many memorable courtroom dramas in the various iterations of *Star Trek*. Kirk is accused of criminal negligence in the death of one of his officers, a Lieutenant Commander Benjamin Finney, and must stand trial for his murder. Prosecuting counsel is yet another old flame of Kirk's.

'All of my old friends look like doctors,' says Bones when he first meets her. 'All of *his* look like you.'

Defence counsel is Elisha Cook Jr, a character actor of the old school, as small and gnarled as a hobbit and several times more voluble. Kirk is innocent: we know this but we cannot prove it. Finney turns out to be alive, another loon with mad, staring eyes, and he and Kirk end up fighting in Engineering. This is the first episode in which the words 'Starfleet' and 'Starfleet Command' are used, and also our first visit to a starbase. Finally vindicated, Kirk smooches with his old girlfriend for old times' sake.

'She's a very good lawyer,' he tells Spock and McCoy.

'Obviously,' says Spock.

'Indeed she is,' says McCoy.

---

* Whitney died in May 2015, aged eighty-five. Although cast in the 'ingénue' role, she was actually older than both Shatner and Nimoy. Might that have been a problem in itself? Advised to lose twenty pounds to fit her costume less snugly, she became addicted to diet pills, which made her more anxious, which made her drink more heavily. In her brief tenure on the show, says Shatner, Whitney was sexually assaulted twice, once by a network executive, once by a 'co-worker'. There's a dark side to this business, as there always was and ever shall be.

Like so much great art, 'The Menagerie' (1.11 and 1.12) came about through desperation and panic. The production was running out of usable scripts, so Bob Justman suggested to Roddenberry that he find some way of making use of 'The Cage', which had cost all that money and was just sitting there doing nothing. Roddenberry wrote the 'envelope' script in four days. In it the events of 'The Cage' become ancient history. Thirteen years have passed since Captain Christopher Pike was captured and escaped from the Talosians, but the recent past has not been kind to him. Grievously injured by extended exposure to delta rays while rescuing cadets from a training vessel, he is now paralysed and disfigured, confined to a wheel-chair and unable to communicate other than with blinking lights: one bleep for 'yes', two bleeps for 'no'. Roddenberry couldn't afford to rehire Jeffrey Hunter, who didn't want to be rehired anyway, but a disfigured Pike could easily be played by another, similar-looking actor, Sean Kenney (whose make-up took five hours to apply). Result: one of the most memorable and disturbing images in the whole of *Star Trek*. We might be mildly scared by monsters, but we are chilled to the marrow by what has happened to Pike. His is a living death, far more appalling than death itself, if only because his brain is unaffected. As McCoy explains:

'The brain is what life is all about. Now, that man can think any thought that we can, and love, hope, dream as much as we can, but he can't reach out, and no one can reach in.'

Spock is the catalyst to action here. The only member of Pike's crew still on the *Enterprise*, he beams Pike up, makes sure Kirk is stranded on Starbase 11 and sets the ship on computer control, whizzing off at maximum warp to an unknown destination. When Kirk and Starbase 11's boss Commander Mendez finally catch up, Spock gives himself up and submits to a court martial. His evidence is 'The Cage' (minus credits and a lot of background music), shown on a viewscreen to the court. How can this be? Spock says he will explain later. We learn the story of Talos IV, and we also learn that Talos IV is now strictly off-limits to Federation citizens, on penalty of death (its inhabitants' powers are too dangerous). In fact we're so gripped by the story up there on the screen in the briefing room that we stop wondering about its high production values, or why Number One looks so much like Nurse Christine Chapel. It is of course the Talosians themselves who are beaming these images to the ship, and to Talos IV that the ship is travelling. It's all smoke and mirrors, but so elegantly orchestrated. At one point we are watching (on television) Kirk and Commodore Mendez watching (on the viewscreen) the Talosians watching (on their viewscreen) the captured Captain Pike and Vina in their cage. As theviewscreen. com's Eugene Myers says, 'it's viewscreens all the way down'.

The themes here are two of *Star Trek*'s favourites, loyalty and sacrifice. What counts for more, Spock's loyalty to his captain and friend Kirk, to his former captain Pike, or to the Federation itself? Pike injured himself rescuing cadets; Spock is now willing to sacrifice his career for Pike's sake. Kirk's career too is under threat, as he is stripped of his command when Starfleet Command learns of the video link with the forbidden Talos IV.

But it's Pike's plight that really sticks in our memories, and the brutal contrast between the young, vibrant Pike up there on the viewscreen and the ruined Pike sitting immobile in the bleep-chair. Spock insists that he acts logically in all this, but we, and Kirk and McCoy, know he is acting emotionally too, and we love him all the more for it.

Halfway through the season, Spock was what we might now call the 'breakout star' of the show. Shatner headed the cast, was paid five thousand dollars an episode, and was reportedly on a small percentage of the profits of the first-run broadcast.*

* He never revealed what percentage he was on, but as there weren't any profits on first-run broadcast, it didn't much matter.

Nimoy was on $1250 and had to wear prosthetic ears every day, but his sacks of fan mail easily outbulged the captain's. Not long before, NBC Sales had insisted that the character be dropped to assuage maniacs in the Bible Belt. In a glossy brochure sent out to potential advertisers, someone had even airbrushed a photo of Spock to round off the ears and normalise the eyebrows. This was all forgotten. NBC's Herb Schlosser rang Solow and told him that New York wanted all major Spock episodes to air as soon as possible.

Hardly surprisingly, this seems to have riled Shatner. One morning a photographer from *Life* magazine came to see Nimoy having his ears put on. Shatner and Jimmy Doohan were there too, but no one paid them any attention. 'Bill's hairpiece was being applied,' said Doohan. 'The top of his head was a lot of skin and a few little odd tufts of hair. The mirrors on the make-up room walls were arranged so that we could all see the laying on of his rug.' According to Solow and Justman, Shatner blew his top, said, 'From now on, *my* make-up will be done in my trailer,' and stormed out.*

In *Star Trek Memories*, Shatner admits he was rattled by Nimoy's success. 'I wasn't proud of these feelings, but they were simply the natural human reaction.' In the end he went to Gene Roddenberry's office to have a moan. 'Don't ever fear having good and popular people around you,' said Roddenberry, 'because they only enhance your own performance. The more you play to these people, the better the show.'

'And he was absolutely right,' says Shatner. 'It suddenly made perfect sense.'

Shatner, of course, had other ways of ensuring that the audience's attention returned to him. In his invaluable *Encyclopedia Shatnerica*, Robert Schnakenberg offers 'Kirk points' for each

---

* Shatner has always denied that he is bald. 'I don't wear a hairpiece,' he told an inquisitive radio DJ in 1994. 'That's the stupidest question I ever heard.'

episode on the following basis: one point if Kirk 'gets action' from a female admirer; one point if Kirk is seen with his shirt off or partially torn; one point if his blood is spilt during the episode; one point if Shatner plays a dual role; one point if Kirk outwits a supercomputer; one point if he gives a long, moralising speech to an alien or an enemy; one point if he is provoked by a nitpicking bureaucrat; one point if he refuses to kill an enemy for moral reasons; and one point if he egregiously violates the Prime Directive. Score five extra points if any five of these conditions are met. Any episode scoring ten or more, says Schnakenberg, 'represents the ultimate in Shatner performances, the nirvana of Shatnerica'.*

For me, the very Shatnerest episodes were those in which he tore his shirt, usually during a fist-fight. In the first season this happened in 'Where No Man Has Gone Before', 'The Corbomite Maneuver', 'The Enemy Within', 'The Naked Time', 'Miri', 'Court Martial', 'Shore Leave' and 'Arena'. That's four of the first six, six of the first fourteen and finally eight of the first nineteen. Very rarely did opponents' shirts suffer damage. Villains' clothes were made of much more hard-wearing material. Strangely enough, Kirk's subordinates never tore their shirts either. Only captains' shirts ripped into rags at the slightest pressure. You would almost have thought it was intentional.

'Shore Leave' (1.15) takes us to a planet that isn't Studio 9 at Desilu but actually has an outdoors. In idyllic parkland on a fresh summer's day, a white rabbit toddles past, followed by a small girl. This week's Yeoman Who Isn't Rand finds a medieval costume, complete with wimple, hanging on a tree, and decides to change into it.

'Don't peek,' she says to Bones.

* *The Encyclopedia Shatnerica: An A to Z Guide to the Man and His Universe* by Robert Schnakenberg (Quirk, 1998) – 'Full of information about me that I can't imagine people find interesting' (W. Shatner). Schnakenberg's next book was *Sci-Fi Baby Names* (2006).

'My dear girl, I am a doctor,' says Bones. 'When I peek, it's in the line of duty.'

She is roughly a thousand years younger than him, but that doesn't stop them flirting in a way that might turn the twenty-first-century stomach.

Meanwhile, Kirk keeps bumping into old friends. There's yet another old flame from years ago – cue the softest of soft focus – and an annoying Irish rival from Starfleet Academy, who taunts the captain from afar to the strains of twiddly-widdly 'Irish' music. This is a planet where whatever you imagine becomes real, although the dangers of this are illustrated when a knight on horseback impales McCoy with his lance and kills him instantly. Are there no safety protocols here? Well, there are certainly no instructions, which is a little careless for a so-called pleasure planet. 'Shore Leave' is a fan favourite but its relentless whimsy soon becomes wearing. Roddenberry was rewriting the script as it was being shot, which helps to explain its bagginess of plot. The fight in which Kirk tears his latest shirt seems to last several days.

(This is the first episode in which a major character is killed but miraculously restored before the end. Sometimes mere peril isn't enough. Only death will do.)

'The Squire of Gothos' (1.17) is equally drenched in whimsy, as the *Enterprise* crew encounter Trelane, the first of many all-powerful child-aliens who treat humans as playthings. Once you know the twist (which itself is a rejig of the one in 'Charlie X'), you might struggle to watch this one again all the way through. Even Spock isn't that impressed.

'Does your logic find this fascinating, Mr Spock?' asks Dr McCoy.

'Fascinating is a word I use for the unexpected,' says Spock. 'In this case, I should think interesting would suffice.'

'Arena' (1.18) was Gene Coon's first solo script. Once again there was nothing else ready to shoot, and Bob Justman was threatening to shut down production until something came in. So Coon went home early on Friday afternoon and bashed it out over the weekend. Small problem: without realising it, he had lifted the idea from a well-known Fredric Brown short story. (When told, Coon's reaction was a horrified 'Oh my God!') Business Affairs rang Brown and told him that *Star Trek* would like to buy one of his stories, and offered him a decent price. Brown was delighted and said yes. 'We never did tell him that the script had already been written,' says Solow.

The *Enterprise* arrives at an Earth outpost in deep space only to find it destroyed and the alien attackers lying in wait, firing their disruptors at the landing party. We don't know who they are but they have bigger and nastier weapons than we have, and Kirk interprets the attack as a prelude to invasion. Back on the *Enterprise*, he pursues the alien ship at maximum warp, snarling quietly to himself. Spock tries to calm him down. The captain will have none of it.

'It's a matter of policy. Out here we're the only policemen around. And a crime has been committed. Do I make myself clear?'

The two ships pass through an uncharted solar system and are brought to a dead stop by an external force. 'We are the Metrons,' say some pretty lights on the viewscreen. The locals, it seems, object to the violent intentions of the two ships buzzing past their homeworld, guns a-blazing. Both captains are thus deposited on a nearby moon, to settle their argument personally. There are no weapons there, but there might be the raw materials for one. Whoever survives the contest will be allowed to leave with his ship, whereas the vessel of the defeated captain will be summarily destroyed. These are the rules. Now off you go.

Kirk's enemy is a Gorn, or a man in a lizard suit. He is bigger and stronger than Kirk, and has even larger, more expressive eyes, although he moves like a nonagenarian. (A very old man in a lizard suit.) Fortunately, our captain finds small piles of minerals lying around the place. These, he realises, are the various substances one would need to make gunpowder. He fashions himself a cannon out of bamboo and fires it at the Gorn. Victory! But what was the Gorn doing for all that time? Having a nap? Snacking on the local wildlife? At the last moment, realising he might earlier have jumped to the wrong conclusion, Kirk spares the wounded Gorn's life. The Metrons, represented by a weedy youth in a toga, spare Kirk's.

'Very good, Captain. There is hope for you. Perhaps in several thousand years, your people and mine shall meet to reach an agreement. You are still half savage, but there is hope. We will contact you when we are ready.'

How many more all-powerful alien races does a galaxy need? And why do they never seem to bump into each other? Instead they only ever bump into the *Enterprise* and its half-savage human crew, and judge them harshly.

'Arena' is considered something of a *Star Trek* classic, mainly because of the combat scenes between Kirk and the Gorn. But the episode is full of holes. Kirk's belligerence at the start of the episode is completely out of character: it's just there to drive the story. When the Metrons stop the two ships in their paths, Kirk and McCoy are amazed by this power, even though something like it happens nearly every week. And I'm afraid I really cannot take seriously an alien race who call themselves the Metrons, which sounds like something out of a 1940s comic book. When you're launching yourself as an alien race in an unexplored sector of the galaxy, the first thing to do before anything is get the marketing men in and decide on a decent brand name.

(The planet scenes were filmed at Vasquez Rocks in California, and have occasionally been referenced in geeky films and TV shows. In *Bill & Ted's Bogus Journey*, the two leads watch 'Arena' on television and then go to Vasquez Rocks to muck about. In *Paul*, Simon Pegg, pretending to be Kirk, and Nick Frost, in a Gorn mask, go to Vasquez Rocks, act out the scene and run away when other tourists spot them. In an episode of *The Big Bang Theory*, the four main male characters, dressed as *Next Generation* characters, stop at Vasquez Rocks while on their way to a comics convention and take daft pictures of each other. While they do this, their car is stolen.)

'The Alternative Factor' (1.27) would be held back for two months, because it was terrible. A lunatic called Lazarus, with a wispy beard, is convinced he is being pursued by someone even madder, 'the devil's own spawn', who turns out to be himself from an alternative antimatter universe. If the two of them should meet in either this universe or that one, they will destroy both universes and any others that happen to be lying around. Fortunately there's a corridor between the two universes, where the two Lazaruses can grapple away without doing anyone any harm. (It's a real corridor, with walls, floor, ceiling and doors.) The only possible solution to this ludicrous set-up is to trap both of them in this corridor for eternity, bashing the stuffing out of each other, although what they will do for food, water and bedding is never made clear. Why not just kill one of them? Or both of them? Job done, universes safe, time for lunch.

(Lazarus, the mad one, steals the *Enterprise*'s dilithium crystals to power his own ship. Fortunately, they fit perfectly in the slot in his ship, like Lego pieces, or something made by Ikea. He doesn't even seem surprised.)

'Tomorrow Is Yesterday' (1.19) is where things begin to look up. Having nearly bumped into a 'black star'* and used every

---

* The term 'black hole' wasn't coined until later that same year, 1967, by the US physicist John Archibald Wheeler. As Stephen Hawking wrote in his introduction to Lawrence Krauss's *The Physics of Star Trek*, 'had they continued with their original names of "frozen stars" or "gravitationally completely collapsed objects", there wouldn't have been half so much written about them.'

last ounce of warp power to escape its gravitational pull, the *Enterprise* finds itself thrown back to 1969, and orbiting the Earth. Caramba! Unfortunately the ship is spotted by an air force pilot, who happens to be flying past, and takes it for a UFO. His plane starts to break up, so they have to beam him aboard. Already, then, the past has been altered and must now be unaltered by some complicated plotting. Captain Christopher may not be a man of great consequence himself – he is a little bit disappointed to be told this – but his as yet unborn son will become a famous astronaut. 'Coo!' thinks Captain Christopher. Kirk and Spock stroke their chins. If we go back in time to the point when we beamed him aboard and beam him back onto his ship, then he will never remember he was on board the ship and everything will be fine. I don't like to use capital letters unnecessarily, but THIS MAKES NO SENSE AT ALL. And do we care? No, because the whole episode is immense fun, perkily written by Dorothy Fontana, with a polish by Gene Coon. Down on Earth, Kirk is captured by the US Air Force and interrogated.

'What is that? Is that a uniform of some kind?' asks Air Force Guy.

'This little thing?' says Kirk. 'Just something I slipped on.'

'I'm going to lock you up for two hundred years,' says Air Force Guy.

'That ought to be just about right,' says Kirk.

But here's a thing: the day after this episode first aired, Apollo 1 exploded on its launchpad, and astronauts Gus Grissom, Ed White and Roger Chaffee were all killed.

'The Return of the Archons' (1.21) was one of Roddenberry's original pitches for the first pilot, much improved in the telling. In their search for the remains of an Earth ship, the *Archon*, that had gone missing a whole *century* previously – better late than never, Starfleet would probably say – the landing party find a planet in which the population wander around in a catatonic daze, like Stepford Wives and Stepford Husbands. Dispensing instant justice are the 'lawgivers', clad in robes and carrying huge electronic rods. In charge, it seems, is the unseen Landru, who appears only as a projection on a wall and tells the landing party that they are to be 'absorbed', as the crew of the *Archon* were all those years ago. McCoy comes back from the absorption chamber as a grinning zombie, talking of the 'joy, peace and tranquillity' you will find if you 'go to Landru'. It will come as no surprise to experienced *Trek* watchers to discover that Landru is a giant computer, with the flashing lights and inability to cope with paradox of all its kind.

'The plug must be pulled,' says Kirk.

Spock (for the first time) reminds his captain of Starfleet's Prime Directive. This prohibits its personnel from interfering with the internal development of alien civilisations.

'That refers to a living, growing culture,' says Kirk.

He talks to the computer for about three minutes, makes it explode and everyone goes home.

Like 'The Squire of Gothos', 'The Return of the Archons' was a defining episode of *Star Trek* in that it created a template that would be reused and reused until we all wanted to scream. Roddenberry had a taste for what might be called High Concept Planets, where human life continued normally except for one curious twist that Kirk usually managed to sort out. On Landru's planet, one has to ask, was the computer running the entire world, or just the Hollywood backlot in which the landing party arrived? On a very large planet it would be remarkable good fortune to land in the same small town that hosted this all-powerful supercomputer. It would be like landing in Kettering and finding the United Nations there.

'A Taste of Armageddon' (1.23) is the one in which two neighbouring planets are fighting a war without actually fighting it. They don't fire missiles at each other; they just conduct a series of computer simulations. Every so often a 'hit' is recorded and large numbers of civilians have to interrupt their day and report to their local disintegration chamber to be atomised. The *Enterprise*, by making contact, becomes a casualty of war and its crew are ordered to beam down and surrender to the authorities. Kirk isn't having it.

'Death, destruction, disease, horror. That's what war is all about, Anan. That's what makes it a thing to be avoided. You've made it neat and painless. So neat and painless, you've had no reason to stop it. And you've had it for five hundred years. Since it seems to be the only way I can save my crew and my ship, I'm going to end it for you, one way or another.'

The Prime Directive is only two episodes old, and he has already broken it twice.

There are some good moments here. For the second episode in a row, Scotty takes command after Kirk and Spock get stuck on the planet's surface, and this time he has an idiot brass-hat ambassador on board to deal with.

'Diplomacy, gentlemen, should be a job left to diplomats,' says idiot brass-hat.

'Diplomats!' says Scotty. 'The best diplomat I know is a fully activated phaser bank.'

On the planet, Spock attempts to distract the guard.

'Sir, there's a multi-legged creature crawling on your shoulder.'

And gives him a Vulcan nerve pinch.

We are now, I believe, in the midst of the greatest run of episodes in *Star Trek* history.

CHAPTER 4

I'M A DOCTOR, NOT A BRICKLAYER

The only problem was the ratings. Too few people were watching. NBC always insisted that the Nielsen ratings were but one tool used to determine the viability of a series. But were there any other tools? If so, they were left rusting in the toolbox. The Nielsens were the basis on which a network determined its pricing structure for advertising agencies, and on which those agencies decided how to spend their clients' money. Low ratings meant low advertising revenue, and less chance of a show being recommissioned for another season.

Star Trek's ratings were low but steady. There were no dramatic fluctuations week on week, depending on whether a decent monster was due to appear. No, the same few people were watching every episode. By and large these people were young and well educated, and some of them were actually female. But no one cared about demographics in 1966. Only raw numbers counted, and *Star Trek* was not delivering them.

Roddenberry sought support from the wider science-fiction community. In December 1966 Harlan Ellison (who hadn't yet fallen out with Roddenberry over 'The City on the Edge of Forever') wrote a letter to fellow SF writers to initiate a 'write-in' campaign. Isaac Asimov spoke in favour of the show. Fans across the US wrote to NBC too. It was the first such campaign to 'save' a beloved TV show, and the new episodes being transmitted showed it was a show worth saving.

In 'Space Seed' (1.22) the *Enterprise* encounters an old, old Earth ship floating in the middle of nowhere. It's the SS *Botany Bay*, and frozen in suspended animation within its cold corridors are the survivors of our planet's deeply destructive Eugenics Wars, which aimed to 'improve the race through selective breeding'. Their leader is Khan Noonien Singh: strong, charismatic, highly intelligent, mad as a box of frogs. He is played by Ricardo Montalban, and he is *Star Trek*'s villain of villains. Lieutenant Marla McGivers quickly takes a shine to him. She is the *Enterprise*'s resident twentieth-century historian, and as such, normally rather underemployed, I would have thought. We learn that in 1993 a group of genetically enhanced maniacs simultaneously took power in more than forty nations.

'The scientists overlooked one fact,' says Spock. 'Superior ability breeds superior ambition.'

So Khan, when he wakes from his long sleep, instantly grabs McCoy and holds a scalpel to his neck.

'Where am I?' asks Khan.

'You're in bed, holding a knife at your doctor's throat.' McCoy does not even blink. 'It would be most effective if you would cut the carotid artery, just under the left ear.'

When Marla McGivers comes into sickbay, however, Khan turns on the charm.

'I've been reading up on starships, but they have one luxury not mentioned in the manuals,' he says.

'I don't understand,' says Marla.

'A beautiful woman. My name is Khan. Please sit and entertain me.'

Only Ricardo Montalban, of any man who has ever lived, could get away with these lines, even in 1967.

Having studied the manuals, Khan finds it the work of a moment to take over the ship.

'Captain, although your abilities intrigue me, you are quite honestly inferior,' he explains. 'Mentally, physically. In fact, I am surprised how little improvement there has been in human evolution. Oh, there has been technical advancement, but how little man himself has changed. Yes, it appears we will do well in your century, Captain.'

But superior ambition breeds superior arrogance. Kirk takes back his ship and dumps Khan and his henchpersons on a nearby planet, Ceti Alpha V, which, according to Spock, is 'habitable, although a bit savage, somewhat inhospitable'. Kirk quotes Milton: 'It is better to rule in hell than to serve in heaven.'

'It would be interesting,' says Spock, 'to return to that world in a hundred years and to learn what crop has sprung from the seed you planted today.'

'Yes, Mr Spock, it would indeed,' says Kirk.

Hmm, yes, well. Or, as Eugene Myers put it, 'it might even be interesting to check things out in fifteen years or so, just to see what's going on with Khan and make sure no nearby planets have exploded or anything.'*

---

* 'Space Seed' is also the first episode in which McCoy's dislike of the transporter becomes apparent: 'I signed aboard this ship to practise medicine, not to have my atoms scattered back and forth across space by this gadget,' he moans, as they are about to beam over to the SS *Botany Bay*. This was an idea first mooted by George Clayton Johnson in his script for 'The Man Trap', but cut by Roddenberry. Who obviously remembered it a few months later and put it back in.

Behind the scenes, Dorothy Fontana had left her job as Gene Roddenberry's secretary, having decided that if she didn't make a go of the writing now, she never would. 'I said to myself, "I think I'll give it a try. I've got some money in the bank, and even if I don't sell *anything*, I'll be okay, and at least I have tried." Actually, I was hoping that Gene might let me write some more *Star Treks*.'*

A fortnight later, Roddenberry rang her up. He had a script by Jerry Sohl called 'The Way of the Spores' and it wasn't working. Could she rewrite it, preferably by yesterday? As a little extra incentive, Roddenberry told her he was in need of a new story editor. If she could turn this one around, the job was hers.†

'The Way of the Spores' would become 'This Side of Paradise' (1.24), which was credited to Fontana from a story by Nathan Butler and Fontana. 'Nathan Butler' was Jerry Sohl, who objected to the changes she had made. Pseudonyms are littered all over *Star Trek*'s writing credits. Each one speaks of a tantrum, argument or grand writerly sulk.

In 'This Side of Paradise' the planet Omicron Ceti III is being bombarded with lethal Berthold rays, and the *Enterprise* flies in to rescue the 150 human colonists there. But they're all fine, in tip-top health, and they don't want to go anywhere. It's a mystery, until someone spots the presence of huge triffid-like flowers, which fire a cloud of spores into your face if you make the mistake of smelling one. The spores bring on a sense of peace and well-being, and make you talk like a hippy. (The spores also protect you from the Berthold rays, which is why the colonists have survived.) Who would have thought Sulu could smile

* Quoted in Shatner and Kreski's *Star Trek Memories*.

† Aged twenty-seven, Fontana would become the youngest story editor in the US television industry.

so widely? Soon everyone on the *Enterprise* is infected and they beam down to the planet to make a new life there. Only Kirk, because he is Kirk, can resist the pull of paradise. How can he counter the effect of the spores before the *Enterprise*'s orbit decays and important bits start to drop off it?

All of which would stick in our minds for barely a nanosecond if it weren't for the effect the spores have on our favourite Vulcan. One of the colonists is Jill Ireland, beautiful, blonde, shot in soft focus and known to Spock of old. She loved him years ago, and once the spores have battered down his Vulcan reserve, he realises he loves her too. Never mind about Sulu: who would have thought Leonard Nimoy could smile so widely? He also kisses Miss Ireland with an enthusiasm many male viewers may have sincerely shared. Her boyfriend in real life, and later husband, was Charles Bronson. Nimoy said he was always hanging around the set to make sure she didn't get up to anything.

All of *Star Trek*'s Edens must come to an end, though, and this one is destroyed by Kirk's discovery that strong emotion nullifies the effect of the spores. Kirk persuades Spock to beam back up to the ship, and insults him, calling a traitor and a half-breed.

'You belong in a circus, Spock, not a starship! Right next to the dog-faced boy!'

Spock, for once, loses his temper, and in so doing, loses the spores. 'They've gone,' he says. 'I don't belong any more.'

The sadness in that sentence is unmeasurable.

You can tell a woman wrote this. It's all about the characters, and in Spock's case it's a 'what if' tale like none other. We see him climbing trees and lying with his head on Jill Ireland's lap, staring at the clouds. And after it's all over, 'I have little to say about it, Captain. Except that for the first time in my life, I was happy.'*

And so to 'The Devil in the Dark' (1.25), my third five-star episode and, in fact, my all-time favourite episode of any kind. A Hungarian actor and stunt performer named Janos Prohaska had made what would become known as the Horta costume, and took it into Gene Coon's office.

'That's great. What is it?' said Coon.

'I don't know. It can be whatever you want,' said Prohaska.

'I'll write a script around it,' said Coon. It took him four days.

We begin beneath the surface of the planet Janus VI, where a Federation mining colony is being terrorised by a murderous monster in Grand Guignol style. You know the sort of thing: anxious man walks down dark corridor sweating, screams, everyone else comes running, sees only a pile of ashes where their colleague was standing only a moment ago. Call the *Enterprise*, which is in the area and has an apparently unlimited supply of redshirts anxious to sacrifice their lives for the good of the plot. The creature zips through solid rock as humans move through air. Kirk and Spock wander separately through the caverns with their phasers at the ready, and it's Kirk who finds a cavern full of strange silver-painted spheres. The monster arrives but does not kill him, possibly because of the colour of his shirt. Spock arrives and mindmelds with the creature, who we learn is a Horta, the last of her kind, looking after her eggs, which are soon to hatch. But the Horta is dying, injured by phaser fire. Enter Dr McCoy, in one of his grumps.

---

* Nimoy had this to say in *I Am Spock*: 'If you put Dorothy's scripts together as a group . . . she gave us, by far, the best stories where we interacted with women who were fully developed characters in their own right. That's not to say that that was her primary intent as a writer, or that that was her only contribution to the show. But *Star Trek* was a product of the sexist sixties, and that was sometimes reflected in the writing, where women characters were often treated as stereotypical love interests or altogether ignored. Dorothy's scenes not only avoided such stereotypes, but were dramatically intriguing.'

'You can't be serious, that thing is virtually made out of stone.'

'Help it,' says Kirk. 'Treat it.'

'I'm a doctor, not a bricklayer,' says McCoy.

Now the miners turn up, seeking vengeance.

'That thing killed fifty of my men,' says the furious miner boss.

'You've killed thousands of her children,' says Kirk.

It's speech time.

'The Horta is intelligent, peaceful, mild. She had no objection to sharing this planet with you, until you broke into her nursery and started destroying her eggs. Then she fought back in the only way she knew how, as any mother would fight when her children are in danger.'

Here, then, is *Star Trek* in microcosm. Expectations are subverted, cooperation replaces antagonism, difference is celebrated. These were bold sentiments to express in late-1960s America, when the Vietnam War was in full swing and everyone thought there were reds under the bed. As Arthur C. Clarke later said, 'it impressed me because it presented the idea, unusual in science fiction then and now, that something weird, and even dangerous, need not be malevolent. That is a lesson that many of today's politicians have yet to learn.'

But 'Devil in the Dark' also works because it has a magnificent story to tell. It's a fable of the far future, executed with wonderful finesse. Every time I see it I blub like a small child, and I have seen it an awful lot of times. There may be no more joyous moment in all *Star Trek* than when McCoy, his hands covered in wet concrete after treating the Horta, says, 'By golly, Jim! I'm beginning to think I can cure a rainy day!'

'Devil in the Dark' first went out on 9 March 1967. Over the closing credits, an NBC announcer had this to say:

'*Star Trek* will be back in the fall. And please, don't write any more letters.'

According to Solow and Justman, this was the first time ever that an American TV network had directly informed viewers that their favourite show would be coming back. A number of them ignored the network's request and wrote simply to say thank you.

Herb Solow was bemused. Why had NBC renewed? It didn't quite make sense to him:

> Sold-out sponsorship? Barely. Passable ratings? Barely. More intelligent viewers? Probably, but meaningless. Hard-core younger audience? Sure, but still meaningless. Viewers with great buying power? Not really. No better series to schedule? There were lots of candidates. Protest calls? Yes, but organised, not spontaneous. Protest letters? Yes, but organised, not spontaneous . . .
>
> Networks make unexpected and seemingly illogical decisions for corporate reasons, not viewer reasons. I never bought the campaign to 'Save *Star Trek*' as the only reason the series was brought back for a second year. Perhaps something else, something more related to money and profit, helped change NBC's mind.

Solow had a theory, and it's an interesting one. By the mid-1960s, colour TV had been around for a while, but the high cost of a set had put people off buying one. Only in 1965 did sales begin to rise. Colour TVs had been developed by RCA, whose development costs were estimated at $130 million, a huge sum at the time. (Quite a lot now.)

In 1966, at the behest of NBC, the Nielsen Company started to research the popularity of shows being viewed on colour TVs. It turned out that shows that did well in colour were, by and large, the same shows that had been doing well in black-and-white. *Bonanza*, for example, was high in the ratings in both lists.

But in December, an NBC executive gave Solow a call. According to the Nielsen research, *Star Trek* was the highest-rated colour series of them all. It was, in Malcolm Gladwell's useful expression, the outlier, the unexpected result that is more powerful than all the other, more expected results. NBC's parent company was RCA. *Star Trek* sold colour TV sets, and that was good news for everyone.*

In Gene Coon's 'Errand of Mercy' (1.26) we meet the Klingons, the alien race we will come to know better than any other. War between the Federation and the Klingon Empire is imminent, and the planet Organia is inconveniently positioned in the middle of the disputed area. Kirk and Spock beam down and try and persuade the Organians, who are gentle and wear long robes, to side with us and not with them. Eventually some Klingons turn up: swarthy, oriental, scenery-chewing villains without, at this stage, much light or shade. John Colicos, as Kor, has some wonderful fruity dialogue, as well as a useful 'truth-finder' machine.

'It's a mind-sifter or mind-ripper, depending on how much force is used. We can record every thought, every bit of knowledge in a man's mind. Of course, when that much force is used, the mind is emptied. Permanently, I'm afraid. What's left is more vegetable than human.'

The Organians appear unworried by this, however, and just smile amiably, as though heavily sedated. Spock reports that Organian society is stagnant. 'This is a laboratory specimen of an arrested culture.' It takes everyone rather too long to work out that the Organians are another super-powerful race of energy aliens who have evolved beyond the need for physical bodies. 'To us, violence is unthinkable,' they say, with the slightly smug wisdom of millennia. Not only do they stop Kirk

---

* Solow later asked NBC's Herb Schlosser, who would have been party to the decision, what he thought of this theory. Very little, it seems. 'Star Trek was renewed because it was good and it was different. And we were proud to have it on NBC.'

and Kor fighting, they impose a galaxy-wide peace between the Federation and the Klingons.

'Well, Commander,' says Kirk, 'I guess that takes care of the war. Obviously the Organians aren't going to let us fight.'

'A shame, Captain,' says Kor. 'It would have been glorious.'

This is an odd episode, and given how important the Klingons will become, it's difficult to watch it again without hindsight getting in the way. In a throwaway comment, the lead Organian tells Kirk, 'In the future, you and the Klingons will become fast friends. You will work together.' Later writers would work together to make sure that this came true. It was John Colicos himself who came up with the Klingons' dark-skinned, moustached look: he said he had Genghis Khan in mind. Dorothy Fontana believed that the Klingons became the show's regular adversaries because they didn't need expensive make-up, unlike the Romulans, who she thought had more potential. At this stage, of course, the Klingons had no forehead ridges, for reasons that have never been adequately explained. Did they have them surgically removed to make them more streamlined? It doesn't seem likely, but we will never know for sure.

Most curiously, 'Errand of Mercy' is a clear rehash of Coon's previous script 'Arena': two warlike races prevented from fighting by a third, super-powerful race.

'I should say the Organians are as far above us on the evolutionary scale as we are above the amoeba,' says Spock.

Unlike the Klingons, the Organians will not become *Star Trek* regulars, because once you have established their boundless superiority, there's little else you can do with them. The Organian Peace Treaty, though, will resound down the ages. And as always with a Coon script, the banter more than makes up for any structural deficiencies.

'What would you say the odds are on our getting out of here?' says Kirk.

'Difficult to be precise, Captain,' says Spock. 'I should say approximately 7824.7 to one.'

And so we arrive at the grand centrepiece of the *Star Trek* legend, the episode that wins polls for best episode so regularly and often, there's hardly any point holding them. 'The City on the Edge of Forever' (1.28) is two stories in one, really: the actual episode, and the way the episode came together. In orbit around an unknown planet, the *Enterprise* notes severe fluctuations in the space-time continuum, and rides them like a plane flying through turbulence. Sulu's console explodes and the doughty helmsman is mildly injured. Enter Dr McCoy with a hypo-spray full of cordrazine, a powerful stimulant. A drop or two is enough to revive Sulu, but more turbulence strikes and Bones accidentally injects the rest of it into his own stomach. 'Killers! Assassins!' he raves, and runs off the bridge. The drug has sent him round the bend, and he beams down to the planet to escape all the people he thinks are trying to kill him.

And he beams, of course, straight to the source of those time ripples. Kirk, Spock, Scotty and Uhura and a couple of very nervous redshirts follow him down. They find a huge, electronic, interplanetary doughnut, which Spock says is 'ten thousand centuries old'.

'What is it?' asks Kirk, not unreasonably.

The doughnut awakes.

'A question. Since before your sun burned hot in space and before your race was born, I have awaited a question.'

The doughnut calls itself the Guardian of Forever, and offers the general public the chance to revisit their planet's past. Ancient film footage from Paramount's vaults can now be seen through the hole in the doughnut. Kirk is intrigued. 'Strangely compelling, isn't it? To step through there and lose oneself in another world.'

At which point we have almost forgotten about poor Dr McCoy, but suddenly there he is, as mad as a conclave of hatters. He leaps into the centre of the Guardian and vanishes.

'He has passed into . . . what was,' explains the Guardian.

Uhura realises she has lost contact with the *Enterprise*, mainly because it is no longer there. Kirk realises that Bones has gone back in time and changed history. The landing party are stranded in a tiny time bubble, with no past and no future. Kirk and Spock must follow their demented medic chum back into the past and change history back to the way it was going to be.

They land in New York in 1930, about a week before Bones is due to arrive. Spock finds the first of many convenient beanie hats, to hide the ears. Fortunately he also has his tricorder, on which he recorded Bones's leap into the past. Now he must build a computer 'using stone knives and bearskins' to access the tricorder's findings. Meanwhile, at the soup kitchen where our boys take their three meals a day, Kirk meets Edith Keeler, played by Joan Collins. She is a woman out of time, a pacifist, a dreamer, with a vision of a shiny, benevolent future not much like our own. She and Kirk fall in love: slowly, rather chastely, very affectingly. Spock establishes from his tricorder that McCoy will save Edith Keeler's life in a traffic accident. She will go on to found a pacifist movement, which will be so success-ful that the United States will delay its entry into the Second World War, and Nazi Germany will take over the world. Only if Edith Keeler dies will the familiar timeline be re-established.

If television drama is usually about jeopardy, well, none plays for higher stakes than this. Kirk, the twenty-third cen-tury's most accomplished crumpeteer, has actually fallen for someone and now he has to see her flattened by a truck. Indeed, it is he who must hold back McCoy from rescuing her.

'You deliberately stopped me, Jim! I could have saved her! Do you know what you just did?'

'He knows, Doctor. He knows,' says Spock.

I am not going to upset any applecarts, or be controversial for the sake of it. 'The City on the Edge of Forever' is a glorious forty-eight minutes of television. Kirk meets his soulmate and loses her in a single reel. Edith Keeler's optimism and idealism are the show's philosophy in capsule form, and her clarity of perception would be unusual in any era. She knows at once that Kirk and Spock are not what they pretend to be.

'Where would you estimate we belong, Miss Keeler?' asks Spock.

'You?' says Edith. 'At his side, as if you've always been there and always will.'

The episode ends with, for *Star Trek*, uncharacteristic bathos. Edith dies, the correct timeline is restored, and Kirk, Spock and McCoy leap back through the portal into the present. The Guardian of Forever offers them another trip into the past. Kirk doesn't want to know. 'Let's get the hell out of here,' he says. And the credits roll.

(The network strongly objected to his line. 'Hell' was not used as an expletive in 1960s primetime television, only as a word to describe where the Devil lived.)

The story of the making of 'The City on the Edge of Forever' is nearly as intriguing as the episode itself. Harlan Ellison's script was one of the first to be commissioned (in March 1966), and the last but one of the first season to be produced. Of his initial story outline, Bob Justman wrote in a memo, 'Don't ever tell Harlan . . . but this outline is beautifully written. The fact that it may have become rather difficult to achieve the effects that he has written into the story is another matter . . . The time vortex is described as a shimmering pillar of light set between grey-silver rocks. It would be nice if we could find a cheaper time vortex.'

History would record that there were two problems with Ellison's script: it was ruinously expensive and it wasn't *Star Trek* enough. For instance, it isn't McCoy who goes through the time portal, but a Lieutenant Beckwith, a nasty piece of work who has been dealing in a weird hallucinogenic drug called the Jewels of Sound. After a fellow officer-cum-addict threatens to shop him, Beckwith murders him and flees to the surface. Roddenberry wasn't having drug-dealing on the *Enterprise*, or indeed an out-and-out villain among the ship's officers.

But as Dorothy Fontana would write many years later, 'Harlan's script was brilliant. Always a master of words, his language conjured the images of the desolate planet "as if some cosmic god had flicked an ash and it had grown into a world".' The Guardians of Forever, plural, aren't a giant stone patisserie but unimaginably old nine-foot men in very long robes, who speak wonderful, gnomic dialogue that betokens great wisdom.

'This place is dead, empty,' says Spock. 'Why do you stay?'

'Only on this world do the million pulse-flows of time and space merge,' says one of the Guardians. 'Only here do the flux lines of forever meet.'

'Have you seen another man, dressed as we are?' says Spock.

'What we see has already been, or is yet to be. No. No other like you.'

'There are legends in space,' says Kirk. 'About you.'

'You are the first visitors we have had for twice two hundred thousand years.'

What to do? It's beautiful, but we must take it on trust from Justman and Co that it was also a bank-breaker. Rewrites were deemed necessary. As Fontana remembers, Gene Coon had the first crack at it. He removed Beckwith and made Dr McCoy the catalyst. In Ellison's original, Kirk and Edith Keeler only met in act three; Coon gave them an extra ten minutes or so of screen time together. Ellison hated the rewrite, and expressed his displeasure in robust terms. This was known behaviour. As Fontana says, Ellison's 'temper burned at such a low firing point and with such high explosivity that it devastated buildings for ten square miles around ground zero when it went off.' And she was a friend of his.

Other drafts followed, from Ellison, Coon again, and Fontana, who introduced cordrazine to send McCoy temporarily round the bend. 'I tried to build the relationship of love between Edith and Kirk gently and meaningfully so her death would be the most wrenching personal moment Kirk would ever know. And I inserted the running joke of Spock's tricorder, which grew larger and more complicated with mechanical additions each time it was seen.' Ellison 'liked this draft a little better, but not much. He thought the characterisation and dialogue showed sensitivity, but it wasn't his script . . . You will notice that every writer who worked on the rewrite was trying very hard to please Harlan, allowing him to read each draft and comment on it. That doesn't happen now – on any show.'

Roddenberry himself wrote the shooting script, dated 1 February 1967. Only two lines from Ellison's original draft survived, both spoken by the Guardian of Forever. On 3 February, the first day of filming, a letter from Ellison's agent arrived, saying he wanted his name taken off the script and replaced by the pseudonym 'Cordwainer Bird'. This would tell the science fiction community that Star Trek could not be trusted, that it was just like any other show, promising much, delivering little. Roddenberry tried soft-soaping Ellison, and when that didn't work, says Ellison, there came an 'absolute threat' to stop him ever working in Hollywood again. He gave in, and 'Cordwainer Bird' reverted to 'Harlan Ellison'.

Anyone else would have retired beaten, licked wounds, moved on. Instead, Ellison submitted his original script to the Writers Guild of America for its annual awards. These are awards decided only by writers, who don't see the film, they just read the script, without knowing who has written it. Even so, Desilu bought a table for the event and everyone donned their dinner jackets. 'The award for the most outstanding script for a dramatic television series is "The City on the Edge of Forever", story and teleplay by Harlan Ellison.' The writer went up to say a few words and, without mentioning anyone by name, berated the studio 'suits' for 'interfering with the writing process'. He ended his speech by shaking his script high above his head and crying, 'Remember, never let THEM rewrite you!'*

Roddenberry would get his own back, and then some. At conventions in the 1970s and 1980s, he would stand up and tell audiences that he personally had had to rewrite Ellison's script for 'The City on the Edge of Forever' because he had Scotty dealing drugs. He even said this in interviews: a blatant untruth, and a powerful one, because many people came to believe it.

Finally, in 1995, Ellison could bear it no longer, and published a book called *The City on the Edge of Forever*, which incorporated his original script, some of the changes he had made in later versions, a handful of supportive afterwords from the likes of Leonard Nimoy and DeForest Kelley,† and a coruscating, invective-packed thirty-thousand-word introductory essay ripping into Roddenberry and his people. It's a wonderful read, marinated in nearly thirty years of rage, and challenges once again Roddenberry's self-aggrandising need to be recognised, admired and possibly even worshipped as *Star Trek*'s sole creator. 'That was Gene. Couldn't write for sour owl poop, but strutted around for the benefit of the gullible Trekkie Nation, explaining how every failure was someone else's fault, and every success was due to his fecund imagination, vast literary ability and CEO-level organisational skills.'

---

* Solow says he looked at the two knives in front of him on the table, the dinner knife and the butter knife, and wondered which he would use to kill Harlan. He chose the butter knife: 'it was sort of dull and would cause more pain'.

† Dorothy Fontana's quotes in this section are taken from her own afterword in this book.

As Fontana says, 'Harlan had the last word. He always does.'

A few last random thoughts on the Ellison script. The dialogue is wonderful: rich, thoughtful, even poetic. But Spock's lines don't sound a lot like Spock. Ellison has captured Kirk's character perfectly but the Vulcan eludes him. Uhura, who gets the most embarrassing line in the final version ('Captain, I'm frightened'), is nowhere to be seen in the original, but Yeoman Rand is there, and she has to do some technical stuff with the transporter that she is obviously perfectly capable of. Remember any other woman doing anything like this in the original series? Nor can I.

'Operation – Annihilate!' (1.29) rounded off the first season with an exclamation mark and a splendidly rubbery alien menace. On the planet Deneva, human colonists are being driven mad by these gelatinous horrors, which sting them in the back and take over their central nervous systems. Kirk's brother Sam, who looks uncannily like Shatner with a false moustache, lives on the planet with his family, but by the time the *Enterprise* arrives, Sam is dead and his wife will die soon after. In the previous episode the captain lost the love of his life; now he mourns most of his extended family. It has not been a great couple of weeks.

Downstairs in a basement, the landing party find a few alien wobblers, which pulsate and fly through the air like frisbees. 'It is not life as we know or understand it,' says Spock, before one of them infects him. The pain, it seems, is unbearable, and that's what has driven the colonists mad. Fortunately Spock's extraordinary powers of mental control enable him to resist the rubbery fronds coursing through his bloodstream. After a lab experiment or two, we discover that they can be killed by intense light. Spock undergoes the treatment.

'I am free of it and the pain. And I am also quite blind. An equitable trade, Doctor, thank you.'

Too late, Bones establishes that the evil blancmanges are

specifically vulnerable to ultraviolet light, which is why they hide in basements. Vast sunlamps are installed in orbit and the aliens quietly sizzle to death. Finally, Spock returns to the bridge, and he can see! He had neglected to mention that Vulcans have an inner eyelid that protects their eyes from the ferocity of their sun. His sight is so fully restored, he won't even need to wear glasses.

'My first sight was the face of Dr McCoy bending over me.'

''Tis a pity your brief blindness did not increase your appreciation for beauty,' says McCoy.

And that's it for the year. Another world saved, another menace extinguished, another slightly creaky subplot resolved a little too quickly. But what wonders we have seen along the way. In its first twenty-nine episodes *Star Trek* achieved a certainty of tone and characterisation, even when dealing with aliens that looked like piles of fake vomit. And they looked like piles of fake vomit because that's what they were, bought from novelty shops and slightly modified to become vicious neural parasites. To know this and still find them scary: that is suspension of disbelief.

CHAPTER 5

LIVE LONG AND PROSPER

Star Trek wasn't just about story, characters and ideas. The whole texture of the show was something to delight in. Here was a world that, for all its wobbly sets and shiny studio floors, had been made with a fine eye for detail. In truth there were many fine eyes, belonging to production designers, set decorators, costumiers and propmasters, as well as to directors, lighting cameramen and, at the centre of it all, associate producer Bob Justman, somehow making sure it all happened on schedule and only slightly over budget. There were also fine ears, for music, sound effects and those weird floaty ambient sounds you heard on strange new planets, even when they had the same boulders as last week's planet.

In the early 1990s, I was browsing in a record shop somewhere in central London, when there were such things as record shops and so many that you couldn't hope to browse through them all, when I found a CD entitled *Star Trek Sound Effects*. Shocked at how much it cost – somewhere north of fifteen pounds, as I remember – I paused for several femtoseconds before taking it to the till. I have it still and although it would be an exaggeration to say that I play it often, I know it is there. *Star Trek Sound Effects* – original series only – has sixty-nine tracks, including 'Transporter Energize' (seven seconds long), 'Dematerialization' (twenty-five seconds), 'Materialization' (twenty-eight seconds), 'Buttons on Bridge' (sixteen seconds), 'Photon Torpedo (3 Blasts)' (twenty seconds), 'Phasers Striking Hull' (ten seconds), 'Sickbay Scanner' (twenty-nine seconds), 'Shuttlecraft Interior' (thirty-two seconds), 'Warp Drive Acceleration & Deceleration' (forty-five seconds) and the unimaginably brilliant 'Warp Drive Malfunctioning' (thirty-six seconds). If my house were burning down and I had saved my family and the cat, this would be the next thing I went back to retrieve.

Sound effects are designed to enhance the action, not to dominate it, but we know these sound effects so well that hearing them separately conjures up all the pictures we would ever need in that greatest of picturehouses, the one inside our heads. For Proust it was a madeleine biscuit that prompted an unstoppable surge of reminiscence. For me, it's the swish! swish! of *Enterprise* doors opening and closing, which is actually the sound of an airgun played in reverse. Phaser fire is the sound of three electric guitars and a harp, again played in reverse.

Here are a few more madeleines. Nearly a whole packetful, in fact.

For such a compact vessel, the *Enterprise* has remarkably wide corridors. This was because there had to be room for the huge, unwieldy cameras of the time, and their many cables, to roll up and down them.

A tricorder – so-called because it had three functions, as sensor, recorder and computer – only had a tiny little TV screen when you looked closely at it, and three minute blue knobs to twiddle. Underneath them were what looked like two little drawers, with handles. And indeed, they were drawers. What did Spock keep in them? A spare pair of socks, maybe? (A plastic tricorder toy, made and sold in the 1970s, featured a cassette recorder instead of the drawers. Much more useful.)

When anyone fired a phaser, they had to keep their hand absolutely still, so that the phaser effect could be added in post-production. And yet, as the cast discovered, it's hard to keep your hand still for any length of time. And there was rarely time to reshoot. That's why there are any number of slightly wobbly phasers in *Star Trek* issuing absolutely straight unwobbly lines of phaser fire.

Some props, like tricorders and phasers, were specially designed and constructed. Others just turned up. For 'The Man Trap', propmaster Irving Feinberg was instructed to go out and buy as many futuristic salt cellars as he could find. (Kirk was going to use them as bait for the salt vampire.) The ones he found were Swedish, chrome-plated and rather oddly shaped. Roddenberry rejected them because they didn't look enough like salt cellars. But Feinberg found another use for them, as Dr McCoy's medical instruments. They appear throughout the series. We think Bones is treating his patients, whereas in reality he is just adding seasoning for lunch.

Art director 'Matt' Jefferies was the main man responsible for the look of *Star Trek*, and the Jefferies tube, which Scotty climbs up to effect repairs in times of great peril, was named after him. Occasionally someone would open a wall panel, and inside would be various wires, pipes, circuits and conduits, one or two of which might be marked 'GNDN'. These letters stood for 'Goes Nowhere, Does Nothing'.

One more initialism: in scripts for the series there were occasional references to the 'FSNP'. This stood for 'Famous Spock Nerve Pinch'.

No official rules were ever formulated for three-dimensional chess, although that didn't stop some fans from making up their own. Spock plays the game in six episodes, and in two of them Kirk beats him. So much for Vulcan logic, as Bones might say.

How did Kirk, Spock and Co communicate with different alien species every week? This was one of Roddenberry's smartest tricks: the universal translator. As Justman said, 'You couldn't see it, you couldn't hear it, but you could depend on it. And you could also forget about it, which is what we did soon after it was introduced.'

(Unlike the communicators. Kirk always taps his when it doesn't work: a very twentieth-century response to malfunctioning technology.)

In their splendid book *Star Trek 365*, Paula M. Block and Terry J. Erdmann ask an important question: 'Have you ever wondered why the *Enterprise* almost always flies from left to right across your TV screen?' Well, no, actually, but now you come to mention it . . .

The explanation is almost comically straightforward. After the second pilot was made, the 11-foot model of the *Enterprise* had a refit, and more running lights were added. But to make this work, the wires for the new lights had to be fed through holes drilled in the other side of the model, which made the other side unsuitable for filming thereafter. So the *Enterprise* always orbited a planet in an anti-clockwise direction. (Except in the parallel universe episode 'Mirror, Mirror', when old, pre-refit footage was used.) What no one could have guessed was how far-reaching this decision would be. In almost all space fiction made since, spacecraft have orbited planets in an anti-clockwise direction. My guess is that they do this because if they didn't, it would somehow look 'wrong'. And that's because the *Enterprise* didn't do it.

When the *Enterprise* flies across the screen in the main titles, it does so to the sound of a huge 'whoosh!', even though we know there's no sound in space. When this sequence was being put together, the sound editors had real problems finding a satisfying whoosh sound. Nothing they tried sounded right. Step forward Alexander Courage, composer of the show's theme tune. He picked up a microphone and made a 'whoosh!' sound into it. Everyone decided it sounded perfect, so that's what they used.

One of Matt Jefferies's signature designs was the shape of the doors. On the *Enterprise* they tended to be rectangular, or what one might call 'door-shaped'. On strange new worlds, by contrast, they were trapezoidal, or triangular, or even hexagonal. Trapezoidal archways were his thing as well. Doors never opened in the old-fashioned way. They slid up or sideways. They didn't slide down, Justman informs us, because that would mean digging a hole in the floor.

On the main bridge set, when actors were looking at the screen, they weren't actually looking at the screen, because that's where the cameras and crew were. To bring in the screen and then shoot from the captain's chair, as it were, took ages and cost money, so one day Bob Justman took some stock shots from the captain's chair viewpoint, with Sulu turning round and looking worried. These could be slotted in whenever, and my god, were they. Sulu turned around looking worried about twice an episode. When Walter Koenig joined the series as Chekov, Justman filmed similar shots with him turning round looking worried, and then some shots of both of them turning round and looking worried. Were your helmsman and navigator supposed to look worried so much of the time? Shouldn't they just get on with the job?

The bridge, of course, was regularly populated by extras, sitting at consoles, walking around importantly, bringing reports for Kirk to sign. But one in particular stood out, a tall, slender, rather bulbous-headed individual who often sat at the navigator's station and never said anything, never showed any reaction, never cracked a smile. In all, William R. 'Billy' Blackburn appeared in sixty-one of the seventy-nine episodes, often as this mute officer (who was later given the name 'Lieutenant Hadley'), but also in other roles. He was the white rabbit in 'Shore Leave', he was a NASA technician in 'Assignment: Earth', an Organian villager in 'Errand of Mercy' and an android in 'I, Mudd'. You always noticed him because, unlike most extras, he was curiously noticeable. Blackburn himself has said that he did speak one or two lines as Hadley, but they were always cut. After *Star Trek* he became a costumier, and ended up working on *T. J. Hooker*, William Shatner's 1970s cop show. According to Blackburn, Shatner always greeted him as 'Billy!' on set, and couldn't understand why he had forsaken acting for costuming. Probably because it allowed him to speak.

For season two there were two notable innovations. DeForest Kelley's name now appeared in the opening credits after Shatner's and Nimoy's, as if to affirm that the focus of storylines would henceforth be on these three characters, with the others picking up the scraps.* And there was a new young navigator on the bridge, Ensign Pavel Chekov, played by Walter Koenig in an unfortunate Beatles wig. The story goes – and it would often be repeated by Roddenberry over the years – that the Soviet newspaper *Pravda* had published an editorial criticising the 'typically capitalistic' mindset behind *Star Trek*. (What,

---

* Quick, easy way of identifying whether an episode comes from the first, second or third season. First season, big yellow writing, no DeForest Kelley in credits. Second season, animated 'Created by Gene Roddenberry' credit tucks under 'Star Trek' logo, DeForest Kelley joins credits. Third season, same as second, except that big yellow writing has become big blue writing.

in a world that saw no need for money, where capitalism had essentially been abolished?) *Pravda*'s real beef, though, was that there wasn't a Russian officer aboard the *Enterprise*. Oriental, yes. Black African, yes. But not a single person anywhere to be seen who couldn't quite pronounce the word 'vessel'. So Roddenberry hired Koenig and gave him the hair in order to attract a younger audience to the show.

Except that it didn't quite happen like that. Chekov came into existence because of the Monkees. Roddenberry saw that the lovable and wacky mop-topped quartet were wildly popular among the young, and Koenig was chosen primarily for his resemblance to the Monkees' Davy Jones. (He was thirty, seven months older than George Takei, and beginning to go bald, but the baby face carried him through.) The wig was a short-term measure until he could grow out what remained of his own hair (into a most un-Monkee-like combover). Then *Pravda* published their editorial, Roddenberry saw an opportunity, and the new character became Russian. Koenig was initially cast as a 'recurring' cast member rather than a regular, on a show-by-show basis. George Takei had won a role on the John Wayne film *The Green Berets* and was eventually away from *Star Trek* for ten weeks. Lines, scenes, whole subplots that would have been given to Sulu ended up with Chekov. Takei admitted in his memoir that he was jealous. 'All right, I'll admit it – I hated him! Sight unseen, I churned with venom for this Walter Koenig!' But the two quickly became friends, and when George Takei married his long-term partner in 2008, Walter Koenig was his best man.*

'Catspaw' (2.7) was Chekov's first appearance, although the episode was specifically made for Halloween and held over until then.

---

* 'I never felt *Star Trek* was silly,' said Koenig years later. 'I felt I was silly. Swallows kept trying to nest in the wig they gave me.' Takei has described him as 'a man damned by his sensitivity and his intelligence'.

'If we weren't missing two officers and a third one dead I'd say someone was playing an elaborate trick or treat on us,' says Kirk.

'Trick or treat, Captain?' says Spock.

'Yes, Mr Spock. You'd be a natural,' says Kirk.

But it's poor stuff. Super-powerful, excessively chatty aliens kidnap Starfleet officers and chain them up in dungeons. At the end we see that the aliens are in fact very tiny insect-like puppets that keel over and die with a pitiful squeak. As does the episode.

Season two is notable for its mix of superb and really quite abysmal shows: at times it must have seemed as though sublime and ridiculous were alternating, week by week. In 'Metamorphosis' (2.9), we find Zefram Cochrane, the inventor of the warp drive, who has been missing for 150 years, but is a young man, living alone on an isolated asteroid with a gaseous entity he calls 'the Companion'. Gene Coon wrote this clever little tale, which we come to realise is a love story: a proper one, and a science-fiction one too. But after that comes 'Friday's Child' (2.11), in which the Klingons and the Federation again bicker over a strategically significant planet. The locals live near the Vasquez Rocks and wear strange pastel headdresses, while a young woman has a baby she names after Dr McCoy. Some high-quality chat barely masks the poverty of the basic idea. Hardware enthusiasts should note that this episode sees the debut of Sulu's personal scanner, emerging and unfurling from within his helm console at the touch of a button. James Blish, in his *Star Trek* novelisations, referred to this piece of kit as a 'gooseneck viewer'.*

---

* This final snippet of information, as so much in this book, was gleaned from the excellent and staggeringly comprehensive *Star Trek* website Memory Alpha, which can tell you everything you want to know about the show and so much more. For instance, this is the only episode in which Uhura and Sulu call the Chief Engineer by his nickname 'Scotty'. I like knowing that fact, although I wouldn't want to have been the one to watch all seventy-nine episodes to check it.

In 'Who Mourns for Adonais?' (2.2), the *Enterprise* meets an all-powerful alien who claims to be the Greek god Apollo. Is he? Do we care? There have already been too many episodes like this, and we have barely started. Meanwhile, Mr Scott is mooning over a comely young female officer like a lovesick teenager, while the comely young female officer develops a *tendresse* for Apollo, as he is (i) a Greek god, and (ii) not a middle-aged Scottish engineer with a smile like a crocodile. In an early draft of the script, Apollo made Lieutenant Comely pregnant, which would have been fun. But it was dropped because it would have been fun.*

The day after they finished that, they started shooting Theodore Sturgeon's 'Amok Time' (2.1): from one star to five in a single bound. Spock is behaving strangely, even for Spock. He is irritable to the point of fury, and when Christine Chapel makes him a bowl of plomeek soup – his favourite – he flings it into the corridor.

'It is undignified for a woman to play servant to a man who is not hers,' he tells Kirk and McCoy.

Spock asks that he be given a leave of absence to return to Vulcan, and McCoy, after examining him, confirms that if he doesn't get back home in eight days, these adrenal surges will kill him. For Spock is undergoing *pon farr*, the Vulcan biological mating urge, which strikes every seven years and requires a salmon-like return home for some green-blooded procreation.

'How do Vulcans choose their mates?' asks Spock. 'Haven't you wondered?'

'I guess the rest of us assume that it's done . . . quite logically,' says Kirk.

'No,' says Spock. 'It is not.'

The rather delicious irony in all this is that sex, which

---

* There's never any accounting for taste. This is Jason Alexander of *Seinfeld*'s all-time favourite episode. He has described it as 'thought-provoking, beautiful and very sad'.

could be much implied on US television in the 1960s but never alluded to specifically, let alone shown, is equally unmentionable in Vulcan society. For such a logical race to lose control of this primal instinct is a source of shame to them. So they dress the whole thing up in ritual which, to the outsider, looks very much like a wedding. Spock is betrothed to T'Pring, and the joining ceremony (the *koon-ut-kal-if-fee*) must take place before his head explodes. Presiding over it is T'Pau, a splendid and eminent old boot who is the only person ever to turn down a seat on the Federation Council.

'He never told us his family was *this* important,' says Kirk.

But T'Pring, who has been Spock's intended since they were both seven, no longer wants him. She favours Stonn, who doesn't gallivant across the galaxy but stays at home, brooding handsomely. T'Pring invokes the *kal-if-fee*, her right to have Spock fight for her. But as her champion she selects not Stonn, whom she is saving for later, but Kirk. Only after the captain accepts the challenge does he learn that it's a fight to the death.

The fight begins and although Spock is weaker than usual, he is stronger than his captain, who is struggling with Vulcan's heat and thin atmosphere. McCoy asks T'Pau if he can inject Kirk with a tri-ox compound to compensate.

'Proceed,' says T'Pau in her vaguely Germanic accent.

'Now be careful,' says McCoy to Kirk as he gives him the shot.

'Sound medical advice,' says Kirk.[*]

Spock then strangles Kirk until he is dead. The shock of this instantly obliterates the madness of the *pon farr*. Spock frees T'Pring from any obligation to him, and prepares to beam back up to the *Enterprise*, expecting to face a court martial for murder.

---

[*] Another wonderful, lunatic fact from the Memory Alpha website. Celia Lovsky, who played T'Pau, was apparently one of only eleven credited guest stars in *Star Trek* who were born in the nineteenth century. She died in 1979, aged eighty-two.

'Live long and prosper,' says T'Pau.

'I shall do neither,' says Spock. 'I have killed my captain and my friend.'

He hasn't, of course. On returning to the ship he sees that McCoy has pulled a fast one with that injection and that Kirk is very much alive. 'Captain! Jim!' he cries, grinning from ear to ear. It's a lovely moment in an episode that never puts a foot wrong. 'Excellent script,' said Leonard Nimoy many years later. 'Very poetic, very dramatic, intense and important, I felt immediately, for Spock and Vulcans . . . It was a very, very exciting episode to shoot and perform.'

'Amok Time' showed us the planet Vulcan for the first time, and the first Vulcans other than Spock. It also introduced the phrase 'Live long and prosper' and what became known as the Vulcan salute. This latter wasn't in Sturgeon's script (or any of the many rewrites): Leonard Nimoy came up with it on the day. He remembered something he had seen as a young boy in synagogue, at a high holy day service. Instructed to cover his eyes during the delivery of the sacred blessing, the naughty young science officer had peeked, and seen the rabbi raise both hands, with a gap between the third and fourth finger of each, to form the Hebrew letter 'shin', which stands for 'Shaddai', or 'Almighty'. Years later he adapted this for his own purposes, and ours. I practised the gesture assiduously as a small boy and can now do it with ease. Celia Lovsky, playing T'Pau, couldn't do it naturally, so she had to use her other hand to put the fingers in the right pattern out of shot, and then raise her hand at the right moment.

'The Doomsday Machine' (2.6) introduces *Star Trek*'s first Trail of Unspeakable Destruction. The *Enterprise* arrives at system L-370 and discovers that all seven planets have been destroyed. Up the road, system L-374 has lost all but its two innermost planets. Floating amongst the rubble is the USS

Constellation, under the command of Commodore Matt Decker. Kirk, Scotty and McCoy beam over to find out what happened. There's no one there at all, except Decker himself, slumped over a desk. They had encountered what he calls a 'planet killer . . . miles long, with a maw that could swallow a dozen starships'. It carves up planets and then uses them to refuel. There's a great, chilling moment in amongst all this exposition, that you never quite forget.

'Matt, where's your crew?' asks Kirk.

'On the third planet,' says Decker.

'There is no third planet,' says Kirk.

A beat, as the truth sinks in.

'Don't you think I know that?' cries Decker. 'There was, but not any more!'

He had beamed them all down for safety, and then watched as the planet killer consumed them as a tasty snack.

We now see the machine itself, and maybe more important, we hear the threatening, doomy music that comes with it. If it continues on its present course, says Spock, it will pass through the most populated part of the galaxy. Indigestion is its manifest destiny. Can the *Enterprise* stop it? The *Constellation* tried, and failed. The hull of the doomsday machine consists of solid neutronium, a fact that has stuck in my mind for forty-six years, while everything I learned at school has dissipated into shadow and dust.

Decker, who is the only sweaty and unshaven starship commander in Starfleet history, now provides a small sub-plot by beaming over to the *Enterprise* and, in Kirk's absence, taking command in order to fight the monster some more. After some argy-bargy, Spock relieves him, and the poor man is compelled by his inner demons to take a shuttlecraft and fly it straight at the planet killer, 'right down its throat'. When the shuttlecraft blows, Sulu notices a very slight drop in the planet killer's power emanations. Might an exploding starship damage it more? Happily, they have a spare one to hand. Kirk, still stuck on the *Constellation* by random transporter problems, must pilot the old crate into the machine's interior and then beam the hell out of there. We know he will do it, but however many times we see the episode, it remains a nail-biter.

William Windom played Matt Decker as though he was in a cartoon, he said later, and only noticed the *Moby-Dick* parallels when he read about them in a magazine. Norman Spinrad, the esteemed SF author who wrote this (at the age of twenty-seven), had been told that Robert Ryan would be available, but in the event he wasn't. Windom is less tragic than Ryan might have been, but probably more sympathetic. He underrates his own performance. Spinrad was unimpressed with the model used for the planet killer, which he imagined would be bristling with weapons. Instead, the props department made something that, to Spinrad, 'looked like a windsock dipped in cement'. This is because it *was* a windsock dipped in cement. It still looks primal and unstoppable. You really can believe that an ancient civilisation built this as a doomsday machine, and was itself destroyed by it.*

'Wolf in the Fold' (2.14) has Scotty accused of a number of Jack the Ripper-style murders, mainly because whenever a body is found, he seems to be in the vicinity holding an enormous knife covered with blood. It isn't him, of course: it's a mild-mannered administrator whose body has been hijacked by an evil fear-eating alien spirit. Robert Bloch's third and final script for the show was pushed back in transmission order until mid-season, possibly because it didn't quite work. John Fiedler, who played the mild-mannered-administrator-cum-mass-murderer, was probably best known for providing the voice of

---

* No accounting for taste, part 2. This was James Doohan's favourite episode in the series, and Dorothy Fontana's least favourite. What, worse than 'Spock's Brain'?

Piglet in Disney's Winnie-the-Pooh animations. But he said he liked playing Jack the Ripper more.

'The Changeling' (2.3), by contrast, was shifted up the transmission order because it did work. Another planet full of people has been found bereft of life, and the culprit turns out to be a little floaty machine called Nomad, which has been whizzing around the galaxy sterilising the populations of planets that do not meet its rather demanding standards of perfection. It would have 'sterilised' the *Enterprise*, only it believes Captain Kirk to be its creator. So it beams aboard the ship and several amusing conversations are had.

'This is one of your units, creator?' says Nomad, of McCoy.

'Yes, he is,' says Kirk.

'It functions irrationally,' says Nomad.

It prefers Spock.

'This unit is different. It is well-ordered.'

As careless in its way as Charlie X, the machine kills Scotty and then brings him back to life, and wipes Uhura's mind. That can't be reversed, but with some remedial education she will be opening hailing frequencies again by next week. Spock tries mind-melding with Nomad, and establishes that the machine started out as an Earth probe sent out to make contact with extraterrestrial life. Damaged in a meteor shower, it met and combined forces with an alien probe whose mission was to collect and sterilise soil samples. They added two and two, and got πr^2. Nomad has mixed up Kirk with its actual creator Jackson Roykirk, long dead. It's the work of a moment for our silver-tongued leader to talk this computer into self-destructing, and all the civilisations it would have gone on to obliterate are thus saved. After 'The Doomsday Machine', it has been an excellent few weeks for preventing billions of unnecessary deaths.

'The Apple' (2.5) is horrendous. In another false paradise, soppy orange child-aliens in huge nappies are controlled by the mysterious Vaal, which might be 'vile' spoken in a South African accent. 'What is love?' asks a tribal elder. 'What are children?' a girl asks, later. Work out the answer to the first, and the answer to the second should become clear.

This is the episode in which the Redshirt Phenomenon really gains traction. Four security bozos beam down to planet Gamma Trianguli VI with the landing party, and not one of them makes it back alive. Hendorff is killed by a poisoned dart, Kaplan is struck by lightning and vaporised, Mallory steps on an exploding rock, and Marple is hit on the head. If you're hit on the head and you're wearing a different-coloured shirt, you get a headache. A red shirt, and it's curtains.*

But why such inconsistency in the scripts? 'Amok Time' and 'The Doomsday Machine' (*pace* Dorothy) are timeless classics; 'The Apple' and 'Who Mourns for Adonais?' (*pace* Jason) are dreary and melodramatic. 'The Apple' is the third or fourth phoney paradise we have encountered, and the fourth or fifth society run by a giant computer. Waving aside the Prime Directive in that airy way of his, Kirk doesn't even talk to the computer in this one: he just gets Scotty to fire full phasers at it from orbit. Vaal glows for a while, then a puff of smoke comes out of its entry portal and it is no more. Everything about the episode is slightly off-kilter: the characterisations, the dialogue, the hokey *Enterprise*-in-jeopardy subplot, the reasons anyone actually does anything. It's painful to watch.

This should have been *Star Trek*'s era of greatest achievement, and occasionally it was. The characters were well set and, though budgets had been cut, you wouldn't necessarily

---

* Someone has done a tally. Over the three years of the series, fifty-nine crew members were killed on-screen. Of these, six wore gold shirts, five wore blue, four wore engineering smocks and the remaining forty-three wore red. That's 79 per cent of all crew deaths. You'd be frightened to get up in the morning.

have known it from what you saw on the screen. Crucially, the show was also now a known quantity, so the two Genes, though still rewriting frantically, were able to take many more pitches from outside writers. Yes, we'll have that; no, go away and try again. Yes, no, yes, no. Add Bob Justman and Dorothy Fontana and, in effect, you have *Star Trek*'s dream team in charge. And still they turned out rubbish like 'The Apple', which suggests that the demands on them all were simply too great.

Gene L. Coon, in particular, was showing signs of burn-out. Halfway through season two he would leave the series, and for years afterwards rumours would abound that he and Roddenberry had had some terrible falling-out, over the names of shuttlecraft, maybe, or the colour of a planet's sky. But there's no evidence of this. The two Genes would remain friends – if rather competitive friends at the poker table – until Coon's death of lung cancer in 1973. His widow believed that he was already ill in 1967. Coon smoked as though there was no tomorrow. Eventually he was proved right.*

But what's this? 'Mirror, Mirror' (2.4) was another startlingly good show. An ion storm creates a trans-port malfunction, and Kirk, Bones, Scotty and Uhura are beamed into a parallel universe, where there is no Federation, but instead an evil empire. Mirror Spock has a villainous goatee beard, everyone does Nazi-like salutes and people are routinely tortured, if not killed, for the tiniest infraction of the rules. Normal Kirk, who finds himself in charge of this madhouse, shows some modest level of mercy, and so Mirror Chekov tries to have him assassinated in a turbolift.

---

* On 3 July 1973, Coon walked into Bob Justman's office with an oxygen cylinder and a mask. 'The goddamned smog is getting worse,' said Coon. 'It's surely not helping my bronchitis.' And put the mask aside and lit up a cigarillo. His friends told him to go to the doctor. Five days later he was dead.

'So you die, Captain, and we all move up in rank,' says Mirror Chekov, cackling. 'No one will question the assassination of a captain who has disobeyed prime orders of the Empire.'

Meanwhile, in our world, Spock has quickly seen through Mirror Kirk and the rest of the landing party and thrown them in the brig.

'Has the whole galaxy gone crazy?' screams Mirror Kirk. 'What kind of uniform is this? Where's your beard? What's going on? Where's my personal guard?'

'Fascinating,' says Spock.

What's wonderful about this is the thoroughness with which the parallel universe has been conceived. The Empire is as mad and threatening as the Federation is benign. We genuinely worry for our landing party's safety as, often, we simply do not. In our universe the *Enterprise* has been trying to negotiate with a planet of dyed-in-the-wool pacifists for dilithium mineral rights. Normal Kirk has been bending over backwards to convince them of his own peaceful intentions. In the parallel world, the *Enterprise* has orders to take what it wants and kill all the planet's inhabitants, possibly for fun.

'Terror must be maintained or the Empire is doomed,' explains Mirror Spock. 'It is the logic of history.'*

But being logical, Mirror Spock helps our party escape, at exactly the same moment that Normal Spock is beaming Mirror Kirk and Co back into their universe. Equilibrium is restored, and normal Kirk, Spock and McCoy chew the fat on the bridge. Spock says that the mirror-universe characters were 'brutal, savage, unprincipled, uncivilised, treacherous, in every way splendid examples of *Homo sapiens*, the very flower of humanity'.

'I'm not sure, but I think we've been insulted,' says Kirk.

---

* Compare with the antimatter universe in 'The Alternative Factor', where the planet just had a different-coloured sky. By the way, is this the same parallel universe as that or a different one? A perpendicular universe, maybe?

'I'm sure,' says McCoy.

As Torie Atkinson points out on theviewscreen.com, this may not be the most popular episode of *Star Trek* but it is surely the most parodied. For a while in the 1980s, there was a progressive rock band called Spock's Beard.* Jerome Bixby based his script on a short story he had written in the early 1950s, although I suspect that many of the defter touches in the final draft were added by Fontana and Coon's rewrites. The crucial thing is that the episode doesn't take itself too seriously, as it would have done if Roddenberry had still been making all the decisions.

In 'The Deadly Years' (2.12), the *Enterprise* encounters a colony of scientists who are ageing with terrifying speed. Accordingly the landing party start adding decades with each few hours and will quickly die unless a cure can be found. Cue masses of prosthetic ageing make-up, except for Spock, who lives twice as long as humans and so adds a little distinguished grey at the temples while Bones and Scotty are contemplating Zimmer frames. According to legend, William Shatner objected to being seen as old and so insisted on rather less ageing make-up than his fellows. What isn't in doubt is that these young men made up to look old looked much older than they would when they actually did become old. In the twenty-second century, it seems, they had forgotten about hair dye.†

Incidentally, we learn in this episode that Kirk is thirty-four. Watching it again now, when I am quite a few years older than that, is not an uncomplicated experience, especially when Kirk falls asleep on the bridge.

'I, Mudd' (2.8) was a sequel to 'Mudd's Women', possibly commissioned as a dare. If you really want a comic *Star Trek*

---

* Since 2010 there has also been a band of Leeds-based jazz improvisers called Shatner's Bassoon, but that requires slightly more explanation.

† Other tonsorial enhancements were clearly available, though. Kirk's hairline recedes in the early part of the show but then advances again as he gets older.

episode, look no further than 'The Trouble with Tribbles' (2.15), and sensibly, few people do.

'Do you know what you get if you feed a tribble too much?' asks Dr McCoy.

'A fat tribble,' says Kirk.

'No, you get a bunch of hungry little tribbles.'

On Deep Space Station K-7, an interstellar con man is trying to sell his modest stock of tribbles, small, purring balls of fluff that everyone adores.

'A most curious creature,' says Spock, stroking one idly. 'Its trilling seems to have a tranquillising effect on the human nervous system. Fortunately, of course ... I am immune ... to its effect ...'

The one snag with tribbles is that about 50 per cent of their anatomy is geared towards reproduction. No one has one tribble for long. The motor of the plot is the transportation of a high-yield crop called quadrotriticale to Sherman's Planet, yet another strategically vital globe on the disputed border of Klingon space. All of which means some more splendid bickering with the latest Klingon antagonist, Koloth, played by William Campbell (who had been Trelane in 'The Squire of Gothos'). We know, whether we have seen this episode before or not, that the tribbles will eat all the quadrotriticale, aiming to beget more tribbles. But before we get there, there is some fine if occasionally arch comedy, including a bar brawl of sublime silliness. Humans and Klingons may not be able to go to war after the Organian Peace Treaty, but they can still beat each other up after a few rounds of brightly coloured alcoholic drinks.

'The Trouble with Tribbles' was the first script sale for twenty-three-year-old David Gerrold, although like everything else it went through subsequent drafts by Fontana and Coon. Not everyone liked it. Bob Justman thought the characters parodied themselves, and that the humour lacked believability.

Samuel A. Peeples said 'it wasn't my idea of what the show should be'. But William Schallert, who played the week's annoying bureaucrat Nilz Baris, said that in his sixty-year career in film and television, this was the role most people remembered him for. William Campbell said that after the episode aired, his neighbour's son started addressing his wife as 'Mrs Klingon'. According to Gerrold, five hundred tribbles were made for the episode, after a design from sculptor and prop wizard Wah Chang.* The tribble-maker, or tribbliste, Jacqueline Cumere, received $350 for her troubles. Most were conveniently stolen just after production, although stragglers would turn up on set or in cupboards for months afterwards.

'Tribbles' wrapped in early September 1967. Gene Coon left the show the same week, and the golden age sputtered to a close.

---

* Who also made the communicators and tricorders to Matt Jefferies's specifications, and designed the Gorn in 'Arena', the salt vampire in 'The Man Trap', the Romulan bird-of-prey craft in 'Balance of Terror' and the fake vomit neural parasites in 'Operation – Annihilate!'

CHAPTER 6

THE ENGINES CANNA TAKE IT

The new producer was John Meredyth Lucas, who had been working as a writer and director on the private eye show *Mannix*. He was an old pro in his late forties, who had already written 'The Changeling' for *Star Trek*, and had another script, 'Patterns of Force', in development. During his brief time on the show, you can feel something in *Star Trek* hardening up, calcifying.

I'm not sure it was his fault. Coon, after all, had been rather more than an old pro. And Lucas had less money to spend. From here on in, new music would be commissioned only rarely. Every snippet of incidental music would be used and reused, until we knew them all backwards, forwards and sideways. Effects shots had to be recycled. Every planet looked the same. Location shooting would be pared to the bone.

It was on one of the rare days out of the studio, in fact, that Lucas was introduced to cast and crew. 'Bread and Circuses' (1.25) was the only script credited jointly to Roddenberry and Coon, and was known to all as 'the Roman show'. Planet 892-IV, according to the captain's log, is 'a heavily industrialised 20th-century-type planet very much like Earth, an amazing example of Hodgkin's Law of Parallel Planetary Development'. Good grief, they even speak American English there. (This is the only episode where this is specified.) The only difference: Rome never fell. And now one of the Federation's own, Captain Merrick, has gone native and become Merikus, First Citizen. The crew of his ship have been labelled 'barbarians' and forced to fight for their lives in gladiatorial combat. This being the twentieth century, though, gladiators are now fighting on TV, with canned applause and catcalls. The Master of the Games tells a pacifist slave that he must still fight convincingly for the cameras:

'You bring this network's ratings down, Flavius, and we'll do a special on you.'

For the 'Roman show' is, in reality, a scabrous satire on 1960s television, with a cynical edge we don't often see on *Star Trek*. It's just a shame that Roddenberry and Coon had to resuscitate the old parallel-Earths idea. Lucas noted on his first day at work that this was not a happy ship: 'Shatner came round the corner, and when he saw Gene, he turned round and went round the other way. And the cast was fighting too. All the actors complained to me about all the other actors.'

Director Ralph Senensky was cheesed off as well:

'The scenes in the arena are the part of "Bread and Circuses" most harmed by the time restrictions imposed by the new management. The sequences were literally shot on the run . . . That set piece should have been the highlight of the production; but those bloodhounds in black suits were nipping at our heels.'

Why the budget cuts? Because the series wasn't making money. In early 1967, Desilu had been bought up by Paramount's owners, the Gulf & Western conglomerate, which couldn't understand why a series continued to be produced when it lost money on every episode filmed. Ratings were still poor, so NBC wasn't selling enough ads at the right price. And for the second season, all the main cast members had negotiated pay rises, so a higher proportion of the budget was eaten up by human costs.

In 'Journey to Babel' (2.10), for instance, Spock's parents arrive on the *Enterprise* by shuttlecraft, rather than just beaming aboard as you might expect. Why so? To save a little money. They already had the stock shot of the shuttle flying into the hangar deck, and the set cost nothing to build. The transporter effect would have taken more time and cost more. This is what happens when you have *2001: A Space Odyssey* ambitions on *Blake's 7* budgets.

'Journey to Babel' is the seventh and last of my five-star episodes, one final day in the sun before the long slow twilight of season three. Dorothy Fontana, kicking around potential story ideas, remembered a line in 'This Side of Paradise'. 'My mother was a schoolteacher,' said Spock, 'my father was an ambassador.' She went to Roddenberry and said, 'We've talked about them, let's show them.' Carry on, said Roddenberry. So she created these characters: Sarek, stern, Vulcan, unimpressed with his son's choice of career, and Amanda, his all-too-human wife. Spock and Sarek, we discover, have not spoken to each other for eighteen years, for Vulcans, as well as being unemotional, are extremely stubborn.

'You don't understand the Vulcan way, Captain,' says Amanda. 'It's logical. It's a better way than ours. But it's not easy.'

'Spock is my best officer, and my friend,' says Kirk.

'I'm glad he has such a friend,' says Amanda. 'It hasn't been easy on Spock. Neither human nor Vulcan. At home nowhere except Starfleet.'

The hairs on the back of your neck shift direction, reverse their polarity.

This character stuff is embedded in an unusually dense narrative. The Vulcan delegation is joined on the *Enterprise* by some Andorians, who are light blue and have comedy antennae sticking out of their heads, and the pig-faced Tellarites, who 'do not argue for reasons,' says Sarek. 'They simply argue.' All are off to a conference somewhere about something, but before we get there, there's a murder, an unidentified wessel (says Chekov) shadowing the ship's every move, some emergency surgery and an awful lot of chat. Some commentators have suggested there's too much plot, but rather that than too little, I say. (What actually *happens* in 'Who Mourns for Adonais?' or 'The Alternative Factor'?)

Sarek was played by Mark Lenard, the Romulan commander in 'Balance of Terror'. He was only forty-three, seven years older than Leonard Nimoy, but a little grey hair and a lot of natural gravitas helped suspend our disbelief. Jane Wyatt, who played Amanda, was the most eminent guest star the show had yet attracted, having starred in *Lost Horizon* in 1937 and been blacklisted in the 1950s for supposed Communist sympathies. As a mark of respect, she was credited as 'Miss Jane Wyatt' in the end titles. Dorothy Fontana had no role in their casting but was delighted by them. 'They were just wonderful and they carried it off so well, even the Vulcanisms that we had to put in.' Lenard and Wyatt asked Leonard Nimoy for guidance on the intricacies of Vulcan culture, and he said he thought Vulcans placed great importance on their hands and hand gestures. So the actors developed the finger-touching gesture they used on-screen. Call me an old softy, but that single gesture says rather more about the solidity and sincerity of their relationship, of their love, than a passionate clinch ever could.*

Nonetheless, it is left to Dr McCoy to ask the truly important questions.

'Spock, I've always suspected that you were a little more human than you let on. Mrs Sarek, I know about the rigorous training of the Vulcan youth, but tell me, did he ever run and play like the human children, even in secret?'

'Well, he did have a pet sehlat he was very fond of,' says Amanda.

'Sehlat?' says Bones.

'It's sort of a fat teddy bear.'

McCoy is delighted by this. Spock elaborates:

'On Vulcan, the teddy bears are alive. And they have six-inch fangs.'

'A Private Little War' (2.19) is a dreary Vietnam allegory with a Gene Roddenberry script of clod-hopping unsubtlety. The good planet-people have blonde hair, the evil planet-people have black hair, and there's a very silly 'ape-like carnivore' called a Mugato. In the script it was called a Gumato, but DeForest Kelley said it wrong so many times they ended up having to change its name.

In 'The Gamesters of Triskelion' (2.16), Kirk, Uhura and Chekov are kidnapped by aliens and forced to engage in gladiatorial combat. Many of the tropes of late-era original-series *Star Trek* are here: mysterious bald figures dressed in black, dungeons, triple-locked pain collars that mete out instant agony if you don't follow orders, all-powerful aliens (here called 'the Providers'). There is simply no compelling reason for this episode to have been made, although it is the first in which a pulchritudinous young alien woman asks

---

* Years later, at a *Star Trek* convention in New York, Jane Wyatt was pressed by an audience member to reveal Spock's first name. After all, who would know better than his mother? 'Harold,' she replied with a smile.

Kirk, 'What is love?' She waits for the answer, and so do
we. On Kirk's face, we can see the internal battle he is fighting. Shall I tell her? Or shall I leap straight to the practical
demonstration?

'Obsession' (2.13) is a considerable improvement, featuring no chatty aliens at all but a gaseous entity, or 'vampire
cloud', that sucks people clean of red corpuscles. Spock's green
blood – based on copper rather than iron – leaves a nasty taste
in the creature's mouth, but everyone else is in great danger.
Thirteen years ago, Kirk encountered this same creature, but
he paused a moment before firing his phaser, and it killed
several of his crewmates, so it's his turn to play Ahab to the
cloud's Moby-Dick. Aren't there any other nineteenth-century
novels to be plundered for ideas? (*Wuthering Heights*? *Pride and
Prejudice*?) In truth 'Obsession' trips along nicely, a mystery to
be solved as well as, in director Ralph Senensky's words, 'a deep
penetration into Kirk's psyche, his inner struggle to overcome
guilt for his actions in a past incident'. Shatner is never better
than when he has to suffer. Four redshirts are killed by the
cloud, and two more are seriously injured: the highest casualty
rate of the series.*

In 'The Immunity Syndrome' (2.18) a giant space amoeba
may or may not be intending to eat the galaxy. The only answer
seems to be to put Spock in a specially modified shuttlecraft
and send him straight into the amoeba to face Almost Certain
Death. How many weeks is it since Commodore Decker did
the same and we all shook our heads and said, what a foolish,
deluded man? But regular cast members constantly survive
situations that would finish off guest stars. In this case, Spock
has a bone to pick with this mammoth single-celled organism,
as one of the ships it had previously consumed was manned by

* The blood of octopuses, or octopodes if we're being picky, is also copper-based, but
unlike Mr Spock's it's blue.

Vulcans. Even though it happened light years away, the science officer felt it in the pit of his vitals.

'What was it you sensed?' says Kirk.

'The touch of death,' says Spock.

'And what do you think they felt?'

'Astonishment.'

This is much the same response as many modern viewers have on first seeing 'A Piece of the Action' (2.17), in which an entire planetary society has based itself on a history book about the Chicago Mobs of the 1920s. After the triumph of 'Tribbles', Roddenberry and Coon had felt the need for another out-and-out comedy episode, but sadly, they were wrong. This is one of those shows in which the plot can be stretched out only by everyone behaving like fools. Kirk is kidnapped on *four* separate occasions. Much as I admire Spock's brown pinstriped gangster suit (with matching orange tie and handkerchief), there's a self-consciousness to the episode that 'Tribbles' managed to avoid. The suits may be sharp, but nothing else is.

As *Star Trek* declined, so the aliens became duller. None could be more boring than the Kelvans, extra-galactic nasties in brightly coloured jumpsuits who take over the *Enterprise* in 'By Any Other Name' (2.22) because they want a ride back to their own galaxy.

'We do not colonise,' says Rojan, the lead Kelvan, whose combover is endlessly distracting. 'We conquer. We rule. There's no other way for us.'

Oh shut up. There's one marvellous idea (Roddenberry's) in an otherwise lacklustre hour. The Kelvans have a useful device that reduces the essence of every crew member to a dehydrated polyhedron, about the size of a human fist. Rojan demonstrates it on a couple of redshirts and crushes one of the polyhedra. The other is restored to life, but the powdery one – Yeoman Thompson, as I recall – is not only extremely dead, but would never even have known she was being killed. Kirk gulps with shock, and so do we.

By now, nearly every new *Star Trek* episode feels like a variation on a previous *Star Trek* episode. There's no surprise to any of it, other than the surprise on the characters' faces when they have to solve the same problems as last week's. In 'Return to Tomorrow' (2.20) the crew encounter yet more hugely powerful, disembodied aliens. There are three of them, as there were on Triskelion, they are kept in an underground chamber hundreds of miles below the surface, as on Triskelion, and they pulse with light whenever they speak, as on Triskelion. Like the Kelvans, they want to take human shape, and like the Kelvans, when they take human shape they will find it's all rather more complicated than they expected. They could inhabit the bodies of androids, as in 'What Are Little Girls Made Of?', but they don't fancy that. So they take over the bodies of three of the *Enterprise* crew members. (This may be the first time this has happened, but it won't be the last.) Otherwise, 'Return to Tomorrow' is notable for the first appearance of Diana Muldaur, as astrobiologist Dr Ann Mulhall. She will become something of a Roddenberry regular, and guest-star in almost every 1970s US drama series ever made. She is so very young here, younger than any of us ever were.

The poor old Prime Directive of non-interference in alien societies has been taking a bit of a battering, too. Kirk keeps finding ways around it, when he doesn't ignore it altogether. Giving rifles to the blonde-haired goodies in 'A Private Little War', fomenting revolution in 'Bread and Circuses' and 'The Gamesters of Triskelion' and claiming a piece of the action in 'A Piece of the Action', he could probably have been court-martialled half a dozen times in as many months. In 'Patterns of Force' (2.21) we find another planet subverted by Federation interference, as some gentle old historian has recreated the Third Reich. This gives the actors relishable opportunities to

(i) overact and (ii) wear Nazi uniforms. No German television station aired this episode until the mid-1990s, and then only late at night on a pay-TV station. For the record, we should probably mention that this is the only episode, in any *Star Trek* series or film, in which Leonard Nimoy appears without a shirt. Vulcans are seen to have hairy chests.

If 'The Ultimate Computer' (2.24) still glistens and gleams, while surrounding episodes have tarnished with age, it's because of another fine Dorothy Fontana script (based on a story by Laurence N. Wolfe). In this one, a supercomputer called M-5 is installed on the *Enterprise*. So fast, powerful and clever is it, says its creator Dr Richard Daystrom, that it renders the role of captain unnecessary. Poor Kirk, humiliated by technology, is determined to prove Daystrom and his tormentors wrong. We dock a star, sadly, because this is the third time *this season* that the captain will talk a computer to death. If M-5 had been running the script department, it would never have allowed that.

'The Omega Glory' (2.23) was one of the original script ideas proposed by Roddenberry at pilot stage. NBC rejected it as too weak, and they were right. Roddenberry waited for a season and a half, and made it anyway. Planet Omega IV is populated by 'Yangs' and 'Kohms', or Yanks and Communists for the hard-of-thinking, and takes racial stereotyping to new levels of idiocy. (Yangs are fair-haired and wear nice warm furs, Kohms are brutal Asiatics from Second World War movies.) Yet again Earth history has been duplicated far across the galaxy for no obvious reason; yet again the Prime Directive has been ignored by a visiting Federation representative. When one of the Yangs finally brings out a tatty old American flag, you know you will never watch this nonsense ever again, unless chained up in a medieval dungeon and compelled to by an alien playing a harpsichord. Roddenberry wrote the script himself and then had the temerity to submit it for an Emmy award. It's one of the most pathetic episodes in any incarnation of the series.

As well as all our hopes and dreams, this episode also marked the end of John Meredyth Lucas's occupation of the producer's chair. For the final episode of the season, Roddenberry reclaimed the role for himself. 'Assignment: Earth' (2.26) was conceived as a pilot of a new series, a two-birds-with-one-stone throw that looks very strange now, not least because the pilot didn't sell. The *Enterprise* travels back to the 1960s again to conduct 'historical research' – i.e. for no sensible reason at all – and makes contact with a man called Gary Seven, played by Robert Lansing, who would have been the lead in the planned new show. Seven, which might not be his real name, is a human trained by benevolent aliens to resolve global political problems during an unusually trouble-filled time in Earth's history. Teri Garr plays his dippy comic-relief secretary, with embarrassing jaunty music every time she appears and nearly trips over something. It is said that Roddenberry took rather too close an interest in the shortness or otherwise of her skirt. She has refused to talk about *Star Trek* in interviews ever since.

Thus did another year's deep-space-exploring, Klingon-foiling, hailing-frequencies-opening and wry-eyebrow-raising come to an end.

The devil, as they say, is in the detail. Much of the detail in *Star Trek* was spellbinding, but some of it made no sense at all. What of stardates? When I was a slightly irritable twelve-year-old, the lack of logic drove me mad. 'The Corbomite Maneuver' begins on stardate 1512.2, and 'The Man Trap' on 1513.1. Isn't that less than a day later? I always assumed so, but I may have been wrong. On other occasions, a few hours would pass but the stardate would leap by eight or ten. The explanation was simple: the writers put in whichever number they fancied and no one else gave it a second thought. Several viewers wrote in to complain. Roddenberry prepared an answer: 'There are no constraints or absolutes in deep outer space. Depending upon what quadrant of the galaxy you're in, and at what speed you're travelling, or in all three dimensions in what direction you're headed, time increases or decreased accordingly relative to time on planet Earth – or anywhere else in the universe.'

Or, in plain English, sod off.

Given the importance of the main theme tune to the series, and its echoes in incidental music and later theme tunes, one might ask why its composer Alexander Courage did so little subsequent work on *Star Trek*. As so often, it came down to money. Every time an episode was run or rerun, Courage received a royalty, and expected to get 100 per cent of it. But Roddenberry, who had never written a music lyric in his life, somehow found the time to write one for this tune. It would never be sung or used in any way, but it would be printed on the sheet music, which entitled him to 50 per cent of the royalties. Solow and Justman reprint a letter from Roddenberry to Courage that is a small master-piece of arse-covering, disingenuous bullshit. For Courage had signed his contract without noticing a two-sentence clause at the end of it, inserted by Roddenberry's attorney, allowing Roddenberry the right to write a lyric to the tune if he wished. And he did wish, for reasons of greed. After the first two episodes – his contractual obligation – Courage barely worked for the show again, and never directly for Roddenberry.

By the end of the first season, Nichelle Nichols was cheesed off. Uhura had already been reduced to little more than opening hailing frequencies, and occasionally closing them again. Off-set, there had been racist insults from studio employees. (When Grace Lee Whitney was fired, one of them said, 'If anyone was let go, it should have been you. Ten of you could never equal one blue-eyed blonde.') Then she found out that someone high up had ordered that she not be given her fan mail. There were sacks of it, lying around in the mailroom. After the final show had been filmed, Nichols went to Roddenberry's office and tendered her resignation. He asked her to reconsider, but she had had enough.

The following evening she was at an NAACP fundraising event, when someone approached and said, 'Nichelle, there is someone who would like to meet you. He's a big fan of *Star Trek* and of Uhura.' She turned round and found herself gazing on the distinguished features of Dr Martin Luther King Jr. She told him that she had resigned.

'You cannot,' he said, 'and you must not. You have opened a door that must not be allowed to close. I am sure you have taken a lot of grief, or probably will for what you're doing. Don't you see that you're not just a role model for little black children? You're more important for people who *don't* look like us.' These are just the edited highlights. He gave her a real mouthful.

After thinking about it over the weekend, Nichols went back to Roddenberry's office and withdrew her resignation.

One thing that definitely worked in season two was the intro-duction of Ensign Pavel Chekov, who fitted in so well and so quickly that viewers quickly forgot that he hadn't been there during season one. One factor in Chekov's success was that he had a joke. Sulu and Uhura, in all their decades of service, never acquired a joke. Chekov's was his touching belief in Russia's innate superiority. During the Cold War, the Soviets often boasted that everything of note had been invented in Russia; Chekov revived the tradition three centuries later. In 'The Apple', the landing party beam down to an earthly paradise.

'It makes me homesick,' says Chekov. 'Just like Russia.'

'More like the Garden of Eden, Ensign,' says Bones.

'Of course, Doctor,' says Chekov. 'The Garden of Eden was just outside Moscow.'

In 'The Trouble with Tribbles', he claims that the new wonder-grain quadrotriticale is 'a Russian inwention'. In the same episode, in the bar, Scotty says that Scotch is a drink for a *man*.

'Scotch? It was inwented by a little old lady from Leningrad,' says Chekov.

In 'Who Mourns for Adonais?' Kirk asks where Apollo has gone.

'He disappeared again, like the cat in that Russian story,' says Chekov.

'Don't you mean the English story, the Cheshire cat?' says Kirk.

'Cheshire?' says Chekov. 'No, sir. Minsk, perhaps.'*

The episodes 'Amok Time' and 'Journey to Babel' prompted much speculation on the history, traditions and fashions

---

* Chekov also had a scream, which he employed to excellent effect in half a dozen episodes and at least two films. Although Uhura screams once or twice, and says 'Captain, I'm frightened' in 'The City on the Edge of Forever', we understand that she is too professional and matter-of-fact to play the femme fatale on a regular basis. Walter Koenig, though, gave good scream. You can imagine the writers rubbing their hands with glee and wondering how to use it next.

in Vulcan proper names. Back in May 1966, Bob Justman had sent a memo to Roddenberry proposing that all Vulcan male names should begin with SP and end in K. Among his suggestions were Splek, Spirk, Spook and Spank. He wasn't serious, but the S---k pattern did actually become part of the *Star Trek* canon for a while. Spock's father was called Sarek, and the founder of Vulcan pacifism was Surak. Stonn, in 'Amok Time', was an exception, but we didn't like him, so it didn't matter.

In *I Am Spock*, Leonard Nimoy noted that Roddenberry often gave his characters names that featured the 'k' sound. Kirk, Spock, McCoy, Pike, Scott, Sarek, Picard, Khan, Riker . . . 'All very tough, strong, short-sounding names,' says Nimoy, 'and certainly very different from Roddenberry. If one wanted to get psychoanalytic about it, a case could be made that these [characters] were part of Gene's fantasy life, representing the "tough leader" he always wanted to be.'

But then Nimoy and Roddenberry didn't get on brilliantly either.

In his 1973 book *The World of Star Trek* (of which more later) David Gerrold described the *Enterprise* bridge as 'one of the best designed science fiction sets in motion picture history'. It is 'a model of logic and efficiency'. The captain's eyes are directly ahead of him, in the shape of a giant viewscreen. Helmsman and navigator are at eleven o'clock and one o'clock, communications right behind, science to his right, engineering to his left. So workable was this design, said Gerrold, that the US Navy sent a delegation to the studio to see if it would work for their new aircraft carrier.

In which case, he continues, why was there only one way in and out? The turbolift connects the bridge with the rest of the ship. There's no spare lift, no emergency stairs, no Jefferies tube, nothing. Knock out the turbolift and you isolate the bridge, and oddly enough, several aliens who take over the ship for their own nefarious ends do just that. Surely Starfleet's engineers would have thought of this. But I suppose Roddenberry, Bob Justman and Matt Jefferies would have had to think of it first.

And we can only take verisimilitude so far without asking ourselves some very awkward questions. How does the artificial gravity work, and why does it not fail once in seventy-nine episodes, a dozen films and four sequel series? (Although there was some floating about on a Klingon ship in *Star Trek VI*.) And if there are no shockwaves in space, why does the ship shake so violently every time a phaser hits her shields?

Years later, a fan asked Bob Justman the $64,000 question: 'Why don't you put seat belts on the chairs?'

'Because if we did, the actors couldn't fall out of them.'

In 'Return to Tomorrow' the disembodied alien Sargon takes over Kirk's body and is delighted by what he finds. 'Your captain has an excellent body, Dr McCoy. I compliment you both on the condition in which you maintain it.'

In truth, Shatner was fighting a constant battle to maintain that body. David Gerrold probably put it most diplomatically: 'Shatner is a very athletic actor, and takes great pride in his ability to do strenuous scenes such as fights; he exercised regularly, but as the strain of each season's production began to tell on him, he would begin slacking off on the exercises, and well . . .'

At one point towards the end of season two, memos were exchanged by the production staff with the subject line, 'William Shatner's Equator'. They discussed the possibility of selecting one or two particularly unflattering film clips, including 'a full belly body view', and sending them to the star without comment. It didn't happen. Maybe a quiet word was said instead. Certainly the message was received and understood. Wrote Gerrold, 'William Shatner is too much of a professional, he took too much pride in his own appearance to allow the show to be damaged. The *Enterprise* was not going to be commanded by "Captain Fatty".'

Well, not yet, anyway.

We now introduce another pivotal figure in *Star Trek*'s bizarre history, someone who never produced or directed or wrote or acted in an episode, but who loved the show dearly, and was determined it should survive. Bjo Trimble (pronounced Bee-jo: it's short for Betty JoAnne) was a pillar of the science fiction community, or what they call a BNF, a Big Name Fan. (At her first-ever convention, aged eighteen in 1952, Harlan Ellison had proposed to her on the spot.) She and her husband John met Roddenberry at a convention in 1966, before any episodes had been aired. Trimble was running a Futuristic Fashion Show, and 'this big handsome man' jollied her into including a couple of costumes from 'Mudd's Women' and one from 'What Are Little Girls Made Of?' A friendship was formed, and the Trimbles became regular visitors to the Desilu set.

By halfway through season two, however, it was becoming clear that NBC did not intend to renew the show for a third. 'We watched the actors do their stuff beautifully in front of the camera,' said Trimble, 'then slump off looking depressed.'* On their way home, John turned to her and said, 'There ought to be something we could do about this.' By

---

* Quotes taken from an interview with Bjo Trimble on startrek.com in August 2011.

the time they arrived, they had mapped out a plan of action. They called Gene Roddenberry, asked for his blessing, and got down to work.

The Trimbles orchestrated a letter-writing campaign, but with a professionalism and an efficiency that may have taken NBC by surprise. Having noticed that many fan letters were poorly written and even offensive, Bjo wrote a 'How-to' memo, including the names and office addresses of the relevant executives, and distributed it through the fan community. Use a legal-size envelope, she said. Don't mention *Star Trek* on the front of the envelope. Don't put a return address on the back of the envelope, because then they have to open it. Don't send a form letter, write it yourself. And above all, be courteous and polite.

The campaign grew. The Trimbles received requests for their memo from all over the United States. Employees from Polaroid, a prominent *Star Trek* sponsor, wrote not just to NBC but to their own executives to canvass their support. The *Kansas City Star Tribune* interviewed the Trimbles, which itself generated more requests for the memo, and thus more letters – although exactly how many letters has long been the subject of quite violent disagreement. NBC's then Director of Program Publicity told Solow and Justman that around twelve thousand letters were received during January and February 1968. Each one received a reply, and they had to hire two extra hands to carry out this task.

But according to Allan Asherman, in 1968 NBC themselves acknowledged the receipt of 115,893 letters, of which 52,358 arrived in February alone.

Bjo Trimble has said that NBC told the *TV Guide* that they had received more than 200,000 letters. She met a man at a party who was in the computer business and had been working at NBC at the time. He told her that her name was very well known at the corporation. Many people would like to meet her.

'Why?' she said.

'Well, you broke down the machines at NBC in New York.' He knew, because he had had to repair them. He said that the talk around the office was that more than a million letters had come in.

On 31 March 1968, the network announced that *Star Trek* would be renewed for a third season.

CHAPTER 7

HE'S DEAD, JIM

Would it really have made such a difference if there hadn't been a third season of *Star Trek*? Creatively, artistically, maybe not. But practically, commercially, historically, very much so. Without a minimum of three seasons in the can, a drama series could not be sold into syndication and would therefore not be shown again. It would effectively disappear. As we shall see, it would be *Star Trek*'s growing popularity in rerun that led to everything else: the films, the TV series, the novels, the mini-figures, the Borg, this book. Bjo and John Trimble didn't just save the show for one season, they saved it for all of us for all time.

What NBC gave with one hand, however, it took away with the other, and then punched you in the face.

Having confirmed the new run, the network told Roddenberry that the show would now be airing in what cast and crew agreed was the perfect time slot: Monday nights at 7.30. This would capture the young, bright audience the show clearly most appealed to. As a result, Gene Roddenberry announced that he would start producing the series again personally, hands on, rewrites a-go-go. There might be no more Gene Coon, and Dorothy Fontana had also decided to move on, but with Roddenberry back at the tiller, quality control could again be guaranteed. (John Meredyth Lucas had been quietly let go. Some histories say that he walked, but Solow and Justman insist that Roddenberry sacked him, and neither they nor Lucas ever found out why.)

In Shatner's characteristically colourful description, 'the adrenaline once again began coursing through Gene Roddenberry's tired veins, the gleam returned to his baggy eyes, the calluses returned to his carpal tunnel syndromed fingertips and he almost immediately got to work on our third season's scripts.'*

Then came the phone call.

'Gene baby!' said Mort Werner of NBC.

Roddenberry always knew he was in trouble when Werner called him 'baby'.

'Gene baby! I've got great news for you. We're moving you to a brand-new time slot. You're going to love it! We're actually going to let you have Friday night at ten.'

This was the kiss of death. Young, bright people are at home on Monday evenings at seven thirty. At ten o'clock on Friday nights they are out doing something else. Only the elderly and the infirm are watching TV, and they don't like Mr Spock.

The original plan had been to put *Star Trek* on Mondays before *Rowan & Martin's Laugh-In*, one of NBC's biggest hits. But this would need *Laugh-In* to move back from eight o'clock to eight thirty. Its producer threw a strategic tantrum, and

---

* From *Star Trek Memories* by Shatner and Kreski.

insisted that *Laugh-In* stay at eight. Whereupon the executives looked at *Laugh-In*'s ratings (huge) and *Star Trek*'s (modest) and made the obvious decision. The rest of the schedule, though, had already been decided. There was only one slot left.

According to Shatner, Roddenberry then threw his own tantrum. If they moved the show to Friday nights, he would renege on his promise to produce the show personally. NBC executives, who had seen 'The Corbomite Maneuver', called his bluff. But Roddenberry did what he said he would do and withdrew to the executive producer's office. His day-to-day involvement with the show essentially came to an end at this moment.

(Solow and Justman say all this is hogwash. NBC never promised Roddenberry Monday night at half past seven. That was just the slot he wanted and argued most strongly for. And when he was given Friday night at ten, there was no threat to resign. Instead, he simply lost interest.)

Whatever the truth of the matter, the worst wound of all was self-inflicted. Roddenberry had all but promised Bob Justman that he would be promoted to producer for season three, but at the last moment he hired another old pro called Fred Freiberger, who had written B-movie scripts in the 1950s and produced *The Wild, Wild West* on TV. Justman was given the consolation job title of 'Co-Producer', but Freiberger was the boss. Unlike John Meredyth Lucas, who had worked under Roddenberry's supervision, this old pro would have a free hand. Roddenberry even gave him his office, and withdrew to a much smaller office at the other end of the lot to plan new projects and think about anything that wasn't *Star Trek*.[*]

---

[*] Justman believed he didn't get the top job because NBC preferred a 'creative', a writer-producer, to a nuts-and-bolts line producer like him. Over the previous two years, though, Justman had written hundreds of pages of script notes, even if he hadn't written a script. Roddenberry could have made a case for him if he had felt so inclined – as Justman told Joel Engel, 'Gene was a wonderful friend, but he was never someone who would fight for someone else.'

Cursed with an unforgettable name, Fred Freiberger would spend the rest of his career, and indeed life, as The Man to Blame for Season Three. 'I thought I could never have a more unpleasant experience in my life than when I, a Jewish kid from the Bronx, parachuted out of a burning B-17 over Germany to land in the middle of eighty million Nazis. But that was before my association with *Star Trek*. My ordeal in a German prison camp only lasted two years. My travail with *Star Trek* has spanned twenty-five years and still counting.'

But if you have watched any third-season episodes recently, you will understand the need to find out who was responsible and have him punished. Freiberger had to operate with even more drastically reduced budgets than previous producers. His executive producer had gone AWOL, and he had lost the services of the series' best writers and rewriters. But if *Star Trek* had hardened and calcified during the second half of the second season, under Freiberger it coarsened and dumbed down. Good ideas were mishandled, bad ideas were mistaken for good ideas, scripts lost their pace and their shape, common sense went out of the window. Freiberger got the programmes made under difficult circumstances, but as a creative producer he was revealed to be utterly inadequate.

When I was eleven or twelve and the Freiberger shows were first broadcast on the BBC, I loved them and looked forward to them. They seemed bigger and bolder and more colourful than the old episodes, which in some ways they were, presumably to make up for the fact that they were all made on standing sets with old costumes and without location shooting of any kind. Even the Vasquez Rocks went unvisited during season three. I'm not sure if Freiberger was consciously trying to gear the series more towards eleven-year-olds, or whether that was just what happened, but I suspect that there was something of Irwin Allen in his make-up. He would have made an excellent producer of *The Time Tunnel*.

What I think settles the verdict against him – and this judge is looking forward to imposing the maximum possible sentence – is that many of the ideas for episodes in season three were really rather good. Take 'Requiem for Methuselah' (3.19), a Jerome Bixby script about a reclusive human man living apparently alone on a planetoid with lots of newly painted Leonardo da Vinci canvases and a newly written Brahms piano piece. He is called Flint because he has been alive since the Iron Age. Vastly intelligent and infinitely wise simply by dint of having lived so long, he has withdrawn from human society for reasons of overpowering millennial tiredness, and built an enormous fortress in the middle of nowhere with nothing more than a floating robot and a beautiful young android woman for company. If you can get past the dodgy sexual politics of a very, very, *very* old man building a luscious young lovely for his own personal satisfaction, it's all just about making sense until now.

But what is Flint wearing? A multicoloured cape that makes him look like an end-of-the-pier stage magician. A tatty, moth-chewed toupee sits atop his ancient bonce, painful in its obviousness. The android girl wears another mad glimmering silver dress, as though permanently dressed for dinner. Spock, armed with only a tricorder, can verify that the paintings are 'da Vincis'* and that the waltz is Brahms's because *he recognises the handwriting.* We don't mind Spock being clever, but most of the time he won't admit that it's Tuesday until he has verified it with the library computer. Who built Flint's

---

* As any fule kno, Leonardo da Vinci's name was Leonardo and he came from the town of Vinci. So to call the paintings 'da Vincis' instead of 'Leonardos' is an entry-level solecism that Spock, if properly scripted, would never make.

enormous fortress, and who does the hoovering? Soon, Flint and Kirk are rivals for the affections of the beautiful baco-foil girl, so how do they settle it? They have a fist-fight. (Or rather, their stunt doubles do.) At one point, armed with a little remote control panel with coloured buttons, Flint can pluck the *Enterprise* out of orbit, reduce it in size to a foot-long model and deposit it on the nearest table, with its crew in suspended animation. That's quite useful technology. Care to share it with the rest of us?*

And so it goes on. Bacofoil girl falls in love with Kirk and that *makes* her human, as McCoy verifies with his medical tricorder and a raised eyebrow. Are we sure about that? Isn't that rather remarkable? Finally, Flint gives the list of all the famous people he has been during his long and action-packed life: 'Solomon, Alexander, Lazarus, Methuselah, Merlin, Abramson, a hundred other names you do not know.' Merlin? *Merlin*? This is utter Freiberger. Why not the Venerable Bede, Franklin D. Roosevelt or Jimmy Greaves? No, a mythic wizard with a long beard it has to be.

As a twelve-year-old, I remember being impressed by this episode; as a grumpy middle-aged man, I'm less so. Even so, there's a pleasing little twist at the end, not quite earned, but nonetheless cherishable. Android girl has died from an overload of humanity – it doesn't do the circuits any good at all – but in the meantime Kirk has fallen in love with her. (What, again?) Back on the *Enterprise*, he sits in his quarters with his head in his hands. Spock is there too. He stands and thinks a moment, then places his hands on the captain's head, as though to mind-meld. And says one word. 'Forget.'

It's all in the performance. Nimoy's sensitivity, Spock's deep regard for his captain, and a skill we didn't know about, but

---

* Also, exactly the same thing happened in 'Catspaw', a season and a half earlier.

can believe. If Kirk hadn't fallen in love half a dozen times since Christmas, it might have a greater emotional impact, but it's still a great scene in an episode that doesn't overflow with them.*

Freiberger's tenure was characterised by these missed and muffed opportunities. David Gerrold went in to pitch a sequel to 'The Trouble with Tribbles'. As Gerrold told Gross and Altman, 'I walk in, Freddy Freiberger is looking at me and his first words are, "I saw 'Tribbles' this morning," because he was having the episode screened for him. The polite thing to say is "Not bad" or "Well done" or "Good job". His words were "I don't like it. *Star Trek* is not a comedy." I said, "Well, Gene said he wanted a sequel," and he said that he had no interest.'

Dorothy Fontana, now freelance, submitted a script called 'Joanna'. Mining the main characters' backstories, as she loved to do, she invented a twenty-one-year-old daughter for Dr McCoy, who came aboard the ship with some rather outré 'space hippies'. Her story eventually became 'The Way to Eden' (3.20), Joanna became Chekov's ex-girlfriend and Fontana took her name off the teleplay. ('Michael Richards', her usual pseudonym, used the middle names of her two brothers.) The reason? Freiberger said that McCoy wasn't old enough to have a twenty-one-year-old daughter, as he was supposed to be Kirk's contemporary. It's one thing to be arrogant and wrong, but it's another not even to have read the show's bible, which explicitly states that McCoy is a decade or so older than his commanding officer.

(For the plot to work, Chekov has to experience a complete change of character, from eager young ingénu to inflexible, rules-obsessed jobsworth, and the space hippies have to take

---

* It also gives rise to a crucial moment in *Star Trek II: The Wrath of Khan* a dozen years later: 'Remember'.

over the *Enterprise* in a minute and a half by flicking a few switches in the auxiliary control room.)*

Margaret Armen, who wrote three episodes over the years, told Gross and Altman that Freiberger wasn't interested in the more thoughtful *Star Trek* shows. 'Fred was looking for all-action pieces. That's why he wasn't crazy about "The Paradise Syndrome". He didn't think that there was enough violent and terrifying action in it. He didn't realise that the suspense would come from the characters, their relationships and so forth.'

'The Paradise Syndrome' (3.3), in which Kirk loses his memory and starts a new life with a tribe of humans who look like Native Americans, except a bit whiter, was one of a dozen or so shows that Roddenberry had commissioned before his disappearing act. Freiberger was stuck with them. Needless to say, all the season's best shows are to be found within these dozen.†

The two best, for me, are 'The Tholian Web' (3.9) and 'The Enterprise Incident' (3.2). In 'The Tholian Web' the *Enterprise* finds another starship, the USS *Defiant*, floating derelict and ruined in a region of space that, according to Spock, is 'literally breaking up'. (If anyone else delivered this line, you'd think: nonsense. From Spock it's authoritative and obviously 100 per cent accurate.) Kirk, Spock, McCoy and Chekov beam over to have a look, but the transporter starts playing up, and Kirk is still on the ship when it appears to 'wink out' of existence. Is the captain a goner?

---

* But the episode does gain an entire star for its inspired use of the insult 'Herbert', to denote any sort of establishment stiff. Captain Kirk, in particular, is highly put out to be so addressed. It's thought that 'Herbert' was a joke at the expense of the recently departed Herb Solow, possibly at the hands of his ever-mischievous friend Bob Justman.

† In 'The Paradise Syndrome' Kirk spends several months on this planet – by far the longest timespan of a single episode – marries a local woman and makes her pregnant. Other than a brief sword-fighting scene in 'All Our Yesterdays' (3.23), this was the only episode in season three that featured location shooting. It seems to have eaten the year's budget for breakfast.

All common sense would say so, but Spock insists on staying in the area in case there's a way of rescuing him from the alternative universe into which he might have slipped. Is he working on a hunch? Please don't use that word in polite Vulcan conversation. Spock calculates the next 'period of spatial interface', when they might have a chance of beaming the (almost certainly deceased) captain back aboard.

There are, however, two complicating factors. One is that this region of space drives men mad. That's what happened to the crew of the *Defiant*, and now Chekov is leaping up and trying to strangle people. The other is that this region is claimed by the Tholians, mysterious but happily inexpensive special-effect beings who are sticklers for the rule of law. The Tholians turn up and tell the *Enterprise* to hoof off. Spock explains why they must stay, and to give them their due, the Tholians listen and respect his wishes. But when circumstances change and the *Enterprise* must stay longer than planned, the Tholians start building a huge energy lattice, or web, around the *Enterprise*. It's one of the most effective and memorable effects in the whole series: pure ticking clock. Kirk is eventually restored, as we know he must be, but in the meantime Spock and McCoy bicker pretty much ceaselessly. Against expectations, it's Spock whose behaviour seems overly emotional, while McCoy, the doctor who has seen death many times, believes it's time to accept that Jim has gone and get the hell out of there. The best moment of all is when the pair of them watch a video message Kirk had left for this very eventuality, in which he tells them to stop arguing and get on with things. They look oddly sheepish, for middle-aged men of such high rank and achievement.*

---

* This was Judy Burns and Chet Richards's first script sale. Burns went on to a long and successful writing career and served as producer on *Airwolf* and co-producer on *Magnum PI*. In Japan this episode was entitled 'Crisis of Captain Kirk, Who Was Thrown Into Different-Dimensional Space'.

'The Enterprise Incident' is one of those shows that cleave fandom in half. Some – and I would imagine Roddenberry would have been in this camp – blanch at the liberties taken with characters, story and the previously unblemished integrity of Starfleet. The rest of us delight in a clever and unexpected spy caper, Dorothy Fontana's last *Star Trek* script under her own name. Kirk has been behaving strangely for a while, as though under intolerable stress. Suddenly, for no apparent reason, he orders the *Enterprise* across the neutral zone and straight into Romulan space. Some Romulan ships show up and demand surrender. Kirk and Spock beam over and meet a female Romulan commander, whose name we never learn. She accuses Kirk of trying to steal the Romulans' exciting new cloaking device. Spock says that, if so, his captain is not following orders and has gone rogue. Kirk, doing bonkers acting, is thrown into a cell. The Romulan commander, who is trying to seduce Spock over to the dark side, proclaims him the new captain of the *Enterprise*. Kirk objects. 'I'll kill you, you filthy traitor! I'll kill you! I'll kill you!'

'He is not sane,' says Spock.

Kirk lunges at him, and Spock responds with what he calls 'the Vulcan death grip'.

'But there's no such thing as the Vulcan death grip,' says Nurse Chapel, back on the *Enterprise*.

'Ah, but the Romulans don't know that,' says Kirk, now no longer bonkers and about to reveal the plot to Bones and Scotty. We learn that the captain and his first officer are acting on secret Starfleet orders, and really are planning to steal the cloaking device. While Spock distracts the Romulan commander over dinner, Kirk will have some pointy ears installed and beam over and nab the device. It's all completely ridiculous, but carried off with great style and humour, and pacily directed by none other than

John Meredyth Lucas. We even learn something new about Vulcans.

'There is a well-known saying,' says the Romulan commander, 'or is it a myth, that Vulcans are incapable of lying.'

'It is no myth,' says Spock.

But hold on: in this episode Spock lies more than once, by omission if not overtly. So when he says that Vulcans do not lie, that itself could be a lie. But if he had said that Vulcans do tell the occasional whopper when labyrinthine plotlines demand it, that would have been the truth, if not the whole truth or nothing but the truth.

'The Enterprise Incident' has generated controversy in fan circles with its portrayal of something approaching romance between Spock and the Romulan commander. In Fontana's first draft, says David Gerrold, they didn't even touch. Spock's most tender line was 'I admire your mind'. A later draft, written by the new story editor Arthur Singer, had Spock 'raining kisses on every square inch above the shoulder'. Fontana sent a strongly worded memo objecting to this, and the scene as shot seems to have been a compromise between the two extremes. Nimoy and Joanne Linville, who played the commander, touch fingers and look longingly into each other's eyes. I think they carry it off, just about, but it's a near thing. Nonetheless Fontana was bombarded by furious letters from viewers, some of whom insisted that, according to 'Amok Time', Vulcans only had sex every seven years. Which, if true, would be yet another reason they never crack a smile.*

On one occasion, the budget cuts actually worked to an episode's advantage. In 'Spectre of the Gun' (3.6), the *Enterprise* has been sent to make contact with the reclusive,

---

* Nimoy loved 'The Enterprise Incident'. 'Scripts like this added to the moral structure of the *Star Trek* universe. The durability of such fine work is endless; I felt that the more of it we were able to do, the more we added to the show's life span.'

xenophobic Melkotians, who are not to be confused with all the other reclusive, xenophobic alien races we have met. Beaming down to a planet apparently populated by fog machines, our landing party are informed that they are trespassing and must die, and that the means of their death will be drawn from the mind of their captain. Who, as we know, is a fan of the old American west, so our five are thrown into a surreal recreation of the Gunfight at the OK Corral, in which they will be the losing side. The idea for this episode (Gene Coon's, written under his pseudonym 'Lee Cronin') had been knocking around since season one, but the cost of building an outdoor western set had always been prohibitive. Matt Jefferies's ingenious solution was to build a set indoors that was clearly a set, as though from the low-budget western B-movie of Kirk's imagination. Buildings have only a front wall, and the sides and backs are open to the elements. Signs and clocks hang in mid-air, and the sign with the word 'Sheriff' uses the same font as the main titles to the show. Its wrongness makes it far creepier and more alien than expensive verisimilitude would have done.*

But now it's time to acknowledge the elephant in the room. 'Spock's Brain' (3.1) has as poor a reputation as any episode, of any show, ever: it has become a byword for silliness within *Star Trek* fandom and without. A mysterious ship approaches the *Enterprise*. A beautiful young woman, only just wearing those clothes, mysteriously appears on the bridge. Mysteriously, she renders everyone unconscious. When they all awake, they find Spock lying in sickbay with a mysterious void in his skull where his brain used to be.

'It's the greatest technical job I've ever seen,' says McCoy.

---

* I wonder, too, whether it had not been at least partly inspired by Patrick McGoohan's folie de grandeur *The Prisoner* (1967–8), one of whose episodes, 'Living in Harmony', was also set in the western B-movie backlot of our imaginations.

'Every nerve ending in the brain must have been neatly sealed. Nothing ripped, nothing torn, no bleeding. It's a medical miracle.' He can keep the brainless husk of Spock alive for twenty-four hours or so, but after that it's curtains. 'In this whole galaxy, where are you going to look for Spock's brain? Where are you going to find it?'

The babe-rocket, though, has left a convenient ion trail, which leads to Sigma Draconis VI, a primitive planet in the midst of an ice age. Kirk and a landing party beam down and bump into some local neanderthals.

'We mean you no harm,' says Kirk, holding a phaser.

'You are small, like the Others,' says the lead caveman.

'Who are the Others?' says Kirk.

'Givers of pain and delight,' says the caveman.

Bones now arrives with Spock's body, which he can operate with a remote control. Walk this way! Walk that way! Before they know it they are all in a high-speed lift masquerading as a cave, zooming down to an underground complex where the 'givers of pain and delight', wearing miniskirts and thigh-length boots, hang out and exchange make-up tips. Spock's brain is running this underground complex, as his voice helpfully informs us via Scotty's communicator. The girls, though comely, know nothing about anything, educational standards having fallen rather sharply in the past few thousand years. Nor do they seem to survive long after the age of twenty-five. McCoy must don 'the Teacher', a spiky helmet connected to a vast database, which gives him the temporary expertise on how to put Spock's brain back in and connect all the bits together. But can he restore the old cabbage before his knowledge runs out?

The case against 'Spock's Brain' rests on one thing: its boundless stupidity. Director Marc Daniels, a regular on the roster throughout season two, was so dismayed by it that he left the series. Bob Justman, whose idea it was to give McCoy the surgical knowledge through 'the Teacher', described it as 'late lamented'. Shatner, in his 2008 book *Up Till Now*, suggested that its plot was a tribute to the NBC execs who had slashed the show's budget and given it the Friday night death slot.

And yet this was another script from the fertile pen of Gene Coon, still writing as Lee Cronin. What's more, Freiberger and NBC liked it well enough to start the season with it.

I have to admit – the slightly smaller elephant accompanying the larger elephant in this now rather crowded room – that when I was little, I loved 'Spock's Brain'. And now that I'm big, I don't dislike it as much as everyone tells me I should. Its idiocy is, somehow, its saving grace. The true one-star episodes are unwatchable for all sorts of reasons, but mainly for their dullness. Despite some longueurs, 'Spock's Brain' is too daft to be dull. If it made more sense, it wouldn't be as much fun.*

Watch any number of Freiberger episodes back to back, as I'm afraid I have just done, and you start noticing certain tics: Freiberger signatures, if you like. One is the Superior Technology Short-Cut. Most of the regular villain races, such as Klingons and Romulans, have technology roughly on a par with the Federation's, so that when the Romulans develop a superior cloaking device, Kirk and Spock have to go to extreme lengths to steal it. But one-off villain races, and even one-off villains, routinely have powers that far exceed our own, without explanation. The partially costumed lovelies in 'Spock's Brain' have ion-propelled spaceships and a little device that knocks everyone out with a single sound effect. In 'Requiem for Methuselah', Flint can turn the *Enterprise* into a coffee-table ornament at

---

* Gene Coon was divorcing his first wife at around the time he wrote it, and about to marry his childhood sweetheart. 'Givers of pain and delight' was a phrase that came from the heart.

the touch of a button. in 'Let That Be Your Last Battlefield' (3.15), a nuance-free racism allegory in which a man with white skin on one side of his face and black skin on the other pursues another man with the same combo, except reversed, one of them can take control of the *Enterprise* by mind control alone. In the truly unwatchable 'Whom Gods Destroy' (3.14), a witless remake of 'Dagger of the Mind', the lead psychopath has learned shapeshifting techniques on his travels, so he can change into anyone whenever he wants to. This isn't just lazy writing, although it is very lazy writing indeed. It's wilfully incompetent, and undermines everything surrounding it.

Another signature is the Freiberger Beat. This is the moment in almost every third-season episode when we learn that there is a new threat, or maybe a renewed threat, to our heroes, and quick action is called for. But presumably to ramp up the tension, no one does anything for about five seconds. There's a great example in 'The Lights of Zetar' (3.18), in which a cherished library planet has been obliterated by an optical effect full of disembodied aliens. The landing party is on the planet, surveying the damage, when back on the *Enterprise* Chekov sees that the optical effect has turned back and is coming back to the planet. Big music!

Kirk and the landing party stand for a while. Mulling it over.

A bit more music.

On the *Enterprise*, the screen shows the optical effect is speeding up.

The planet has no defences. If they're still there, the landing party will be killed.

They stand a bit longer. Time to act now, surely.

Finally, like an elderly man covered in treacle, Kirk calls Scotty and asks him to beam them up.

Phew! That was a close one!

The only possible explanation is that Freiberger thought the audience were stupid. But you would have to be quite stupid yourself to think they were as stupid as that.

Any more elephants? Just the one. 'Plato's Stepchildren' (3.10), a turgid slab of drivel set on a planet whose inhabitants claim to be the unimaginably long-lived followers of a certain Greek philosopher, was the episode of the Interracial Kiss. These aliens have psychokinetic powers, so can force the *Enterprise* crew to do anything they want them to, partly because they are bored, but also because they want us to be too. Kirk and Uhura are compelled into an embrace, which was said to be the first interracial kiss ever seen on American network television. NBC were nervous. The southern states, they expected, might run riot, and burn effigies of prominent network executives.

The legend has been a little simplified. 'Interracial' seems to be defined here only as black and white. Kirk himself had kissed the Vietnamese actress France Nguyen only a few weeks earlier, in 'Elaan of Troyius' (filmed first, but shown later). David McCallum had kissed an Asian actress in *The Man From U.N.C.L.E.* back in 1966. And in the more lax arena of light entertainment, the notably white Nancy Sinatra and the unambiguously black Sammy Davis Jr had greeted each other on-stage with a friendly slobber over a year earlier in a variety special called *Movin' With Nancy*. That was on NBC too.*

So as the Memory Alpha website prefers, this was 'the first kiss between a fictional white male and a fictional black female to premiere on American television'. In the first draft of the

---

* I first heard that as 'Move In with Nancy'. Which would have been far more controversial, and possibly more entertaining.

script it had been Spock who kissed Uhura. Nichelle Nichols said that Shatner didn't like that. 'If anyone's gonna get to kiss Nichelle, it's going to be me . . . I mean, Captain Kirk.'

But did the kiss take place at all? Shatner insists not. Their lips, he says, did not actually touch; they just appeared to, thanks to an ingenious camera angle. As the scene was shot, NBC executives stood on the sidelines, making sure the kiss didn't happen. As Nichols told Shatner for *Star Trek Memories*: 'It was bullshit! Bullshit! It was simply and clearly racism standing in the door . . . in suits. Strange how a twenty-third-century space opera could be so mired in antiquated hang-ups.'

In her own autobiography, though, Nichols insists that they did kiss in every take, all thirty-six of them. A few others were shot in which they nearly kissed but didn't, and Shatner and Nichols pulled faces or flubbed them intentionally to ensure that they couldn't be used.

The fans were not bothered. 'We received one of the largest batches of fan mail ever,' says Nichols, 'all of it very positive, with many addressed to me from girls wondering how it felt to kiss Captain Kirk, and many to him from guys wondering the same thing about me.' The only 'negative' letter ran as follows:

> I'm a white Southern gentleman, and I like *Star Trek*. I am totally opposed to the mixing of the races. However, any time a red-blooded American boy like Captain Kirk gets a beautiful dame in his arms that looks like Uhura, he ain't gonna fight it.

Spock would get to kiss Uhura eventually, but not for another forty-one of your Earth years.

Two-thirds of the way through the season, Bob Justman resigned. He could bear it no longer. Cancellation was now a certainty. There was no saving the show this time. Even the cast had run out of patience. As Nimoy told Shatner for *Star Trek Memories*, 'I felt we were really on a downhill slide throughout the third year, and when we weren't renewed, I have to say I felt a sense of relief, in that we wouldn't have to worry about the fourth season being even worse than the third.' Spock had become most un-Spock-like over the course of the year, sneering out sarcastic orders in 'That Which Survives' (3.17), jamming with the hippies on his Vulcan lute in 'The Way of Eden', and falling in love nearly as often and as randomly as his priapic commanding officer.

On 9 January 1969, after the final scene of the final episode, 'Turnabout Intruder' (3.24), had been completed to no one's great satisfaction, the series wrapped for the final time, and everyone went home and wondered what to do next.

CHAPTER 8

HE'S STILL DEAD, JIM

Gene Roddenberry spent much of *Star Trek*'s final year writing a film called *Pretty Maids All in a Row* for Herb Solow, who had moved to MGM. 'It was a favour to Gene,' Solow told Joel Engel. 'But he was also perfect for the material.' Based on a novel by Francis Pollini, it was a story about a handsome teacher who slept with his female students. 'He loved young girls,' said Solow, not talking about Pollini or the teacher. That old charlatan Roger Vadim directed, and the result, according to one old NBC colleague of Roddenberry's, was one of the worst films he had ever seen.

By the time the series was cancelled, Roddenberry had moved off the lot altogether to write a new Tarzan film.

Immediately after cancellation, Leonard Nimoy was invited to replace Martin Landau on *Mission: Impossible*. He stayed with the show for two years. To watch these episodes again is to see a man whose emotions appear to have shut down. In 1973, Nimoy was guest murderer on an episode of *Columbo*, and again, restrained to the point of inertia. On the *Star Trek* set Nimoy had been known to stay in character, as Shatner put it, 'never smiling, never telling a joke and worst of all, never laughing at mine'. Nimoy wasn't enjoying it much either: 'I was, in a way, in deep isolation, and having a tough time. The character isolated me, and I think that during the course of a day on the set, I probably projected a certain kind of indifference, intolerance, frigidity, whatever. I remember one day we were sitting around waiting for a set to be lit, and I was sitting there totally stone-faced and out of it. One of our actresses said, Uh-oh, Leonard's in his Spock bag.'

The twin Vulcan suns cast a long shadow.

In the meantime, *Star Trek*'s seventy-nine episodes went into syndication, and were soon being rerun on local stations around the country. Each station, having bought the episodes as a job lot, could do what it liked with them, and many chose to 'strip' the episodes, running an episode every weeknight in the same slot. But these stations, knowing something that NBC didn't, usually stripped them in the early evening: 5, 6 or 7 p.m. A new audience was introduced to the show: the young. Wherever it was shown, *Star Trek* quickly built an audience and often overwhelmed the competition. Its reach began to expand.

In 1971, a couple of New York fans decided to mount a *Star Trek* convention.

Science-fiction conventions were nothing new: since the 1950s, SF obsessives had been congregating in large groups and small, to talk, share and gossip, free from the lofty indifference of the uncommitted. These fans found a venue, the Statler Hilton Hotel in Manhattan, booked it for a weekend in January 1972, and decided to charge $3.50 a ticket, with a dollar off if you booked in advance. How many people might turn up? They thought around six hundred. On Friday 21 January more than two hundred were queuing for entry six hours before the convention opened. By Sunday afternoon, more than three thousand tickets had been sold, after which they gave up and let everyone else in for free. Speakers included Gene and Majel Barrett Roddenberry (they had married in 1969), Dorothy Fontana and Isaac Asimov. People dressed up in Starfleet costumes they had made themselves. Hucksters flogged memorabilia. Everyone had a glorious time, and asked when the next one would be.

In time a whole string of *Star Trek* conventions would come into being, across America and then across the world, as the show's fans realised that they were not alone, that there were others like them. 'Live long and prosper,' they would say to each other in hushed tones at schools and colleges, in bars and workplaces: the secret sign.*

In February 1972, in the cartoon strip *Peanuts*, Linus says to Snoopy, 'I should think you'd get bored just sitting on a doghouse all day . . . '

'On the contrary,' replies Snoopy. 'Who could get bored flying the starship *Enterprise*?'

In June 1972, the *Los Angeles Times* described *Star Trek* as 'the show that wouldn't die'.

Gene Roddenberry, whose Tarzan script was sitting in a drawer somewhere, was now making his living primarily through convention appearances and college lectures. The *Star Trek* revival gave him renewed access to network money,

---

* Not surprisingly, the stars of the show would not always feel comfortable with the fervour of their more devoted fans. In 1989 *Playboy* asked William Shatner to provide the 'early warning sign of a Trekkie'. 'It's the wild-eyed look,' said Shatner, 'the hands lifted above the ears and the shambling walk that breaks into a run as they approach me.'

and the chance to try and develop some new TV shows. Four
of them would be produced as pilots: *Genesis II* (1973), which
was then reworked into *Planet Earth* (1974); *The Questor Tapes*
(1974), which he co-wrote with Gene Coon; and *Spectre* (1977),
which he co-wrote with Sam Peeples. None led to a series.* At
the same time, Roddenberry was working hard to convince
Paramount that *Star Trek* should be given another go. It could
be a motion picture, he said, or maybe a series of ninety-minute
TV movies, or it could return to the old format. The one given
was that Roddenberry should be the man in charge. Perhaps
surprisingly, Paramount seemed comfortable with this.

Star Trek fans were turning up everywhere. The head of the
animation house Filmation pitched a Saturday-morning cartoon
series to Paramount and won the contract, giving Roddenberry
complete creative control. Which he instantly ceded to Dorothy
Fontana, who acted as associate producer and showrunner.
Most of the original cast lent their voices to the project, Walter
Koenig wrote an episode and David Gerrold finally sold his
Tribbles sequel. The animation, though, was feeble and the
seriousness of the show hopelessly compromised. Fans such as
I fell upon The Animated Series, as it became known, with a
desperate hunger, and tried our utmost to ignore its manifest
weaknesses. It ran for twenty-two episodes.

Also in 1973 came a book that may prove to have been the
most influential of the hundreds, if not thousands, of books
ever published about *Star Trek*. David Gerrold had written 'The

---

* They are all worth watching, although possibly no more than once. Played by Robert
Foxworth, Questor in *The Questor Tapes* is an android, and a clear inspiration for Data in
The Next Generation. In a scene in a casino, Questor spots that the dice are loaded, and
manages to realign them by pressing them together in his hands. Data does the same
thing in a second-season TNG episode, 'The Royale'.

Trouble with Tribbles', and co-written the story for 'The Cloud Minders' in season three. *The World of Star Trek* was a cogent and thoughtful analysis of the show, and more: a hard-hitting critique, simultaneously loving and brutal. Gerrold could see why and how the show had worked, but also why it had declined so precipitously. And he was furious about it. Where the rest of us saw a qualified success, he saw a missed opportunity. Could anyone care this deeply about an old TV show that had been and gone and wouldn't come back? Only as much as the rest of us did.

Gerrold recognised that Roddenberry (with Coon, Fontana, Peeples, Justman, Jefferies et al.) had done something extraordinary. 'Whatever else one might say about *Star Trek* and how well it accomplished its goals, one cannot deny that it established *a new genre for television* – a genre as distinct and rigid as the western, the cop show, the private eye, the doctor series and the situation comedy. Gene Roddenberry developed "the *Star Trek* format".' Any later series about spacefarers would be made in the shadow of *Star Trek*, and would be unavoidably compared with the original.

It was all in the writing. As Gene Coon said, 'All of your production problems can be solved best in the typewriter.' Talented actors and directors could not rescue a duff script. *Star Trek's* best stories, said Gerrold, were about people, 'one or two individuals caught in a trying situation'. All my favourite episodes, and I'm sure yours too, could be described thus, and in this case 'people' includes silicon-based subterranean rock monsters protecting millions of unborn baby rock monsters. There's none more human than the Horta.

In seasons two and three, however, the series lost this focus on the real and the personal. In Gerrold's memorable phrase, Format became Formula. Format, he said, is the flight plan for whatever is to come later. But like any other kind of flight plan, 'the slightest error will magnify itself over a period of time if it isn't corrected or compensated for'. One such error, in his eyes, was the transporter beam. We know why this was included: to save time, money and shuttlecraft launches. It was ingenious, and to this day I would still like a personal transporter device to save me all those hours in planes, trains and automobiles. As would you, and everyone we know.

Gerrold believed that the transporter unbalanced the stories fatally. As well as getting our heroes into the story faster, it could also get them out of it too. So if Kirk was going to be captured and menaced by aliens, one of three things had to happen. Either the aliens had such superior technology they could nullify the transporter. Or the aliens took away his communicator and locked it in a cupboard. Or contact between Kirk and the *Enterprise* had to be cut off by some unseen force thought up at the last moment by a writer who had drunk fourteen cups of coffee and was seriously considering running off to join the Foreign Legion.

How many episodes do those explanations cover? A dozen? Two dozen?

What they should have been doing was writing a story in which Kirk was not captured and menaced by aliens. But the network liked its strange new worlds and its monsters, and Freiberger liked action-adventure. Jeopardy was a necessary constant, even when it was phoney, schematic jeopardy. As Gerrold said, 'It's adventure all right, but it isn't real drama.'

As *Star Trek*'s arteries hardened, so a character's 'personal involvement' in a story boiled down to whether they fell in love or not. If the whole story is about Kirk falling in love, and having to lose the woman he loves, as in 'The City on the Edge of Forever', then we will remember the episode for the rest of our lives. Whereas if Kirk falls in love as a subplot, because the girl is wearing an aluminium dress and has had her hair coiffed into the shape of a bread basket, we will have forgotten we have ever seen the episode by lunchtime tomorrow.

The second and third seasons showed several ways in which format can decline into formula. Regular characters apparently dying but shown to be alive after all. Aliens taking over the *Enterprise* for their own nefarious purposes, until Kirk bamboozles them into defeat. Dungeons. Outbreaks of space madness. Parallel Earths. More dungeons. And endless pain bracelets, or pain headbands, or pain cummerbunds, so that when Kirk doesn't comply with an alien's wishes, random agony can be enforced at the touch of a button.

'If *Star Trek* had been a truly dramatic series,' says Gerrold, 'the essential *Star Trek* story would not have had to have been "Kirk in Danger" but "Kirk Has a Decision to Make".'

As it happens, Kirk did have decisions to make, but they were usually facile ones. Racism? A bad thing. Let's nip it in the bud. A society recreating Nazi Germany? Definitely a bad thing. A lunatic asylum run by lunatics? Probably not entirely desirable, now you come to mention it.

The great episodes were about difficult, if not impossible, decisions. Do you follow a hunch that Spock and the rest of the shuttlecraft crew are still alive? Should we kill the scary rock monster rather than finding out what it wants? Do you let the love of your life walk under a lorry to save the world as you know it?

One of the more charming aspects of Gerrold's book is the series of extended interviews he undertook with the main cast members, while the show was still fresh in their minds and before all their anecdotes were burnished to a gleam by endless repetition. DeForest Kelley remembered pretending to operate on Mark Lenard as Sarek in 'Journey to Babel', and pulling out a tribble. Barely four years after the show's cancellation, he was bemused by the fans' continuing interest: 'The shows that are mentioned to me when I go back east are "The Trouble with Tribbles", "City on the Edge of Forever" and there was another one, "Shore Leave". I've never seen it where fans remember individual episodes of a show before, they remember them by the titles, who was in them, everything.'

I would have pleaded guilty to that too. But one quiet way in which *Star Trek* excelled was in its episode titles. 'The City on the Edge of Forever' comes from a line in Harlan Ellison's original script, in which there was more than just a glowing time portal on a dead planet, but a real city on the edge of forever, which was of course far too expensive to make or show. 'Dagger of the Mind', as we have said, took its title from *Macbeth*, and other Shakespearean titles include 'The Conscience of the King' (*Hamlet*), 'By Any Other Name' (*Romeo and Juliet*) and 'All Our Yesterdays' (*Macbeth* again). In addition, Harry Mudd quotes Jaques in *As You Like It* ('And thereby hangs a tale'), Spock and Miranda trade lines from *The Tempest* in 'Is There in Truth No Beauty?' (itself a quote from a poem by George Herbert), and there are three *Macbeth*-style witches in 'Catspaw'. 'Wink of an Eye' is a phrase whose first recorded use was in *A Winter's Tale*: 'Who would be thence that has the benefit of access? Every wink of an eye some new grace will be born.' 'This Side of Paradise' was also the title of F. Scott Fitzgerald's first novel, itself taken from a line in a poem by Rupert Brooke; 'Wolf in the Fold' is a minor misquote from Byron; 'Bread and Circuses' is from the Roman satirist Juvenal; and 'Who Mourns for Adonais?' comes from Shelley's 'Adonais: An Elegy on the Death of John Keats'.

Possibly my favourite title, however, is that of an episode that isn't up to much in itself: a third-season show in which the inhabitants of a planetoid fail to realise they are living inside it, rather than on its surface. All except for an old man, who once climbed a mountain, even though it is forbidden. 'For the world is hollow,' he says, 'and I have touched the sky!' It's a beautiful little moment, slightly ruined by his painful death immediately afterwards. But making that phrase the episode title as well was a masterstroke. Was it Freiberger's?

With the unforgiving rigour of the young – he was twenty-eight when he wrote his book – David Gerrold saw Roddenberry's *Star Trek* not as a landmark, but as a challenge. The series would be recognised as the best of its kind until someone came along and bettered it. And someone surely would. Someday. 'Television demands that it continue to top itself.'

The first serious challenger to the throne appeared in the autumn of 1975. *Space: 1999* was a British production from the stable of Gerry Anderson, who had made his name on kids' puppet shows like *Thunderbirds* and *Captain Scarlet and the Mysterons*. This 24-part series, though, was much more ambitious: live-action, high-concept, big-budget (for the time) and aimed clearly at the US market. *Mission: Impossible*'s Martin Landau and Barbara Bain were the stars in a predominantly British cast that included Barry Morse, who had spent much of the 1960s pursuing David Janssen across small-town America in *The Fugitive*. Landau, Bain and Morse were respectively the commander, chief medical officer and scientific expert on Moonbase Alpha in the year 1999, when a nuclear explosion had propelled our moon out of Earth orbit, and into deep space and all sorts of wild adventures.

(Remember that happening in 1999? No, me neither.)

It was nonsense, of course. No one on the show had stopped to wonder what would actually happen if the Moon did this. (It would mean the end of all life on Earth.) Nor had anyone given much thought to the Moon's path through the cosmos. In the show, the crew of Moonbase Alpha encounter strange new worlds and new lifeforms with bewildering regularity. In real life, they might float through space for several lifetimes without seeing a single planet. Suspension of disbelief, then, depended on your knowing nothing about astronomy or cosmology whatsoever.

Given these caveats, though, *Space: 1999* had something special about it. Here was a series with a touch of grandeur, ambitious design, high-quality special effects and a questing, mystical edge that spoke to the adolescent in me. If you happened to be looking for a cross between *Star Trek* and *2001: A Space Odyssey*, you had come to the right place. Episodes such as 'Earthbound', 'War Games' and 'Dragon's Domain' still stand up very well.*

In the US, the show was not a success. It had failed to gain a primetime network slot, and hadn't much troubled the now mighty *Star Trek* on local stations. By the skin of its teeth, its backers agreed to fund the show for a second season, but with a brand-new producer: none other than Fred Freiberger. The old pro arrived wearing a creative polo neck† and promising action-adventure instead of the more metaphysical themes of before. The tone was lightened, popular characters from season one disappeared without explanation, and monsters of the week became the norm. 'All That Glisters', for instance, featured a sentient boulder with malevolent intent.

The second season of *Space: 1999* was as bad as television can get. Not only had they thrown the baby out with the bathwater, but the bath had gone as well. There was scarcely a scene in these twenty-four episodes that wasn't glib, foolish, patronising and deadly boring. Needless to say, there was no third season of *Space: 1999*. Freiberger went on to produce the fifth season of *The Six Million Dollar Man*, which was also cancelled on his

---

* And let's not forget Barry Gray's epic theme music, which captured the show's tone to perfection.

† As photographed in Tim Heald's book *The Making of Space: 1999* (1976).

watch. In SF fandom circles he became known as 'the Series Killer'. He died in 2003, possibly of action-adventure.

The *Star Trek* revival continued. Paramount made it known that they would not be averse to the prospect of a feature film. Roddenberry pitched several ideas, wrote treatments, even wrote scripts. John D. F. Black and Harlan Ellison were among writers approached to see if they would like to have a go. Black had a story about a black hole that planets were using as an interstellar garbage dump, and was now threatening to consume half the galaxy. Ellison's story involved alien snake creatures that had gone back in time to assert their superiority in Pleistocene-period Earth, and stop humankind in its tracks. Robert Silverberg pitched a tale called 'The Billion Year Voyage', in which the *Enterprise* discovered the ruins of an ancient and advanced civilisation and had to battle other aliens to gain its spoils.

Paramount said no to everything. Some stories 'weren't big enough'. Others may have been too big. None was just right.

At around this time, according to director Phil Kaufman (another who was briefly attached to the putative *Trek* film), George Lucas made a few discreet inquiries, asking whether *Star Trek* was for sale. Paramount said no to that as well, so Lucas went off and made *Star Wars* instead.

In real space, the Space Shuttle programme was up and running. The first craft to be built wouldn't actually leave the Earth's atmosphere: it would be a prototype, used for training and flight testing. Knowing it would be ready for 1976, the year of the US Bicentennial, NASA's top man was minded to christen it the *Constitution*. Bjo Trimble, whom you wouldn't want to meet down a dark alley, had other ideas. After months of ferocious lobbying, with many thousands of letters sent by fans to the White House, President Gerald R. Ford announced that the first shuttle would be called *Enterprise*. On 17 September 1976 the craft made its public debut at the Rockwell plant in California. In attendance were Roddenberry and most of the cast (bar Shatner, for some reason). The photograph, if you can find it, is worth seeing, if only for the cast's clothes, which, in mutually clashing shades of beige, brown and orange, look far weirder now than any Starfleet uniform.

In 1977 Paramount changed tack. For a while its executives had been dreaming of creating a fourth television network to rival NBC, CBS and ABC. Now they decided to make it happen, by linking up independent stations across the country for one night a week of brand-new programming. The main attraction would be *Star Trek: Phase II*, as it would be called.* Roddenberry would executive-produce, and all the original cast would return, bar Leonard Nimoy, who was suing Paramount over unpaid merchandising royalties. Paramount ordered a two-hour movie to start and thirteen one-hour episodes thereafter. Saturday night would be *Star Trek* night in this brave new televisual world.

A lot of thought and work went into *Phase II*. In *The World of Star Trek*, one of David Gerrold's fiercest criticisms had been the tendency of the captain *and* first officer to beam into troublespots and leave their subordinates back on the ship to clear up the mess. Gerrold's point was this: 'A captain, whether he be the captain of a starship or of an aircraft carrier, simply does not place himself in danger. Ever.' He is too important, his training is too expensive, his skills are too vital. Send in others to take the risks.

Roddenberry had read the book too. For *Phase II*, Kirk would be ten years older and less likely to be gallivanting around the

---

* Sometimes *Star Trek II*. I shall stick with *Phase II* to avoid confusion with *Star Trek II: The Wrath of Khan*.

galaxy in his old cavalier fashion. So he would have a new, younger First Officer, Commander Will Decker, to gallivant on his behalf. There would be a new Vulcan science officer named Xon, and a new female character, Lieutenant Ilia, a Deltan, who would be completely hairless. According to the new series' bible, dated 12 August 1977:

> Just as Vulcans have a problem with emotions, Ilia has a problem that accompanies her aboard the starship. On 114-Delta V, almost everything in life is sex-oriented – it is a part of every friendship, every social engagement, every profession. It is simply the normal way to relate with others there. Since constant sex is *not* the pattern of humans and others aboard this starship, Ilia has totally repressed this emotion drive and social pattern.

Do we need to ask who might have written that?

Spock, by the way, had 'returned in high honour to Vulcan to head the Science Academy there'. Roddenberry offered Nimoy a couple of guest spots. Affronted, he said no.

Scripts were commissioned and written, and for the two-hour movie to kick things off, an Alan Dean Foster treatment called 'In Thy Image' was chosen. This told the story of an old NASA probe that returned to Earth after hundreds of years but now threatened the planet's very existence. Paramount executives loved it. None of them had seen 'The Changeling', but never mind: the decision was made.

Earlier that summer, *Star Wars* had been released, and as *Phase II* was gearing up for production, the world was falling in love with Han Solo and Princess Leia and small boys of every age craved their own light sabre. Legend has it that the unimaginable success of George Lucas's film influenced Paramount's executives to cancel *Phase II* and transform its pilot into a full ocean-going motion picture, but the truth is more prosaic. The US economy had begun to experience one of its periodic downturns, and suddenly it didn't seem such a good time to be launching a risky and expensive new TV network. Paramount's parent company Gulf & Western nixed the idea, and with the network went the *raison d'être* for *Phase II*.

But given how much cash Obi-Wan Kenobi seemed to be generating, there might be room for a moderately priced feature. Small scale, nothing too ambitious, cash in while the going's good. This space thing would probably be over in a year or two. And since we've got this script here, why not go with that?

Why not indeed.

CHAPTER 9

HE PUT CREATURES IN OUR BODIES

What had the others been up to in the intervening years? In most cases, not a lot. 'Hollywood has such a type-casting mentality,' said James Doohan in his autobiography. 'Casting directors and the Hollywood business world think only in terms of "He can do this and nothing else".' Doohan could do every accent and then some: after *Star Trek* he was only ever asked for one. DeForest Kelley, who had made dozens of films in his youth, worked only intermittently after *Star Trek*, and barely at all after the movies began. Possibly the most humbling decline was that of William Shatner himself, who found himself typecast into apparently permanent unemployment in the early 1970s. After an expensive divorce, he lost his home and lived for a while in a camper van in the San Fernando Valley. Shatner has since referred to this time in his life as 'that period'. He says he can barely remember it. But work picked up eventually, and like his former first officer, Shatner was cast as a guest murderer in *Columbo*, turning in as camp a performance by an avowedly heterosexual actor as can ever have been seen on American television. In 1975 he was cast opposite Doug McClure in the western-themed secret agent show *Barbary Coast*. I remember this as good fun, but American audiences were harder to please. The show lasted thirteen episodes.*

When did it dawn on the cast that *Star Trek* would be the defining work in their lives, the shadow from which they would never escape? Leonard Nimoy's 1975 autobiography was called *I Am Not Spock*; his 1995 follow-up was called *I Am Spock*.†　It's analogous, I think, to the pop star who has one great hit, and performs it and performs it and can then bear to perform it no longer, and says in interviews, I hope I'm not just going to be remembered for this song. Twenty years later he is performing the song again because that's what the audience wants, and he has come to terms with that. The *Star Trek* actors knew that, in some ways, they had been lucky. The feature films would enable them to stay in well-paid work, while they also enjoyed the unfettered admiration of possibly the most dedicated fans in the world.‡

Star Trek's greatest casualty may have been Gene Roddenberry. Ambitious possibly beyond the bounds of his

---

* When John Carpenter was shooting his 1978 horror film *Halloween*, the props department needed a mask for mad slasher Michael Myers to wear but they had no money to spend. So they went to the local costume store, bought the cheapest mask they could find and spray-painted it white. The cheapest mask they could find was a William Shatner mask.

† In the second book, he says that calling the first book *I Am Not Spock* was 'an enormous mistake . . . I've made a lot of mistakes in my lifetime, but this one was a biggie and right out there in public.' People mistakenly believed that there was no more *Star Trek* because he couldn't bear to play the character again. The second book is, in some ways, a mea culpa for the first.

‡ Or would that be *Doctor Who* fans? Discuss.

talent, the Great Bird had been always looking to expand his creative empire. *Star Trek* was always conceived as the first show of many. Roddenberry absented himself from season three partly because he had lost interest, and partly because he knew the show was doomed. James Doohan blamed him unequivocally for the season's failure. Freiberger might not have been up to the job, but it was Roddenberry who had hired him and who left him to take the flak.

By the late 1970s, though, Roddenberry hadn't had a series on TV for a decade. *Star Trek* was all he had left, and maintaining control over it became the primary purpose of his life. By the time *Star Trek: Phase II* was in pre-production, Gene Coon was dead, Dorothy Fontana was writing for every series in town, and Bob Justman, having walked out in high dudgeon in 1969, was still *persona non grata* on the Paramount lot. The only link between the old production team and the new was Gene Roddenberry.

His friends outside *Star Trek* frequently spoke of Roddenberry as a warm companion and a loyal friend. But he could be a difficult man to work with, and the older he got, the more difficult he became. On *Phase II*, Harold Livingston was hired as creative producer, another old pro who had scripted episodes of *Mission: Impossible*, *Mannix* and the previously mentioned *Barbary Coast*. He and Roddenberry fell out almost immediately. 'I noticed he either drank a lot or was on dope,' said Livingston later. Other witnesses say that Roddenberry was also snorting a fair amount of cocaine at the time. Alan Dean Foster's treatment for 'In Thy Image' needed to be expanded into a script, and Livingston took on the job himself. Roddenberry's subsequent rewrite, says Engel, was 'unanimously considered inept by the production staff', and Livingston made the mistake of telling him. (What he said, precisely, was 'Why did you do this? When something works, you don't piss in it to make it better!') This sparked off a war between producer and executive producer

that continued through draft after draft after draft over the
best part of a year. 'He wanted what *he* thought was the best
product,' said Livingston. 'It didn't matter what anybody else
thought.' Eventually the producer resigned in disgust and went
off to work with Aaron Spelling.

Star Trek: Phase II had now become *Star Trek: The Motion
Picture*, and Robert Wise had been hired to direct. Wise was a
heavyweight, laden with awards. He had edited *Citizen Kane*,
and directed *The Sound of Music* and *The Day the Earth Stood Still*,
The Andromeda Strain and *West Side Story*. Although he didn't
know much about *Star Trek*, he knew enough, when he read the
most recent draft of 'In Thy Image', to notice that there wasn't
any Spock in it. Wise's wife and her father, both Trekkies,
read it too, and were aghast. 'What's this?' they yelled. 'You
can't possibly do *Star Trek* without Spock! It just won't work,
because he and Captain Kirk have such a thing going!'* Wise
insisted that Paramount find some way of involving Leonard
Nimoy, who wouldn't even read a script until his legal problems with the studio had been resolved. So a young executive
named Jeffrey Katzenberg was sent to mollify Nimoy, who was
appearing on Broadway in Peter Schaffer's *Equus*. Katzenberg
saw him perform, and afterwards listened to his complaints.
Agreement was reached, hands were shaken and cheques
signed. Nimoy declared himself available. In March 1978 a
press conference was held to announce the impending production of *Star Trek: The Motion Picture*. All the originals would be
involved, the budget had been set at $15 million, and release
date was June 1979.

Battles over the script continued, however. Livingston's replace-
ment had been and gone, and Paramount told Roddenberry to get
Livingston back. As Livingston told Shatner and Kreski: 'I met
with him the following morning, and afterwards he messengered

---

* Quoted in Shatner and Kreski's *Star Trek Movie Memories* (1995).

me a script, which I read. One day later, I went back in to meet with him and Robert Wise and I told him that they might as well go jump off the bridge, because there was no way they could have shot this fucking thing. Still, in the end, I came back because they offered me a huge raise and I'm really greedy.'

Livingston said he would return as long as he had a guarantee that Roddenberry would not rewrite his work. A few weeks later, Livingston sent off his first draft. Michael Eisner, head of Paramount, rang up from Paris. 'What is this shit?' Livingston checked with Eisner's secretary that he had received the right draft. Leafing through it, he realised that Roddenberry had intercepted his version, done a quick rewrite and submitted that instead.

This went on, and on, and on. In the end the script would be rewritten throughout the film's production, with Livingston and Roddenberry continuously correcting each other's work. Rewritten scenes were not just dated, but *timed*. Livingston thought that Roddenberry was a great ideas man and a good story man. He just couldn't execute. Or as Livingston told Roddenberry himself, 'Gene, you wouldn't know a good story if it was tattooed on the end of your prick.'

On top of this, there were endless delays and problems with the special effects. The first effects house they employed spent five million dollars and produced almost nothing. FX maestros Douglas Trumbull (*2001: A Space Odyssey*) and John Dykstra (*Star Wars*) were brought in to clear up the mess. They did so, but expensively.

To Michael Eisner, the production was a nightmare.

'On a scale of one to ten,' said Jeffrey Katzenberg, 'the anxiety level on that film fluctuated somewhere between eleven and thirteen.'*

---

* Eisner would go on to run Disney between 1984 and 2005. Katzenberg ran its motion picture division between 1984 and 1994, before becoming one of the founding partners of DreamWorks.

A June release proved too ambitious. *Star Trek: The Motion Picture* opened on 7 December 1979: Pearl Harbor Day. It was, in essence, a rough cut. No one, not even the director, had actually seen the finished film the whole way through before the premiere audience. 'Never in the history of motion pictures,' said Katzenberg, 'has there been a film that came closer to not making it to the theatres on its release date.'

The strange thing is that it starts so well. Three Klingon cruisers bump into the huge V'Ger cloud and make the mistake of firing at it. In quick succession we see the ships' exteriors for the first time in glorious big-budget detail; we see their interiors, whose design will be the template for all future Klingon ships (hot, dark, smoky, sweaty); we see the Klingons' forehead ridges for the first time;* we hear Klingon being spoken (a few words that James Doohan came up with, and which later formed the basis for the entire Klingon language); we see our old friend Mark Lenard as the Klingon captain, almost unrecognisable under prosthetics; we hear Jerry Goldsmith's menacing V'Ger music, with its distorted clangs of synthesised guitar; and huge plasma balls attack and destroy the Klingon vessels, and leave no trace that they had ever been there. Fantastic!

It's the highlight of the film.

From there we flip back to Earth, where the *Enterprise* is in space-dock after a two-and-a-half-year refit. Admiral James T. Kirk, sporting natty new threads and a more bouffant wig, has been Starfleet's Head of Desks for a while, but for this terrifying new threat from deep space he wants the *Enterprise* back. Standing in his way is Stephen Collins's Will Decker, who may or may not be the son of Commodore Matt Decker from 'The Doomsday Machine' (he is, but no one ever mentions it), and is

---

* Make-up artist Fred Phillips, who had worked on the original series, said that this was the way he had always wanted Klingons to look, but TV budgets had stymied him.

the actual captain of the *Enterprise*. The pair of them will bicker tediously for about an hour: old git versus lantern-jawed new young git. Most of the rest of the crew are still *in situ*, looking much the same, despite the unflattering new costumes, for pastel slacks have made a comeback in the late twenty-third century. Only Spock is absent, having left Starfleet and returned to Vulcan to undertake the ancient ritual of Kolinahr, which purges all remaining vestiges of emotion. Just as he is about to complete the course, and receive a natty medal for his troubles, he hears the call of V'Ger from thousands of light years away.

'Your answer lies elsewhere,' says the high priestess.

The medal jangles uselessly on the ground.

Gradually, the crew comes together. Lieutenant Ilia, bald as an egg, played by the Indian actress Persis Khambatta, reports for duty and settles into the navigator's chair.

'My oath of celibacy *is* on record, Captain.'

She has no personality, but we do know that she and Decker were lovers, once long ago. Bones is back, with a huge false beard and most of the best lines.

'Your revered Admiral Nogura invoked a little-known, seldom used reserve activation clause. In simpler language, Captain, they drafted me.'

'Bones, there's a thing out there . . . ' says Kirk.

'Why is any object we don't understand always called "a thing"?'

But Kirk needs him.

'Dammit, Bones, I need you. Badly.' (Even in 1979 this made me titter.)

So there are moments of humanity to be enjoyed, but only in between long, weary, expensive special-effects sequences. When Kirk arrives on the *Enterprise*, he does so via a tiny shuttle piloted by Scotty. We are meant to share Kirk's wonder and stare at this new, detailed, luxuriously overhauled starship, but after seven or eight minutes of this we are bored beyond endurance. Later it will take about as long for the ship to leave its dock: every little movement is invested with so much significance you want to scream. Yes, we liked *Star Trek*. Yes, we're happy to see it back. But no one liked it this much. No one could.

These two sequences apart, though, the first hour of *The Motion Picture* isn't bad. It's just the last seven hours that drag a bit.

The *Enterprise* flies out to the V'Ger cloud, which is heading straight for Earth, possibly with global destruction in mind. But instead of anything happening, the ship flies past ever duller and more pointless special effects, all of which cost millions of dollars. Ilia is swiftly killed and replaced by an Ilia-shaped android probe, which refers to the crew of the *Enterprise* as 'carbon-based units' and demands to see 'the Creator'. Everyone in the audience has seen 'The Changeling' on rerun a hundred times, but Kirk and Spock and Co were actually there and they don't remember it at all. Not for nothing was this film nicknamed 'Where Nomad Has Gone Before'.*

The climax arrives eventually, but the reveal is well done, for 'V'Ger' is, in truth, *Voyager VI*, which had been sent out by NASA in the 1980s to gather information and is now returning to download its findings, having gained consciousness some-where along the way.† The only way this will work, it seems, is for Decker and the Ilia probe to 'merge' in a deranged Roman candle of mutual desire, and enable V'Ger to transcend its cor-poreal state or some other such nonsense. This is convenient, as it sees off Decker, the dullest new character introduced in living memory. He has one good line.

---

* Other nicknames are available, including 'Star Trek: The Slow Motion Picture'.

† This idea was Roddenberry's. Livingston could never come up with a suitable ending for the picture, but Roddenberry hadn't just seen 'The Changeling', he had executive-produced it.

'Jim, I want this. As much as you wanted the *Enterprise*, I want this.'

The Earth is saved, as we were rather hoping it would be.

At $45 million, *Star Trek: The Motion Picture* was the most expensive film Paramount had yet made. (*Star Wars* had cost $10 million.) If it hadn't been for the boundless generosity of the fans, some of whom went to see it three or four times just to confirm how bad it was, it would surely have ended the franchise and might have scuppered the studio as well. Why did we all see it again? Partly because of the glorious familiarity of it all. Shatner is reassuringly Shatner: his Kirk is slightly more weather-beaten but still decisive, risk-taking, bold. Spock starts the film as cauterised and withdrawn, but a close encounter with V'Ger frees him from his Vulcan shackles. Bones complains. Chekov screams. Scotty has a moustache. Uhura opens hailing frequencies. All is as it should be.

The other reason we went to see it again was its last line. Kirk sits in the captain's chair and prepares to take the *Enterprise* out of orbit.

'Heading, sir?' says the new navigator.

'Out there,' says Kirk. 'Thataway.'

That's what we really wanted. Next week's episode, the one they weren't going to make.

Star Trek: The Motion Picture made money, but reviews were terrible and word-of-mouth was worse.* But its most serious sin was a budget that had gone out of control. Katzenberg called it 'the beast that is eating the entire corporation'. Eisner is said to have come close to firing him. If the film hadn't made money, Eisner might have been fired himself.

Scapegoats were sought, and found. Harold Livingston,

---

* At the pre niere, Doohan admits he fell asleep, and says Shatner did too.

who had demanded sole screenwriting credit, and won it after a battle of wills (and lawyers) with Roddenberry, never had a movie script produced again. But it was Roddenberry who copped most of the blame. 'Gene simply didn't have the skills to be a film producer in terms of the size and scale of these things,' said Katzenberg. For the next film – and the good news was that there would be a next film – Roddenberry would be relieved of duty. He would be given the title 'Executive Consultant', which meant nothing, of course. He had no power, only a voice no one would listen to. Future films would go ahead without him.

The very slight irony behind all this is that for three decades *Star Trek: The Motion Picture* remained the best-performing film of the series at the box office, after figures had been adjusted for inflation. Only the 2009 reboot has since beaten it.

Back on the Paramount lot, a TV producer called Harve Bennett was called into a meeting with some of the studio's top brass. Michael Eisner was there, as was his boss Barry Diller, as was *his* boss, Charles Bluhdorn, the chairman of Gulf & Western. Bennett was a little taken aback. He had only been working there a week. His track record, though, was impressive, for at Universal he had executive-produced *The Six Million Dollar Man*, *The Bionic Woman* and *Rich Man Poor Man*, among other hits.

Bluhdorn was in the biggest chair.

'Sit down,' he said. 'What did you think of *Star Trek*, the movie?'

Bennett wondered whether he should tell the truth. Then he remembered his two children getting up from their seats half a dozen times to go to the loo or to buy ice creams.

'Well,' he said, 'I thought it was boring.'

This was the correct answer.

'Can you make a better movie?' asked Bluhdorn.

'Oh yes,' said Bennett. 'Yes, I can certainly make a better movie.'

'Can you make it for less than forty-five fucking million dollars?'

'Mr Bluhdorn . . .'

'Call me Charlie.'

'Charlie, where I come from I could make five or six movies for that.'

'Fine. Do it.'

Thus ended the job interview.*

Bennett found himself a screening room and immersed himself in *Star Trek*, spending three months watching (and rewatching) the seventy-nine episodes. The one that leapt out at him was 'Space Seed', with Ricardo Montalban as Khan Noonien Singh, the proud and arrogant survivor of Earth's Eugenics Wars, marooned with his glowing team of supermen and superwomen on a planet in the Ceti Alpha system towards the end of season one. Fifteen years had passed. Would Khan still be there? Might he be getting a little cross with Kirk, the man who had marooned him?

As ever, though, there were several false starts with the script, and although Jack B. Sowards is credited with the final screenplay (from a story by Sowards and Bennett), it is generally acknowledged that the final draft was the work of Nicholas Meyer, cigar-chomping novelist and screenwriter, who had been hired to direct.† Bennett had promised to send him the

---

* It is reported thus by Joel Engel, but slightly different versions of this meeting appear in several different books. I think we should presume that Chinese whispers have honed it down to this rather elegant exchange.

† Meyer had written *The Seven-Per-Cent Solution*, in which Sherlock Holmes meets Sigmund Freud, as both novel and screenplay, and written and directed *Time After Time*, in which H. G. Wells and Jack the Ripper travel through time to twentieth-century San Francisco.

latest draft when he signed on, but it never seemed to arrive. Meyer rang him up.

'I can't send it to you,' said Bennett. 'It isn't any good.'

'Well, what about draft four?' asked Meyer, remembering that he had referred to the current pass as draft five.

'Kid, you don't get it. Draft four, draft three and all the rest: these are unrelated attempts to get a second *Star Trek* script, and none of them works.'

'Let me read them,' said Meyer.

'There's no point,' said Bennett.[*]

Meyer did read them, and found 'bits and pieces of interest in each of the five. But no theme, character or situation was sustained such as it added up to anything.' But then he had an idea.

'Hornblower!'

(The inspiration came in the middle of the night. He woke up and said the word out loud.)

In his teens, Meyer had been a fan of C. S. Forester's novels of Napoleonic derring-do, featuring the English sea captain Horatio Hornblower. 'Like Hornblower, whose gruff exterior conceals a heart of humanity, Kirk is the sort of captain any crew would like to serve under. He is intelligent but real, compassionate but fearless, attractive to women but not precisely a rake.' He had no idea that Roddenberry was another Hornblower nut, that he had reached the same conclusions nearly twenty years before. Meyer arranged a meeting with Bennett and his producing partner Robert Sallin to tell them the good news.

'And the script?' asked Bennett, quietly.

'Well, here's my other idea,' said Meyer, taking out a pad of paper. 'Why don't we make a list of everything we like in these five drafts? Could be a plot, a subplot, a sequence, a scene, a character, a line even . . .'

---

[*] This conversation is extracted verbatim from Meyer's hugely entertaining if grumpy memoir, *The View from the Bridge* (2009).

'Yes?'

'And then I will write a new script and cobble together all the things we choose.'

They stared at him blankly.

'What's wrong with that?' asked Meyer.

'The problem,' said Bennett, 'is that unless we turn over a shooting script of some sort to ILM [Industrial Light & Magic] in twelve days, they cannot guarantee delivery of the FX shots in time for the June release.'

'June release? What June release?' asked Meyer. That was when the film was booked into cinemas. He hadn't quite appreciated the urgency of the situation. 'All right,' he said. 'I think I can do this in twelve days.'

Bennett and Sallin didn't respond.

'What's wrong with that?' asked Meyer.

'What's wrong is that we couldn't even make your *deal* in twelve days,' said Bennett.

All this is recorded in Meyer's book, published twenty-seven years after the event, but even if this isn't exactly the way it happened, it only confirms that he can write cracking dialogue. The upshot was that Meyer volunteered to forgo a writing credit, wrote the script in twelve days and ended up making what, for me, remains the greatest of the *Star Trek* films and, if I am going to be wholly honest, possibly my favourite film of any kind.*

We begin with Lieutenant Saavik in the big chair, guiding the *Enterprise* into the Romulan neutral zone to rescue a stricken Federation ship, the *Kobayashi Maru*, and succeeding only in having the Romulans attack and destroy the ship. It's a simulation, of course, only the first case of sleight of hand in this sublimely wriggly narrative. Saavik – Kirstie Alley in her first major role, and I fell badly in love with her in those few

---

* In 2014, *Empire* magazine placed *Star Trek II: The Wrath of Khan* at eighty-ninth in its list of the 301 greatest movies of all time. If I had been invited to vote, I'm sure my influence alone would have lifted it to at least eighty-eighth.

minutes – has failed the test. The lights come up, the crew members we thought were dead open their eyes, and Admiral Kirk walks in, heroically backlit, to pass judgement on her attempt. The *Kobayashi Maru* scenario, he reveals, is a no-win situation, although we will soon discover that he doesn't believe in such things. In Meyer's ingenious script, everything eventually links up to everything else. It's a narrative jigsaw in which every line counts, and every echo and every twist comes as a surprise, however many times you see it. If this isn't a set text on screenwriting courses, why the hell not?*

The themes are ageing, friendship and death. In *The Motion Picture*, everyone's encroaching age was not so much denied as ignored. Here, it's the meat of the story. Kirk is fifty and feeling it. He has to wear reading glasses because he is allergic to Retinox. Spock, now promoted to captain, seems easier in his skin than before. The tortured young Spock has been replaced by a dry, witty, mature man who acknowledges his human half, and declares friendship for Kirk in a way we haven't heard before. ('I am, and always shall be, your friend.') You can almost hear Leonard Nimoy exhale with relief.

Leaving space dock once again (with the same footage as last time, edited down to seconds), the *Enterprise* embarks on a three-week training run, with all but the principals (Spock, McCoy, Uhura, Scotty, Sulu) replaced by young cadets. The ship's status has been subtly reduced since the first film, as though acknowledging that both she and her crew are slightly past their best. Out in deep space a new ship, the USS *Reliant*, led by Captain Terrell (Paul Winfield) and with our own Pavel Chekov as First Officer, is scouting for a planet on which to unleash the Genesis Device, a sort of instant terraforming machine (i.e. weapon of unimaginable power).

---

* In her audition for Saavik, Kirstie Alley told Meyer that she had long been fixated on Spock. And then, during production, admitted that she would sleep wearing her Vulcan ears.

They beam down to one godforsaken rock to check out some anomalous lifesigns ('I suppose it could be some pre-animate matter caught in the matrix') and find a wrecked ship, empty but clearly inhabited. We know whose ship it is because we watched 'Space Seed' again last week, but Chekov doesn't. He sees a buckle with the words 'Botany Bay' emblazoned on it.

'Botany Bay? . . . Botany Bay! Oh no!'*

(On the bookshelf next to the buckle, there are hardback copies of *Paradise Lost*, *King Lear* and *Moby-Dick*. Khan has had fifteen years to read and reread these books. He has absorbed them into the very core of his being.)

At the end of 'Space Seed', Khan and his genetically superior acolytes were left on Ceti Alpha V to make a new life. Six months later, the neighbouring planet exploded and their home was turned into a lifeless wasteland. Did anyone think to check up on them? It has been fifteen years. For sixteen years, ever since 'The Corbomite Maneuver', Lieutenant Bailey has been sitting in that little room with Balok drinking tranya. For all his qualities, Kirk is prone to carelessness. Khan feels hard done by.

'Admiral!' he whispers, with shock and loathing, on finding that his enemy has been promoted. 'Admiral!'†

Ceti Alpha V still has one form of indigenous life, however, a sort of truth-serum maggot that makes people do what Khan tells them to. Chekov and Terrell each get one in the ear, thus unleashing the great Chekov scream. This enables Khan to take over the

---

* One small problem: 'Space Seed' was a season-one episode and Pavel Chekov didn't join the cast until season two. The SS *Botany Bay* should mean nothing to him. Nicholas Meyer knew this but didn't think it mattered. Walter Koenig knew this but didn't say anything for fear that his scenes would be given to someone else. When Khan sees Chekov he says, 'I never forget a face,' so to save our sanity, let's all pretend that Chekov was on the Enterprise in season one: we just didn't see him. Khan did and that's the main thing.

† Marla McGivers, the Starfleet officer who had accompanied Khan into exile, was originally supposed to be there too, until Harve Bennett discovered that the actress who had played her, Madlyn Rhue, had multiple sclerosis and was now confined to a wheelchair. (She eventually died of complications from the disease.) Bennett thought it would be unfair to recast, so the character was written out.

Reliant and hop over to the space station where the Genesis Device is now ready to go. Did I mention that the scientists in charge of this are an old girlfriend of Kirk's and his rather bitter curly-haired son? This film is never knowingly underplotted.

Much of the rest of the film is a cat-and-mouse chase between Kirk and Khan. Once Khan has captured the Genesis Device, his far-too-young acolytes (all still in their twenties, while he is comfortably middle-aged) tell him that he could go anywhere and do anything with it. But Captain Ahab cannot stop himself chasing the whale. The one weakness in the structure is that Kirk and Khan never meet face-to-face. They talk to each other over communicators and viewscreens, unceasingly, but are never in the same room at the same time. A scene in which they met and fought was written but not filmed.

(Incidentally, Khan's absurdly muscular chest, assumed by most of us to have been a prosthetic, was Montalban's own. During filming he celebrated his sixty-first birthday.)

The film's great non-secret was that Spock would die. This was before the internet, before the age of the spoiler, when plot-shocks could be kept from the cinema-going public. But not this time, as Harve Bennett told Shatner and Kreski:

> When the news leaked, I immediately began looking for the person responsible, and I ultimately came up with enough evidence to indicate that it was Roddenberry ... The reason I'm daring to say this on the record is because there was a memo that went out to only seven people ... It was about ten pages long, and it was the first written notice that Spock would die ... Within hours, Gene wrote an ardent memo back, saying 'You cannot do this!!!' Within three days, the letters from the fans started arriving. I rest my case, Your Honour.

(Nicholas Meyer would receive one letter that read, 'If Spock dies, you die.')

Of the regular cast, Leonard Nimoy had been the most reluctant to participate in the new film. He had been dismayed by *The Motion Picture*, and saw no point in continuing the series if its only purpose was to make money for Paramount. His first response to Harve Bennett's overtures, therefore, had been a firm 'No'. Then, at a party, Bennett came up to him and said, 'Leonard, how would you like to have a great death scene?'

'He caught me completely by surprise with that one,' Nimoy told Gross and Altman. 'The more I thought about it, the more I thought, "Well, maybe that's the honest thing to do. Finish it properly rather than turn your back on it."'

In early drafts the death scene came at the beginning of the film, and moved further and further back until it reached its proper place as the film's climax. At the last minute Nick Meyer added the teaser in the *Kobayashi Maru* scene, where it looks as though Spock has been killed. A few moments after this, Kirk bumps into Spock in the corridor and says, 'Aren't you dead?' The wit and knowingness in this line are typical of the film as a whole. As Shatner wrote in *Star Trek Movie Memories*, 'Our characters seemed alive again, perhaps more vibrant than ever before. Our exchanges seemed more genuine, less formal, less preachy, and humour for the first time in a long time was given its due as one of the truly important elements of the best of *Star Trek*.' Humour, and *Moby-Dick*.

'From hell's heart, I stab at thee. For hate's sake, I spit my last breath at thee.'*

'It was as if the years between this film and the old show never existed,' said Shatner afterwards. 'They've captured the essence of what made the show wonderful,' said Nichelle Nichols. 'I think that if you can point to one single element that makes the film successful,' said Walter Koenig, 'it is the

---

* When they met for lunch before shooting, Meyer gave Montalban a copy of *Moby-Dick* and said, 'It's all in this book.'

presence of a formidable, worthy antagonist . . . Nick Meyer was quoted as saying that he would like to direct Montalban in *King Lear*,' and I can believe it.' James Doohan thought Montalban should have been nominated for an Oscar. Meyer himself said, 'I have never driven a Lamborghini but I imagine that directing Ricardo Montalban is as close as I will ever come.'

I went to see the film on its first Saturday night, and was so thrilled by it I took time off work and went to see it again the following Monday afternoon. And then again a few days later. Neither before nor since have I felt compelled to see the same film three times within a week. And having just watched it again on DVD for this book, I found it at times almost unbearably moving. As it happens, I'm a year or two older now than Kirk was supposed to be then.

It's the most quotable film in the series.

'He put creatures in our bodies to control our minds,' says Chekov, explaining the plot to Captain Kirk.

'I've done far worse than kill you,' says Khan a little later. 'I've hurt you. And I wish to go on hurting you. I shall leave you as you left me. As you left her. Marooned for all eternity in the centre of a dead planet. Buried alive. Buried alive.'

'KHAAAAAAAAAAAAANNNNN!!!'

And best of all, Scott and McCoy holding Kirk back when he arrives in Engineering to see that Spock has saved the ship, at the expense of his own life.

'No! You'll flood the whole compartment!' says McCoy.

'He'll die!' says Kirk.

'Sir! He's dead already,' says Scott.

Only once, I think, does Meyer go too far. As Spock's coffin is wrapped in the Federation flag, and Kirk speaks the funeral oration, our eyes catch sight of Scotty puffing out his cheeks to play the bagpipes. Every time I have seen this in the cinema, the audience has guffawed. It must have something to do with his face.

Funnily enough, there was one person who didn't like *The Wrath of Khan* at all. 'I thought they were very lucky they had the actor they did in Ricardo Montalban to play Khan, since it was not a well-written part,' Gene Roddenberry told waiting reporters. 'I also objected to other little things. Remember when the eel came out of Chekov's ear? What did Kirk do? He had a look of disgust on his face and grabbed his phaser and went "zap". Now, how dare he destroy a life-form that had never been seen before! It needs studying.'

But you can't please everyone.

CHAPTER 10

THERE BE WHALES HERE!

Even before *The Wrath of Khan* was released, Harve Bennett was thinking: sequel. He knew they had made a good film, and early screenings confirmed it. There was just one tiny structural problem. In the print Nick Meyer had delivered, Spock died and that was it. He was unequivocally deceased.

At these screenings, audiences who whooped and hollered with delight during the film were left numb and bereft by the end. Meyer later reflected that there's nothing American audiences like more than a tragedy with a happy ending, and so it was decreed that this ending would be lightened somewhat. Meyer was furious. He didn't want his bleak film leavened by unsustainable hope. But Bennett overruled him and arranged some minor reshoots, without Meyer's participation. This is what he added:

- Spock's two-second mind-meld with McCoy in Engineering, with the voiceover 'Remember'.
- A new voiceover for Kirk for the final scene on the bridge. 'All is well,' says Kirk, 'and yet I can't help wondering about the friend I've left behind. "There are always possibilities," Spock said, and if Genesis is indeed life from death, I must return to this place again.'
- And then the final scene on the Genesis planet, in which it is shown that Spock's coffin hasn't burnt up in the atmosphere, but landed safely and softly on some well-cushioned tropical foliage.

As Shatner put it, 'By now the test audience had gone from mourning Spock's death, to hoping he might return, to basically *expecting* same.'

And, as if to remove any final ambiguity, Nimoy provides the final voiceover: 'Space, the final frontier . . . '

For Nimoy, too, had been having second thoughts. He had had his death scene, but when it came to shoot it, he had been nervous and distracted, as though reluctant to kill off the character just as things were getting interesting. When he watched the completed film and saw the coffin lying on the planet's surface, he thought, 'Wow, this could go anywhere'. And then waited to receive a phone call from the studio about *Star Trek III*.

In Shatner's words, the rest of the *Enterprise* crew 'virtually danced back onto the bridge'. Nicholas Meyer, smarting after the last-minute changes to his film, said no, but Harve Bennett (who had described himself as the wing-commander to Meyer's squadron leader) was in for the long haul. Within days of *II*'s release, he was told to start writing *III*. Paramount green-lighted this film faster than any other film he ever worked on.

Nimoy and his agent were summoned to a meeting. As before, his first thought was 'Okay, I'll do your *Star Trek* picture, but what are you going to do for me in return?' While sitting in the lobby, reading a glowing review of the new film, Nimoy had a thought. Why not ask to direct the next one? 'It was an entirely spur-of-the-moment idea.'*

So he told Gary Nardino, the new executive producer, what he had in mind and Nardino said, 'Oh I think that's terrific, I've been thinking about that myself! You'd be great!' Had you really been thinking about that yourself, Gary? Are you sure?

A few days later Nimoy was summoned to see Nardino's boss, Michael Eisner. Did Eisner know what he had in mind? 'Absolutely not,' said Nardino. 'He has no idea. I have not told him a thing. *You* are going to do that right now.' This was wonderfully shifty. Nardino had given unequivocal support to Nimoy, up to the point of saying or doing anything about it. Fortunately Eisner liked the idea too. 'What a great hook! Marketing will *love* that!' Nimoy walked out of his office feeling elated. For the next six weeks not a single person at Paramount would return his calls.

The reality was that Nimoy directing the next movie was the last thing they wanted. Not only would he be a first-time director but worse, he was an actor. Producers call actors 'the talent' not as a mark of respect, but because they think that actors are foolish and vain enough to be flattered by being called 'the talent'. They distrust them nearly as much as they distrust and dislike writers, although at least they don't have to be polite to writers. No one is polite to writers.

As everyone in authority quietly tried to talk him out of it, Nimoy rang Nick Meyer to ask his advice. Meyer's reply was simple.

'Are you prepared to let this ship sail without you?'

---

* From *Star Trek Movie Memories*.

'Absolutely,' said Nimoy.

'Then sit tight. You're gonna direct the movie.'*

He was right, and by April 1983 Nimoy and Harve Bennett were hard at work, thrashing out ideas for the film's storyline, for Bennett to go off afterwards and write the script. Bennett said later that it was the easiest writing job he had ever had. *The Search for Spock* would take up the action from where *The Wrath of Khan* had left off, and add one new complication: what would happen if the Klingons found out about the Genesis Device?

Just as the second film stripped back the huge unwieldy structure created for the first, so the third simplifies matters yet further. Khan is gone, not even mentioned, all the cadets are reassigned and the *Enterprise* limps back to Earth for repair. Or so the remaining crew think. In fact, the ship is to be decommissioned, for being old and past it. The crew look at each other and think, are we old and past it too?

Sarek now shows up and asks Kirk for Spock's *katra*, his living spirit, but he doesn't have it. This, we realise, was the purpose of the brief mind-meld with McCoy at the end of the previous film. What is left of Spock is stored in the doctor, and he is not happy about it.

'The green-blooded son of a bitch! It's his revenge for all those arguments he lost.'

Sarek explains that Spock's body must be returned to Vulcan as soon as possible, and there McCoy can be liberated of the *katra*, which is beginning to affect his personality: he keeps calling things 'illogical' and trying to nerve-pinch people. Kirk and his crew must get back to the Genesis planet, where they have left Saavik and Kirk's son David, and get the body back. But the Genesis planet is now strictly out of bounds, so our chums must disobey orders and steal the *Enterprise*, which Scotty has conveniently automated in about five minutes flat. What was once the

* From Meyer's *The View from the Bridge*.

gang of three – Kirk, Spock and McCoy – has now become the gang of six or seven – Kirk, McCoy, Scotty, Sulu, Chekov and Uhura, with Spock to join later. An important shift has taken place in the group dynamic. Just as these actors found themselves bound together for life, whether they wished to be or not, so the characters now form a tight little band, who will stand or fall together. This also means slightly more opportunities for the second string, beyond aye, aye, sir and warp factor two.

Back at the Genesis planet, Christopher Lloyd's Klingon commander is creating suitable havoc, and the *Enterprise* will arrive in the nick of time. The problem is that the planet isn't stable. David used some protomatter in the matrix, which is bad, bad stuff, as all cooks know. The planet is ageing fast. So is the now revived Spock body, which is rather more animated than that in 'Spock's Brain' and goes so far as to engage in carnal relations off-screen with Lieutenant Saavik when his teenage *pon farr* strikes. Saavik, by the way, is played by a different actress, Robin Curtis, who suffers horribly for not being Kirstie Alley. As indeed do we, who wish that Alley's increased salary demands could have been met.*

Harve Bennett now unveils his great surprise. With the *Enterprise* further damaged in a skirmish with the Klingons, Kirk has no choice but to surrender. So he sets up the self-destruct command and beams off with his crew just as the Klingons beam on, to be blown to kingdom come.

'My God, Bones, what have I done?' asks Kirk, down on the planet as they watch what's left of the ship burning up in the atmosphere.

'What you had to do,' says Bones. 'What you always do. Turn death into a fighting chance to live.'

---

* According to Robert Schnakenberg, Alley did not care for the amorous advances of her commanding officer during the filming of *The Wrath of Khan*. During production, Shatner trod on a round styrofoam prop and playfully shouted, 'I've crushed a ball.' Alley expressed regret that it wasn't one of his own.

Gene Roddenberry hated this. Destroying the *Enterprise*, in his opinion, was pure vandalism. Enraged memos surged from his typewriter. But Bennett felt that something shocking was needed to spice up the film, which otherwise progressed on quite predictable lines. We know we will get Spock back in the end, but the question has to be, at what cost? Kirk and his crew sacrifice their careers and their ship, and Kirk loses his son David, who is stabbed by one of the Klingons. The stakes have never been higher, because they have never been more personal. Shatner, one has to say, is superb. It seems extraordinary that the day after filming wrapped on *The Search for Spock*, he went off to film the next series of *T. J. Hooker*, a police procedural TV show of startling mediocrity, through which he usually seemed to be sleepwalking. In *The Wrath of Khan* and *The Search for Spock*, by contrast, he is a genuine movie star.

Popular opinion decided long ago that the even-numbered *Star Trek* films are worth watching, while the odd-numbered ones are not. There is a kernel of truth in this. But *The Search for Spock* does what needs to be done. On the DVD commentary, Nimoy said that he had wanted the film to be 'operatic' in scope. 'I wanted the emotions to be very large, very broad, life and death themes . . . And the [look of the film] and everything about it derives everything from sizeable characters playing out a large story on a large canvas.' And you have got to love a film in which Scotty can cripple the brand-new transwarp drive, supposedly powering the shiny new USS *Excelsior*, by taking out half a dozen metal widgets the size of spanners. That's the kind of engineering we all understand.*

---

* Strangely, or maybe not so strangely, we will never hear another peep out of the 'transwarp' drive, so let's assume, kindly, that it doesn't work. Nor are there any future mentions of 'protomatter'. Most disappointingly, we never saw any more of Captain Styles, the prissy, pompous captain of the *Excelsior*, played by James B. Sikking. He was very entertaining, and had definite potential as a comic foil for Kirk.

The Search for Spock showed Nimoy's talent for directing actors – Doohan said he was the best they ever worked with – and made $87 million at the box office. The economics of these films were becoming straightforward: as long as it didn't cost too much in the first place, a *Star Trek* film was almost certain to pay back its costs. Studios like films like these. When would the next one be ready? Soon, please.

It also had to be soon because this cast was ageing. On 1 June 1984, the day of *The Search for Spock's* release, DeForest Kelley and James Doohan were sixty-four, William Shatner and Leonard Nimoy were fifty-three, Nichelle Nichols was fifty-one, and even thrusting young Walter Koenig and George Takei were forty-seven. Maybe that's why they hired Dame Judith Anderson to play the Vulcan high priestess. She was eighty-seven.

Nimoy and Bennett agreed that they wanted a change of tone for *Star Trek IV*. No villain, no space battles, but a different sort of challenge for our quietly maturing crew. Nimoy would tell Nick Meyer, 'The idea is to do something nice.'

The film would start with a huge deep-space probe arriving at Earth in the twenty-third century making loud whale noises. It is expecting an answer, but none comes, for the humpback whales it is there to make contact with became extinct a long time ago. Kirk, Spock and Co are returning in the Klingon bird of prey they acquired at the end of the last film, and realise that the only way they can save Earth – the probe is getting a little cross now – is to go back in time, find some whales and bring them back to the future. *Star Trek* is never better than when there is some moral dimension to its stories, just as long as it does not overwhelm everything else. *The Voyage Home* is an ecological parable, but obviously more. As Nimoy said, 'I wanted people to really have a great time watching this film, to really sit back, lose themselves and enjoy it. That was the main goal, and if somewhere in the mix we lobbed a couple of bigger ideas at them, well, then that would be even better.*

The *Star Trek* crew had been back to the 1930s in 'The City on the Edge of Forever' and the 1960s in 'Tomorrow Is Yesterday' and 'Assignment Earth'. Now they would visit 1980s San Francisco, where they would be fish out of water, looking for whales. Bennett and Nimoy thought that a contemporary setting might draw more potential viewers to the film than the fans alone. (They were right.) They knew there would be fun to be had by depositing these characters in such an unusual and unfamiliar environment. (Right again.) And purely practically, they could escape the confinement of spaceship and planetary sets, and go out on location, which they had never been able to do before, unless you counted the Vasquez Rocks, which at this stage no one did.

A complication now occurred. Eddie Murphy, fresh from his success on *Beverly Hills Cop* and thus one of the biggest stars of the moment, turned out to be a huge *Star Trek* fan and lobbied hard for a role in the new film. Nimoy and Bennett happily acquiesced, and Murphy was cast as an eccentric professor who believed in extraterrestrials, and thus became the *Enterprise* crew's primary ally when they landed on Earth. For seven months in 1985, this was the film. Then Murphy dropped out. Either he chose instead to make *The Golden Child*, or he was persuaded by the Paramount suits that it made no business sense to mix their main two franchises. If every Murphy film made $100 million, and every *Trek* feature banked $80 million, why combine the two and halve your take?† But time again was running short. The script, by two outside scriptwriters,

* In *Star Trek Movie Memories*.

† Whatever the reason for the decision, Murphy admitted later that it had been a mistake. *The Golden Child* was a stinker.

Steve Meerson and Peter Krikes, was felt not to work without Murphy in it.

It was time to call Nick Meyer.

Happily, he had a few weeks to spare and he loved the idea. ('I rarely get ideas myself and when I do, most of them stink. I am a pretty shrewd judge of other people's ideas, however, and I was convinced this one was a doozy.')* He and Bennett decided to split the script in half. Bennett would take Acts I and IV, the space stuff, and Meyer would write Acts II and III, the twentieth-century stuff. His first line in the script is just after the time-travel sequence, when someone says, 'When are we?' and Spock says, 'Judging by the pollution content of the atmosphere, I believe we have arrived at the latter half of the twentieth century.' When Kirk quotes D. H. Lawrence's 'Whales Weep Not!' – 'They say the sea is cold but the sea contains the hottest blood of all' – that's Bennett taking over again.

The film is a delight. People who don't much like *Star Trek* still love *The Voyage Home*. But people who loved *Star Trek* also loved *The Voyage Home*, for Nimoy, Bennett and Meyer remained true to the spirit of the show. Indeed, the benefits of writing for familiar characters with decades of backstory, played by talented actors at ease in their roles, can rarely have been better illustrated. Take this sequence, early on, on the Bird of Prey, when the crew have worked out the problem (probes, whales etc.) and now need a solution.

'Does the species exist on any other planet?' says Kirk.

'Negative. Humpbacks were indigenous to Earth. Earth of the past,' says Spock.

(We're seeing Spock, the wise adviser, plant the idea in Kirk's head. It's then up to Kirk, the leader, to make the decision.)

'There must be an alternative,' says Kirk.

'There is one possibility but of course I cannot guarantee

* Again, from *The View from the Bridge*.

success,' says Spock. 'We could attempt to find some humpback whales.'

'You just said there aren't any,' says McCoy, 'except on Earth of the past.'

'Yes, Doctor, that is exactly what I said,' says Spock.

'Well in that case . . . ' says McCoy, who suddenly realises that not only is Kirk a beat ahead of him, but he has already made up his mind. 'Now just wait a damn minute . . . '

'Spock, start your computations for time warp,' says Kirk.

They are superb, these three. All you ever have to do is write decent lines for them.

The three lead the seven, and everyone gets their moment in the sun. Scotty tries to speak into a computer mouse, and will later get the second-best line in the film: 'Admiral! There be whales here!'* No one mentions that he has grown increasingly cetacean himself since the last film ended. God knows what the food must be like on Vulcan, but it's possible that he has eaten all of it.

Chekov and Uhura, meanwhile, are out looking for nuclear fuel to regenerate the dilithium crystals.

'Excuse me, sir,' says Chekov to a San Francisco police officer. 'Can you direct me to the naval base in Alameda? It's where they keep the nuclear wessels.'

The policeman goggles.

'Nu-cle-ar wes-sels,' says Chekov, as if to an idiot.†

If anyone is unlucky it is again Sulu, whose fate it is in these films to be marginally underemployed. In fact George Takei had dreamt up a clever subplot for his character, and

---

* The best line, arguably, being Kirk's when they leave the cloaked Klingon Bird of Prey in Golden Gate Park: 'Everybody remember where we parked.'

† Chekov and Uhura try and attract the attention of several passers-by, who were paid extras and had been instructed not to speak. But one of them, a young woman with rather lovely long brown hair, did answer them. Nimoy liked what she was doing and kept shooting, and the production team had to have her hurriedly inducted into the Screen Actors' Guild as a result.

Harve Bennett had quickly written it in. On the streets of San Francisco, where Sulu was born, he would meet a small Asian boy who, he would realise, was his great-grandfather. On the day of shooting, however, the boy who had been cast in the role seized up with nerves. The scene was never shot. 'I could have cried,' said Takei, 'but I didn't, because you know, it's happened to me so often.'*

(Another idea not pursued was even more promising. Lieutenant Saavik, again played by Robin Curtis, is left on Vulcan at the beginning of the film, never to reappear. But in Meerson and Krikes's drafts of the script, she was pregnant with Spock's child, after his *pon farr* on the Genesis planet. What a terrific storyline, and what a waste not to use it.)

Replacing Eddie Murphy, after a fashion, was Catherine Hicks as Dr Gillian Taylor, attractive young whale scientist and slightly-too-young love interest for Kirk, who hasn't had a girlfriend in *decades*. Fortunately for us all, this one never develops beyond slightly uncomfortable flirtation.

'Don't tell me,' says Gillian over pizza. 'You're from outer space.'

'No, I'm from Iowa,' says Kirk. 'I only work in outer space.'

We see, from her point of view, just how daft these people look, slightly paunchy in their ridiculous costumes, not knowing what 'exact change' means on the bus. And yet at times we marvel, not least when Kirk swims underwater at the end of the film to free the whales into San Francisco bay. His wig actually looks like real hair. Every time I see the scene, this distracts me from what he is doing, and from everything else.

---

* Even if he doesn't have anything very interesting to say, *The Voyage Home* does reveal the full flowering of Takei's extraordinarily rich, deep voice, which now sounds as though he has been gargling with molasses non-stop for several years. It is a magnificent instrument by any standards, and it's only a shame that the franchise rarely found an interesting way of using it.

By all accounts this was an unusually happy production, but one surprising casualty was Leonard Nimoy and Harve Bennett's working relationship. Nimoy suspected later that Paramount had been playing them off against each other, in classic divide-and-rule corporate Machiavellian style. But the disagreements mounted, and by the end of filming they were scarcely speaking. The last straw, it seems, came when Paramount's Dawn Steel said that the dialogue between the whales and the probe should have subtitles. She was worried that audiences would be put off by not knowing what was being said. Nimoy and Nick Meyer disagreed passionately. 'We are better off not explaining it,' said Nimoy. 'Let it be mysterious and magical.' Or as Meyer put it, 'In art, questions are always more interesting than answers. Once you give the answer, the gas goes out of the balloon.' It may have been bad strategy to use words like 'art' in negotiation with a studio executive. Steel's inclination, and maybe even her job, was to assume that the audience was full of idiots. Every i was there to be dotted and every t to be crossed, maybe twice to be on the safe side.

The argument raged, then, but Nimoy was horrified to receive a memo from Bennett supporting Dawn Steel and the subtitles. 'I was furious, furious!' Nimoy later realised that Bennett was only doing his job as a good company man, but at the time it felt like a betrayal. Nimoy got his way in the end: the subtitles were abandoned, the mystery remained. But he and Bennett would not work together again.*

* One cast member who had no time at all for Bennett was Nichelle Nichols. 'Like too many other people in whose hands the fate of *Star Trek* has fallen, Harve refused to accept or respect the fans . . . [His] smooth, friendly manner masked a propensity for arrogance and cruelty that would grate on more than a few nerves.'

With hindsight, *The Voyage Home* can be seen as a high-water mark for *Star Trek*, both critically and commercially. Nothing lasts for ever, and this cast certainly wouldn't. The film grossed over $109 million in the US alone, although only about a quarter of that overseas. But Paramount were already thinking ahead. In October 1986, a month before *The Voyage Home* reached cinemas, a studio suit called Mel Harris made an announcement at a press conference.

'Twenty years ago, the genius of one man brought to television a programme that has transcended the medium,' said Harris, who may have been holding an onion at the time. 'We are enormously pleased that that man, Gene Roddenberry, is going to do it again. Just as public demand kept the original series on the air, this new series is also a result of grass-roots support for Gene and his vision.'

Paramount, in short, could smell money, and Roddenberry had the second, or third, or fourth chance that he had craved for so long. The new TV series, to be entitled *Star Trek: The Next Generation*, would adhere to Roddenberry's 'vision, credibility and approach'. It would be set seventy-eight years after the original series. None of the original cast would be involved, but there would be a new *Enterprise*, new characters, new (younger, cheaper) actors, new alien races.

'I'm not at all sure we'll have a retread Vulcan,' said the Great Bird of the Galaxy. 'I would hate to think our imagination is so slender that there aren't other possibilities to think about.'

Other possibilities were also being considered by Harve Bennett, who after a bruising experience on *The Search for Spock* wanted nothing more to do with the franchise. He wanted a long holiday, possibly followed by another long holiday. (He would later admit that on the three films he had worked on, he had used all the narrative tricks he had learned in twenty years of TV production.) But the director of the next film wanted him to stay. Indeed, he went to Bennett's house and spent four hours trying to talk him back. That director was William Shatner.*

Many years before – so long ago, in fact, that only lawyers could remember when – Shatner and Nimoy's contracts with Paramount had both acquired a 'favoured nations' clause. If one of them had a pay rise, so did the other. It worked well for both, as they had become good friends in real life and would take it in turns, as each film was made, to demand more and more money, to play bad cop while the other played good cop and feigned innocence.

As *Star Trek IV* wound down (says Shatner), Nimoy mentioned to him over lunch that, as he had directed a couple of the films, Shatner could use the favoured nations clause to insist that it was his turn. Other sources say that Shatner had already insisted on directing *V* as a condition for appearing in *IV*. But whatever the truth behind the story, the option was there, and he took it.

For Shatner had an idea. Fascinated by the tele-evangelists who were now clogging up the US airwaves, he wanted his antagonist to be a holy man of extraordinary charisma, who would claim that God had spoken to him. And what had God said? 'I need many followers, and I need a vehicle to spread my word through the universe.' This character would become Sybok, Spock's previously unmentioned half-brother, and the vehicle would be the gleaming new *Enterprise-A*, which Kirk had been given as a reward for saving the Earth from the whale-probe. Sybok, who enjoyed Freiberger-style mind control techniques that enabled him to have his way most of the time, would take the *Enterprise-A* to the centre of the galaxy to meet 'God',

* On learning that Shatner was to direct, George Takei is said to have cried, 'Oh my God! What are we going to do?'

who, despite his fluffy beard, would turn out not to be God at all but a villainous alien.

As Bennett told the magazine *Cinefantastique*, 'the real problem with *V* was that the premise was faulty.' If you're told that the crew are going to find God, 'automatically, and unconsciously, you know you're not going to because no one has and no one will, and no one would be so arrogant to say what they're depicting on screen is actually God, because others will say "No it's not".' So we know that this is a trick, and it will therefore be an anticlimax. Shatner, says Bennett, saw it as 'the greatest adventure of all', but Bennett said no, it's not an adventure because everyone is ahead of you. 'So what we have to do is make getting there as interesting as possible.'

Unfortunately they couldn't do this either. Bennett, working with a young screenwriter named David Loughery, discovered that the ancient rule still applied: you can't polish a turd. Released in the early summer of 1989, *Star Trek V: The Final Frontier* was an ungodly mess, full of inconsistencies, bad calls, dodgy effects and jokes that didn't work. Early drafts of the script had been too dark for the studio's taste, and more humour was requested. But Shatner did not have Nimoy's light touch as a director, and there was no Nick Meyer around to write imperishable lines about nuclear wessels. One 'joke' has Scotty saying that he knows this ship like the back of his hand, before walking into a bulkhead and being knocked out. Jimmy Doohan took forty takes to get it right. 'I found that very, very hard to do because I felt – whether it was Bill's intention or not – that he had constructed the scene just to put me down.' It was, as he said, 'humour at the expense of the character'. Fans hated it – I hated it – because we knew that Scotty *did* know the ship like the back of his hand, and would never do something so daft. As I have recently discovered, *The Final Frontier* is not an easy film to watch a second time, and its modest gross suggested that even the show's most loyal fans only saw it once.

At the tenth Golden Raspberry awards in March 1990, it won Worst Picture, and Shatner won awards for Worst Actor and Worst Director. It was also nominated for Worst Picture of the Decade, but lost out to 1981's *Mommie Dearest*. One can only assume that it was a very close call.

CHAPTER 11

MAKE IT SO

While Bennett and Shatner were inadvertently doing their best to kill off the film series, Gene Roddenberry was starting work on the new TV show. Posterity remembers us for our successes, if it remembers us at all, but the harsh reality of creative lives is that we must somehow manage to cope with all the failures that come in-between. Roddenberry had breakfasted, lunched and dined on failure for twenty years. *Star Trek: The Next Generation* – one of sixty titles his production team considered – was his last shot. Roddenberry was sixty-six when production started, and according to at least one source was on the verge of retirement. But when he heard that Paramount were gearing up to produce a new series, he insisted he was the only person who could do it properly.*

Paramount offered the show to all four US networks, and all four said no.† None was willing to commit to a twenty-six-episode first season in a guaranteed time slot with serious promotional expenditure. As yet uneroded by competition from cable and the internet, the networks still enjoyed a powerful oligopoly. However good or interesting or profitable a new show might promise to be, they would rather not be involved than cede any of that power. Paramount therefore decided to go it alone, and put the show straight into syndication. The studio would effectively create its own ad hoc network out of local TV stations that would broadcast the new show on the same night every week at the same time. There were enough mad old fans to make this work, at least to start with, and if the series went as well as everyone hoped, mad new fans would surely emerge. And without the pressures a network customarily imposed, Roddenberry could make the show as he wished. He would have a creative freedom neither he nor any other TV producer had previously enjoyed.

Even so, it all had to be put together at some speed. Episode one was due on screen almost exactly a year after that first press conference. By the end of November 1986 Roddenberry had produced a twenty-two-page writers' bible for *The Next Generation*, with the extensive assistance (unacknowledged) of David Gerrold. This sought to correct the more obvious flaws of the original series, before instituting any exciting new flaws of its own. No longer would a gung-ho captain

---

* He hadn't been Paramount's first choice for the job. Leonard Nimoy had been sounded out, but did not want to tie himself to a weekly TV show just as his film-directing career was taking off. The studio returned to Roddenberry with reluctance, as everyone knew how 'difficult' he could be. To keep him in check, they imposed on him a co-executive producer of their own, a bouffant-haired young studio suit called Rick Berman.

† Fox had recently joined the magic trinity of NBC, CBS and ABC.

beam down into danger every week. That was the first officer's job. The captain would be more of a CEO, running everything from the bridge. Nor would the new series rely on failing technology as a regular plot device. (Well, not to begin with, it wouldn't.) Machines now worked, and if they didn't there had to be an especially good reason. The new *Enterprise* would still be boldly going where no one (rather than 'no man') had gone before. In this century, 19 per cent of the galaxy had been charted, as opposed to 4 per cent when Kirk was in charge. The five-year mission was no more: this mission would be open-ended, and *Enterprise* crew would be encouraged to bring their families with them. To house this larger complement, the new ship would be twice as long as the old one, and eight times its volume. 'Most 25th-century [*sic*] humans believe that "Life should be lived, not postponed,"' wrote Roddenberry (or possibly Gerrold). 'People need people . . . in both family and community life, as well as other agreeable forms of human bonding.' The *Enterprise*, in short, was to be more domesticated, less 'battleship-sterile'. Although Roddenberry's 'other agreeable forms of human bonding' suggested that many of the women would still be wearing short skirts.*

The new production team featured several old hands. Bob Justman returned as supervising producer, and Dorothy Fontana, installed as associate producer, was given the task of writing the two-hour pilot, 'Encounter at Farpoint'.† It was Justman who found the man to play the new captain, Jean-Luc Picard. Roddenberry had imagined a French actor in the

---

* In an early memo, he proposed that the character of Deanna Troi should be 'a four-breasted, oversexed hermaphrodite'. Dorothy Fontana knocked that one on the head.

† Fontana had been incredibly busy in the intervening years. Among the series she had written for were *The High Chaparral* (two episodes), *Bonanza* (two), *The Six Million Dollar Man* (two), *Kung Fu* (one), *The Streets of San Francisco* (four), *The Waltons* (three), *Buck Rogers in the 25th Century* (one) and *Dallas* (two).

role. 'We saw some rather good actors,' Justman later told the
BBC. 'But we couldn't find that magical person.' In their spare
time Justman and his wife were taking a course at UCLA,
and one evening they attended a Shakespeare reading. One
of two actors taking part was a slender, bald, fortysomething
Englishman named Patrick Stewart. 'He read his first line and
I went crazy,' said Justman. 'I turned to my wife and I said, I
think I've found our new captain.'

Stewart came in for a meeting. Roddenberry was unimpressed. 'I won't have him,' he said. The more Justman pressed
his case, the more stubborn Roddenberry became. Captain
Picard wasn't just French in his mind, he was extremely hairy.
Roddenberry had already had one bald captain. As Oscar Wilde
once said, to hire one starship captain with no hair may be
regarded as a misfortune; to hire two looks like carelessness.

Only by pretending he had changed his mind and didn't want
Stewart at all did Justman manage to change Roddenberry's.
'Every time anyone mentioned Patrick Stewart's name to me, I
would explode and say, "I don't want to hear that. Don't tell me
Patrick Stewart any more." Finally our last possible candidate
came to audition for us. And the guy, whoever he was, read for
us and talked with us and he left the room, the door closed and
we were all silent. And finally Gene Roddenberry heaved a big
sigh. He said, "All right, I'll go with Patrick."'

A week or two before shooting began, Roddenberry and
Justman were asked to present their new captain to the suits at
Paramount. 'We figured they would not go for a bald man,' said
Justman. Patrick Stewart had his toupee sent over from London.
'He put it on and turned to us and it was so ratty, so awful-
looking it really looked like what it was.' Gene Roddenberry
said, 'For God's sakes take it off!' So they took him upstairs *sans*
rug, and the suits 'bought him immediately. They were thrilled
to hear that wonderful voice. It made everything seem better
and more exciting, more intense and entrancing.'

The voice. The actor's instrument. In the 1970s and 80s an actor could still become well known and make a decent living in the UK through stage work alone. Stewart had been a member of the Royal Shakespeare Company between 1968 and 1982, and had then moved to the National Theatre. He had also made a couple of notable contributions to the Golden Age of British TV drama. In Jack Pulman's *I, Claudius* (1976) he had played Sejanus, bodyguard and confidant of the Emperor Tiberius. And in Arthur Hopcraft's dramatisations of John Le Carré's novels *Tinker Tailor Soldier Spy* (1979) and *Smiley's People* (1982), he had been George Smiley's Russian nemesis Karla. In each series, Stewart had been seen in only one scene, never said a word, and yet left an indelible impression of ruthless, implacable malevolence. On each occasion he was playing opposite Sir Alec Guinness. Stewart lost nothing in comparison.

In 1987, Patrick Stewart was forty-seven years old. Despite a long list of credits, his reputation was not strong enough to bring a production of *Who's Afraid of Virginia Woolf?* into London's West End. *Star Trek* was not what he had aspired to. He knew nothing about the show, had never knowingly watched an episode. The idea of signing a six-year contract worried him. But his agent told him, don't worry, that's how the industry operates, it's just a precaution. The show won't work. You'll do a year or two, collect a big pile of cash and then you can come back to England and go back to the work you love. Stewart signed on the dotted line.

The *Los Angeles Times*, announcing his recruitment, described him as 'an unknown British Shakespearean actor'.

Most of the rest of the cast were equally obscure, but that's not so surprising in American TV, which is notorious for filling its shows with slightly bland, interchangeably good-looking young people whose acting skills have yet to be tested, and may never be. Early publicity shots did not look promising.

Oh look, there's a Klingon. There's a man with a white face and yellow eyes who might be some sort of Spock substitute. There's a man with a plastic hairband over his eyes. There's a teenage boy. And there's a woman in a short skirt. It's definitely *Star Trek*.

But wait a moment. Did you say 'teenage boy'? I cannot have been the only old-school fan who felt disturbed by this development. We did not need teenage boys in *Star Trek*. We recognised that the youth demographic needed to be pursued, preferably with dogs. But *Star Trek* was for grown-ups. It was manned (and womanned) by grown-ups, it dealt with grown-up themes and it solved its problems in grown-up ways. It might be watched by teenage boys (such as me, the previous decade), but we had never wanted to be Chekov, we had wanted to be Captain Kirk. Now we would want to be Captain Picard, or at a pinch Commander Riker. No one would ever want to be Wesley Crusher.

Even Wil Wheaton, who played him, didn't want to be Wesley Crusher in the end.*

Casts for new shows often look unfeasibly young because they may have to grow old in the role. Jonathan Frakes, as Commander Will Riker, the first officer, was a big, broad-shouldered man with a baby face and a slightly disconcerting vulnerability. His best-known role had been as someone's older brother in the Civil War mini-series *North and South*. Brent Spiner, as the android Lieutenant Commander Data, had come up the hard way through Broadway and off-Broadway musicals. LeVar Burton, wearing the plastic hairband over his eyes as Lieutenant Geordi LaForge, was probably the best known member of the cast, having starred as the young Kunta Kinte in the miniseries *Roots*. Marina Sirtis,

---

* It's worth noting here the full name of the show's executive producer: Eugene Wesley Roddenberr *y*.

as Counsellor Deanna Troi, was a north Londoner of Greek extraction, who had played the air hostess in the famous TV ad for Cinzano Bianco in which Leonard Rossiter spattered Joan Collins with drink. Denise Crosby, as gung-ho security chief Tasha Yar, was Bing's granddaughter and had originally read for the Troi role, while Sirtis had originally read for Tasha Yar. Roddenberry and Justman liked them both, but swapped them over at the last minute. Gates McFadden, as chief medical officer Dr Beverly Crusher, had a background in dance and mime, and had served as choreographer and 'director of puppet movement' on Jim Henson's film *Labyrinth*. Even her 'son' Wheaton had an impressive CV, having appeared in his first TV ad aged seven and starred the previous year in Rob Reiner's coming-of-age film *Stand by Me*.

The most difficult part to cast turned out to be Worf, the Klingon lieutenant, for one of the great steps forward of the intervening seventy-eight years was that the Federation had made its peace with the Klingon Empire. Mainly for make-up reasons, the producers had decided they needed a black actor. Only when Michael Dorn walked in did they find what they hadn't known they were looking for. 'I did not wear make-up,' Dorn said later, 'but I took on the psychological guise of a Klingon. I walked into Paramount in character. No jokes. No laughing with the other actors. When my turn came, I walked in, didn't smile, did the reading, thanked them, and walked right out.'

(Worf wasn't even intended as a regular character: he was to appear in only seven of the first thirteen episodes. But after filming 'Encounter at Farpoint', the team decided that Dorn had 'presence' and promoted him to series regular. Dorn would end up making 282 appearances as Worf over two separate shows and five feature films, the most by any actor in *Star Trek* history.)

'Encounter at Farpoint', two hours in commercial TV time,

eighty-four minutes without the commercials, would first air on American TV in September 1987. Dorothy Fontana had delivered her first script treatment on 5 December the previous year. First draft 17 February, second draft 16 March, final draft 13 April. Rehearsals 26 to 28 May. Shooting schedule 1 to 25 June. Special effects shot 16 July. In that time, all the decisions that would come to define the series – how it looked, sounded, felt, was – had to be made.

So if the pilot now looks a little stiff, the televisual equivalent of an uncleared throat, we should be neither surprised nor too critical. Everyone is grasping for the correct tone. Patrick Stewart's Picard is prone to pomposity, his accent oddly transatlantic, his defining quality a dislike of children.

'I'm not a family man, Riker, and yet Starfleet has seen fit to give me a ship with children aboard.'

'Yes, sir.'

'And I'm . . . not comfortable with children. But since a captain is supposed to project an image of geniality, you're to see that's what I project.'

'Yes, sir.'

This skin would be shed so fast we would forget it had ever been there.

The new 'Galaxy Class' *Enterprise*, flatter and more streamlined than the original, but just as prone to go 'whoosh' through silent space, is on its way to the planet Deneb IV, on the very edge of explored territory. On their way they encounter another of Roddenberry's all-powerful alien superbeings, Q, played by John de Lancie with pantomime relish. Q tells Captain Picard that humanity has already expanded too far beyond its origins and must go no further. 'You are still a dangerous, savage child race,' he says, although like the Squire of Gothos he seems to behave more like a wilful child than any of the humans on display. Picard must defend humanity's honour in a kangaroo court and, in the process, expound his executive producer's philosophy of peace, civilisation and endless chat. Captain Kirk, in his first episode, spent a lot of time fighting. Captain Picard spends most of his first episode talking.

'We have no fear what the true facts about us will reveal!'

It's a fairly arid debate, but it was shoved in because the original Farpoint story didn't stretch to two hours. Even with the new material, the edited pilot wasn't long enough, and they had to recut it slightly baggier. Watch it now and you can almost see the joins.

Farpoint, then, is the name of an impressive new station that has been built on Deneb IV, and apparently defined only by its great distance from anywhere else. The planet's inhabitants are a simple people who sell pastel fabrics to each other all day long. How could they have built such a marvel? We will soon discover that the new station is in fact a captured space creature, and the *Enterprise* will set it free in a lovely and heartwarming SFX sequence that clearly cost a bob or two. 'A feeling of great joy and gratitude!' says Counsellor Troi, who is half-Betazoid, and adept at reading the feelings of huge multi-limbed interstellar jellyfish. It's a satisfying little conundrum, neatly solved by the *Enterprise* command crew, many of whom have only just met each other, although others are old friends. Commander Riker and Counsellor Troi, for instance, are former lovers, and stare at each other meaningfully, while exchanging gnomic telepathic conversations. In scripting terms, they are the long-lost descendants of the doomed Decker and Ilia from *Star Trek: Phase II* and *The Motion Picture*.

In fact, there are definite resemblances between 'Encounter at Farpoint' – formal, overlit, not quite comfortable in its skin – and *The Motion Picture*, which was the last *Star Trek* production Roddenberry had worked on. It was as though the later, grungier, more human films had never happened. This was clearly Roddenberry's intention, to bring *Star Trek* back to what it used to be, or rather to what he'd wanted it to turn into. *The Motion Picture*, in his eyes, had not been a gigantic mistake, but the way of the future. This was his second chance to create that future.

As a pilot, 'Farpoint' sets the template efficiently enough. Q will return, but future writers will make more of the twinkle in De Lancie's eye. Maybe the most memorable moment of the pilot is a brief cameo by DeForest Kelley as 137-year-old Admiral McCoy, hobbling through the new ship supposedly to 'check medical layouts'. Lieutenant Commander Data accompanies him back to his shuttlecraft.

'I don't see no points on your ears, boy, but you sound like a Vulcan.'

'No, sir, I am an android.'

'Hmph. Almost as bad.'

It's a sweet scene, although we could have done without the violins telling us so. On the call sheets, the old country doctor was referred to merely as 'Admiral', to keep his appearance a secret until the show was broadcast.

It seems hardly believable to say this now, but in Britain we had to wait three years for this pleasure. 'Encounter at Farpoint' was first shown on BBC2 on 26 September 1990. Why so long? In the 1970s American films often came out in the UK six months, nine months, even a year after their Stateside release. But a three-year delay was over the top. While we waited, the first season of *TNG* was briefly made available in 1988 on rental video. The video shop at the top of my road had the first seven tapes, with 'Farpoint' on no. 1 and two shows per tape thereafter. I rented and watched them countless times. It took Paramount another two years to wise up to the potential in the video sales market. In April 1990, six months before its TV transmission, 'Farpoint' was released for sale on VHS at £14.99. Every few weeks more episodes would appear, again in batches of two. I bought them all. In time, I would buy every *Deep Space Nine* tape and every *Voyager* tape as well. At first they were put on shelves. Then there were no more shelves. Eventually I stored them in huge boxes in the loft. One day, not long ago, my video recorder breathed its last. With a manly tear in my eye, I took the boxes of tapes to the local dump. No one has a use for them any more; they have a resale value of £0.00. 'Videotapes?' asked the man at the dump. I nodded. He tutted. 'Bigger landfill problem than disposable nappies.' From novelty to necessity to liability in a generation: a sad fate.

The original *Star Trek* found its tone and established its characters in a trice. *The Next Generation* was a slower burn. 'The Naked Now' (episode 1.2) is a retread of the original series' 'The Naked Time': *Enterprise* crew fall prey to a strange water-borne virus that makes them all behave without inhibition. Picard and Dr Crusher breathe meaningfully at each other, and Tasha Yar and Data actually engage in intimate human-to-android relations. 'Haven' (1.4) introduces Deanna Troi's meddlesome mother Lwaxana, played by Mrs Roddenberry herself, Majel Barrett; 'Where No One Has Gone Before' (1.5) establishes the Mozart-like genius of Wesley Crusher, and sees him promoted to Acting Ensign; while 'The Last Outpost' (1.6) introduces the Ferengi, an alien race of traders who are motivated exclusively by profit and whom Roddenberry intended as the main new threat to the Federation. Unfortunately, they are not very threatening. 'Pygmy cretins,' says Worf, which pretty much sees them off. With their squinty little eyes and enormous ears, the Ferengi will soon be recast as comic relief, an unfortunate fate for any species.

Several early episodes, though, centre on that familiar Roddenberry trope, the Planet of the Week. On this world, you are sentenced to death if you inadvertently break even the smallest rule; on that one, women with fluffy 1980s hairstyles are in charge and men with mullets are an oppressed minority. The *Enterprise* crew, professional and unruffled, resolve these problems and move on. If it all seems a little bloodless, that was the intention. Roddenberry believed that by the twenty-fourth century, humanity would have outgrown its taste for needless conflict, and the sort of bickering that Spock and McCoy once enjoyed was now out of place. Writing this stuff must have been like having both of your hands tied behind your back and having to type with your toes. Years later, in William Shatner's excellent documentary *Chaos on the Bridge*, several noted *Star Trek* scribes would shake their heads in wonderment.

Ronald D. Moore: 'When you look at the original series, there's a lot of conflict between those characters.'

Melinda Snodgrass: 'The essence of drama is conflict.'

Dorothy Fontana: 'If our people are perfect and have no problems or conflicts between them, there is no story here.'

But as Brannon Braga said, 'That was Gene's vision of *Star Trek: The Next Generation*. Take it or leave it. And work within it or don't.'

Many left it. In that first season, staff writers came and went from the show with bewildering regularity. (The term 'revolving door' is frequently used in descriptions of this period.) Quite a few scripts appear under pseudonyms, after their writers objected to Roddenberry's endless rewrites. By halfway through the season, Justman, Fontana and David Gerrold had all fallen out with him and left the series, never to return.

In fact, Roddenberry seems to have treated his old colleagues particularly harshly: underpaying them, stealing their ideas, taking all the credit, badmouthing them to others.* It was as though he felt threatened by their creativity and expertise, for wasn't he the great Gene Roddenberry, who had created *Star*

---

* These are not exaggerations. Joel Engel relates it all in rather depressing detail.

Trek single-handedly? After twenty years of being worshipped
by fans at conventions, Roddenberry's ego had expanded, rather
in the manner of a red giant star before it turns into a white
dwarf. He saw himself as a great visionary, portraying the
human race's utopian future. But if conflict in the future was
unacceptable, it was perfectly OK in the present. Roddenberry
started bringing his attorney, Leonard Maizlish, to meetings,
an abrasive character who alienated writers and studio executives alike. Writers would get scripts back from Roddenberry,
but the comments were in Maizlish's handwriting. David
Gerrold fantasised about pushing him out of a window. In the
early 1970s, Roddenberry had told Gerrold, 'Every time I sit
down at the typewriter, I feel like this is the time that they're
going to find out I'm faking it.' They know now.*

Somehow, despite everything, this first season just
about hangs together, although some might consider that
a generous assessment. George Takei reports that the old
generation were keeping a close eye on the new. 'What we
saw in the first season gave us unexpected secret pleasures.
Not because we thought the shows were good. Quite to the
contrary: we felt an evil gratification because their opening
shows were so disappointing, delightfully disappointing.'
He may have been thinking of 'Too Short a Season' (1.15),
in which a grouchy old admiral takes a reverse-ageing elixir,
and gradually turns into an annoying young man. But you
never believed he was an old man in the first place, because
he can't do the old-man voice and his old-man make-up
doesn't convince anyone, except Picard and everybody else
on the *Enterprise*.

Other episodes were more solidly constructed. 'The Big
Goodbye' (1.11) gives us our first long look at the holodeck,

---

* In an incandescent afterword to Harlan Ellison's *The City on the Edge of Forever*, written
in 1995, Gerrold calls Roddenberry 'the steamroller of lies'.

a brand-new entertainment system apparently exclusive to Galaxy-class starships, which may explain why it is always going wrong. The holodeck creates fully fledged three-dimensional environments out of lights and mirrors, which in practical terms means location shooting or judicious use of the permanent old sets on the Paramount backlot. In this one Picard takes time off from his captaining duties to pretend to be Dixon Hill, a Marlowe-like 1940s PI, who has a dusty old office and a secretary called Madeleine, and is constantly pursued by mobsters who want his blood. A long-range alien scan then removes the holodeck's 'safety protocols', which means those bullets can kill. Echoes of 'Spectre of the Gun'? A little, but it's played with a nice light touch.

In '11001001' (1.14), the ship's computer is upgraded by a race called the Bynars, small people with enormous heads who have become so dependent on computer technology that they communicate in binary code. The Bynars steal the ship with only Picard and Riker left on it, and Riker is too busy flirting with a sentient holodeck character called Minuet to be of much use. 'What's a knockout like you doing in a computer-generated gin joint like this?' he asks with a wolflike grin. Roddenberry had it in mind that Riker should take over from Kirk as the ship's official chaser of skirts, but he always looks as though he wants to eat them rather than make love to them. Later on there's the first auto-destruct sequence of the new series, safely cancelled with seconds to go. It's like greeting an old friend.

In 'Coming of Age' (1.18) Picard's 'old friend' Admiral Quinn comes aboard and, with his slimy aide de camp Remmick, subjects the senior officers to a searching interrogation. Quinn believes that a conspiracy is operating in Starfleet, and he wants to make absolutely sure that Picard and his people aren't part of it. This is the series' first attempt at a running storyline, which will reach a climax only a few weeks later. Before then, though, came the first shock of the series, and possibly the first genuine shock in *Star Trek* history, when one of the main characters was permanently written out.

'Skin of Evil' (1.22) isn't much of a show. On a generic backlot planet, the crew encounter a malevolent oil slick that laughs like a Bond villain and feeds off people's fear.* There's too much chat and the special effects don't quite work. But the episode is notable because, in a moment of random and senseless violence, the monster kills Tasha Yar. Oh yes, we think, they'll get her back. Beam her up and Dr Crusher will find a way. But no, she's dead, in the way that you or I would be if someone killed us.

Behind the scenes, Denise Crosby had grown frustrated by the lack of development in her character, and had asked to be released from her contract. Hers was not the only role that the revolving door of writers hadn't got to grips with. Worf, poor man, seemed to do little more than growl, while Deanna Troi missed four episodes altogether because they didn't have anything for her to do. But Tasha took the bullet and became the first *Trek* regular ever to leave the show in a bodybag. There's a touching scene at the end of the episode in which her hologram tells her friends how much they had meant to her. Marina Sirtis is seen crying throughout, and her tears were real. The cast were sad to see Crosby go.

She had acted too hastily. Scripts would improve and characterisations would strengthen. A couple of years later, the sound of Denise Crosby kicking herself could probably have been heard from one end of Los Angeles to the other. At the same time, Tasha Yar's early-doors departure gave some of the

---

* As in 'Wolf in the Fold' and 'Day of the Dove' from the original series. Another alien that feeds off fear.

other characters room to breathe. The bridge had been looking crowded. Maybe the most galling thing for Crosby was that it wasn't deemed necessary to replace her.

In among these ructions, we could enjoy the first genuinely distinctive episode of the new series. 'Conspiracy' (1.24) took the hints and suspicions expressed by Admiral Quinn in 'Coming of Age' and made them scarily real. Picard is summoned to a secret meeting with another 'old friend', Walker Keel, who tells him he believes there's a conspiracy at the highest level of Starfleet. About three minutes later Keel and his ship are blown to smithereens, and Data's trawl through the records reveals that there has been a lot of 'uncustomary reshuffling of personnel [at Starfleet], usually in the command areas'. The *Enterprise* goes back to Earth to find out what is going on. At Starfleet HQ, which looks like a business-class lounge at a slightly rundown airport, three senior admirals greet Picard and invite him to dinner to discuss his concerns, while Admiral Quinn beams up to the *Enterprise* to say hello. Quinn brings with him a natty little briefcase, in which he has a pink scorpion-like parasite. Picard, meanwhile, has walked into a trap. All the admirals and the senior staff are now controlled by these parasites and eat bowlfuls of live grubs for dinner.

'Patience is one of our virtues,' says one of them. 'We didn't go after you. We allowed you to come after us.'

'More dramatic that way, don't you think?' says another.

Hokey dialogue aside, though, this is all thoroughly menacing, as is the revelation that the slimy aide de camp Remmick houses the mother creature. Indeed, his neck positively bulges with baby scorpions.

'You don't understand!' he cries. 'We mean you no harm! We seek peaceful coexistence.' Picard and Riker, very sensibly, blow his head off. (This sequence was so wonderfully gory the BBC simply edited it out.) Kill the mother creature, it seems, and you kill all the other parasites. The conspiracy is foiled just in time for the final credits.

One can pick holes. If Quinn and Remmick were warning of conspiracy six weeks before, how come they are at the centre of it now? Makes no sense at all, and nor does the idea that one concentrated burst of phaser fire will see off the entire expeditionary scorpion force. It's a messy end to a set-up of some promise. Later in the show's run, this would surely have been a two-parter, with a spine-tingling cliffhanger halfway through.

Back on the ship, Data reports that before being blown apart Remmick had been sending a signal to 'an unexplored sector of our galaxy'. What kind of signal?

'I believe it was a beacon,' says Data.

'A beacon?' says Picard.

'Yes sir. A homing beacon, sent from Earth,' says Data, and the camera cuts to deep space, and a beeping signal, slowly fading out. Creepy.

But the parasites would never appear again, and would only be referred to once, in passing, two or three years later. Maybe being so easy to destroy was their dramatic Achilles heel as well.

The first season ended with a brief sighting of the Romulans, who announced they were 'back' after seventy-five years of unexplained silence. New lead writer Maurice Hurley had wanted to introduce the Borg at this stage, but a number of factors – shortage of time and money and a Writers Guild strike among them – prevented him from doing so. The return of the Romulans also represented the erosion of Roddenberry's promise not to bring back familiar old adversaries, and may have signified a slight loosening of his iron grip on the show. According to Joel Engel, he had the first manifestations of cerebral vascular disease and encephalopathy, which may or may not have come about thanks to longstanding 'recreational abuse' of prescription drugs, alcohol, marijuana and cocaine.

His diabetes, high blood pressure and antidepressant prescriptions didn't help. He was taking drugs to treat problems created by the drugs he had taken to treat problems created by taking drugs. And drinking from first thing in the morning. 'I don't know how much he drank,' said David Gerrold, 'because I'm not sure I ever saw him sober.'

It wasn't an obvious recipe for longevity.

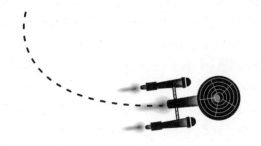

CHAPTER 12

RESISTANCE IS FUTILE

The mother of my children, who doesn't like science fiction anyway, has told me that she can't watch *Star Trek* in any of its incarnations because there are no trees in it. During the first season of *The Next Generation* one could have pointed at Jonathan Frakes, who was about the right size and certainly made of wood. But when cast and crew returned from their holidays to start filming season two, Frakes came back with added beard. As if by magic, the puppyish lunk of before had acquired authority, even substance. At a convention, Gene Roddenberry dragged the young actor on stage and asked the assembled multitudes what they thought of the new face fungus. They cheered, they whooped, they hollered. Frakes was instructed to retain the beard, and has it to this day.

In fact, quite a few off-screen changes had taken place on the *Enterprise* during the hiatus. Deanna Troi had a new, less severe hairstyle, possibly because her fellow cast members had taken to calling her 'Old Bunhead'. Worf had been permanently promoted to Security Chief, and Geordi LaForge was the new Chief Engineer. (Having both worn red in year one, they were now bedecked in mustard.) And there was a new doctor, replacing Gates McFadden, who had been 'promoted' to become head of Starfleet Medical, i.e. sacked. Several years later, Rick Berman, the former studio suit who would succeed Roddenberry as executive producer, explained all. 'There were those who believed at the end of the first season that they didn't like the way the character was developing, vis-à-vis Gates's performance, and managed to convince Mr Roddenberry of that. I was not a fan of that decision.'

Nor were the cast. As Patrick Stewart said, 'She was adored. And suddenly she was gone.'

Dr Crusher was replaced by Dr Katherine Pulaski, played by Roddenberry's old favourite Diana Muldaur. Eleven years older than McFadden, Muldaur would portray a crustier, more McCoy-like medic, sparring with Picard rather than flirting with him. You can see the reasoning, but it still felt like an odd decision, change for the sake of change. The fanbase agreed, for the dismissal of McFadden sparked off the first serious letter-writing campaign of the new era. Maybe some of them felt that the wrong Crusher had been banished. For youthful genius Wesley had survived the cull, and was still sitting at Ops with a perky smile on his face. Except when things became serious and needed to be taken seriously, whereupon he put on his serious face.

The real headline for season two, though, was the arrival of the show's first dedicated bartender, tending at the first bar ever seen on a starship. Whoopi Goldberg was a lifelong

Star Trek fan, who had watched the show as a child, turned to her mother and shouted, 'Come quick, come quick. There's a black lady on TV and she ain't no maid.' After Denise Crosby left the show, Goldberg quietly let the producers know that she might be available to join the cast in a recurring role. When they had picked themselves up off the floor, they created the role of Guinan, the immeasurably long-lived alien chatelaine of the Ten-Forward lounge. Thus was filled another important gap in the *Star Trek* universe. For years we had been wondering where the *Enterprise* crew went to let their hair down. Everyone needs time off from being perfect once in a while. Had Ten-Forward, or its equivalent, always been there? I think we must assume that it had, and that only budget restraints had prevented us seeing it before. (It was called Ten-Forward because it was on deck ten, at the widest point of the saucer section, at the very front of the ship. If the *Enterprise* ever crashed into anything, it would be the bar that went first.)

Season two was hamstrung by a Writers Guild strike, which reduced the scheduled twenty-six episodes to twenty-two, and could easily have caused the show's cancellation. Somehow, in the midst of chaos, a genuine five-star episode came to be made. 'The Measure of a Man' (2.9) is that old standby of episodic television, a courtroom drama. A cyberneticist arrives on the *Enterprise* wanting to switch off Data and disassemble him, with a view to finding out how he works and thus building a whole battalion of Datas. But he is not entirely sure he can put him back together again. Data refuses to comply with the procedure, and resigns from Starfleet to avoid it. The cyberneticist establishes that by a three-hundred-year-old law, Data cannot resign as he is Starfleet property. Can a calculator resign? Can an abacus? Picard challenges this ruling on Starbase 934912, but the judge advocate general is an ex-girlfriend of his, and will do him no favours. What's more, owing to a convenient shortage of legal staff, the cyberneticist chooses Riker to represent him at the hearing. So complications abound, but what it all boils down to is *Star Trek* to its core: a knotty moral dilemma solved by an enormous amount of talking. The script, by Melinda Snodgrass (a former attorney herself), gave Patrick Stewart everything he needed to work with, and Brent Spiner captures perfectly Data's gradually encroaching humanity. He may not be able to feel anything, but we can feel it for him.

The other outstanding episode of the year was 'Q Who?' (2.16), in which John de Lancie's playful superbeing returned with some grave warnings of what was to come. This was the Borg, producer Maurice Hurley's new villains, a cybernetically enhanced race of humanoids with grey skin, implanted tubes and wires and all trace of individuality expunged, living as units in a hive mind, relentlessly roaming the galaxy assimilating other races and destroying anything that didn't interest them. They were originally conceived as an insectoid race, but that cost too much. Unlike the poor Ferengi, though, the Borg were genuinely scary, and their vast cuboid ship was a masterpiece of design.

'The Borg are the ultimate user,' explains Q, in gloat mode even more than usual. 'They're unlike any threat your Federation has ever faced. They're not interested in political conquest, wealth or power as you know it. They're simply interested in your ship, its technology. They've identified it as something they can consume.' Guinan, too, has encountered them before: indeed, the Borg had virtually killed off her own people over a century earlier. The name 'Borg', incidentally, is derived from 'cyborg', and not from the surname of a notably robotic Swedish tennis player of the 1970s and early 1980s.

Elsewhere there's some broadening and enrichment of the regular characters, as backstories begin to be explored. In 'The Emissary' (2.20) we encounter Worf's old girlfriend K'Ehleyr, memorably played by Suzie Plakson with great wit and a certain feral sex appeal.

'Worf, we're alone now. You don't have to act like a Klingon glacier, I don't bite. Well, that's wrong, I do bite.'

In 'The Icarus Factor' (2.14), Riker's father comes into town, and Riker pouts and sulks like a teenager who isn't allowed to use the car. In 'The Dauphin' (2.10) Wesley briefly acquires a girlfriend, who turns out to be a shapeshifting alien in a tatty monster suit. At the age of sixteen, Wil Wheaton has his first screen kiss. In 'Contagion' (2.11), as an alien probe messes with the *Enterprise*'s inner workings, Picard uses one of his catchphrases for the first time, when addressing the replicator: 'Tea, Earl Grey, hot.'*

But this was an uneven year's work, with several shows that verged on the unwatchable. 'The Outrageous Okona' (2.4) introduces a charming rogue played by William O. Campbell, who had been runner-up to Frakes in the auditions for Riker.† Okona charms the birds from the trees and wastes forty-two minutes of our lives. 'The Royale' (2.12) finds an away team trapped on a hostile planet in an alien re-creation of a twentieth-century Las Vegas hotel, a miserably feeble idea that harked back to any number of Fred Freiberger shows in the 1960s. And 'Shades of Grey' (2.24) was, bluntly, a clip show. Riker battles for his life with some unknown disease, and remembers every scene he has been in during the previous forty-seven episodes. General fan consensus is that this is the worst episode of *Star Trek* ever made. Producer Maurice

---

* The replicator is a useful piece of kit that rearranges molecules to make any sort of food, drink or luxury item you want. Which is one reason why money has become redundant: if you can create as much gold as you need, who needs it at all?

† Not to be confused with William Campbell who played the Squire of Gothos.

Hurley wrote 'Shades of Grey' in a rush, having decided to leave the series, so maybe it was a particularly twisted form of revenge. It certainly might have been a sacking offence had he stayed.

'Shades of Grey' also saw the back of Diana Muldaur's Dr Pulaski. For all her snap and crackle, she didn't quite fit in, although her insistence on being given a 'Special Guest Appearance' credit rather than being listed in the main credits may suggest that she was never planning to stay for long. Here's Rick Berman again: 'It was our opinion, Gene's and mine, that the Pulaski role was not working out either. And rather than going and looking for a third doctor in three years, we approached Gates about coming back, and she very graciously did.' Dr Crusher, then, returned from Starfleet Medical; during her year away she had also found time to star in an off-Broadway play and take a small part in *The Hunt for Red October*. Equilibrium was restored.

Maybe the more far-reaching appointment, though, was that of Michael Piller as head of the writing staff to replace Hurley. In his early forties, Piller had worked as a broadcast journalist and network executive before selling his first script to *Cagney & Lacey*, and then serving as writer-producer on the detective series *Simon & Simon*. With Berman's support, he moved the show away from Planet of the Week and concentrated more on the characters. He also, very unusually for Hollywood, implemented an open-door policy on script submission. Anyone could pitch an idea, not just established or favoured writers. Some fine episodes emerged from this policy, and one or two fine writers as well. In short, the series now gets better.

In 'The Survivors' (3.3) the *Enterprise* arrives at a planet where all life in a once-thriving colony has been obliterated. Except for one house, and the elderly couple who live there, who have no idea why they were spared. For half an hour or so, Picard scratches his head in wonderment, for none of it makes sense. John Anderson, a grizzled and magisterially eyebrowed character actor, plays the male half of the couple, who must eventually reveal the bizarre truth. He is not actually human but a Douwd, an immortal and all-powerful alien who has chosen to live as a human. Ah, you think, we have seen this before once or twice, but the twist in Michael Wagner's script is ingenious. The Douwd is a pacifist; he will not kill. An alien race called the Husnock arrived at the planet and laid waste to it. He could have defended the planet against their attacks but chose not to. In the end, everyone, even his beloved wife of fifty-three years, was killed.

'I saw her broken body . . . I went insane. My hatred exploded. And in an instant of grief . . . I killed the Husnock.'

Understandable, says Picard, given the circumstances.

'No, no, no, no, you don't understand the scope of my crime,' says the Douwd. 'I didn't kill just one Husnock, or a hundred, or a thousand. I killed them all. All Husnock, everywhere.' Fifty billion of them.

A beat. We look to Picard, and wait to see how he will respond.

'We are not qualified to be your judges,' he says. 'We have no law to fit your crime.' And the Douwd returns to the planet to resume his life with the image of his dead wife that he has created, in his unassuageable grief and guilt.

Only science fiction can do this: place you in a storyline that is self-evidently ridiculous and yet make you care about the protagonists and shock you with the enormity of a crime that could never have happened. And it's why the actors are everything. John Anderson and Patrick Stewart are superb. They are utterly in the moment.

'Who Watches the Watchers?' (3.4) is a Prime Directive

episode, and one of the best. On a planet called Mintaka III, a team of Federation anthropologists observes and studies the inhabitants, proto-Vulcan humanoids at roughly a Bronze Age level of development. They watch from behind a holographic 'wall' in the mountain, a sort of duck-blind, but this fails, and the locals become aware of their existence. The *Enterprise* turns up to clear up the mess, but everything they do makes it worse. Soon the Mintakans come to believe there are gods in the sky, and they are led by a great 'overseer' called 'the Picard'. With a neat Roddenberryesque touch, we learn that, being rational beings above all, they had given up their belief in gods generations before. Picard has no wish to 'send them back into the dark ages of superstition and ignorance and fear'. He must persuade the Mintakans that he is as human as they are, but merely a millennium or two ahead in the great evolutionary story. The Prime Directive, in short, must go out of the window. The elegance with which scriptwriters Richard Manning and Hans Beimler shape and direct all this is a joy to watch, and as always Patrick Stewart provides the intelligence and the integrity the situation demands. As the scripts improve we begin to enjoy what I can only call the Picard Beat (rather more than we did the dreaded Freiberger Beat). Something happens, Picard has to respond, he has a beat to think about it, he breathes in, he pulls down his tunic and then he says *exactly* the right thing.

(The tunic pulling, a useful tic of the captain's, became easier now with the delivery of new uniforms. The spandex one-pieces used in the first two seasons, though elegant and clean in line, were rather warm under the lights and gave the actors pains in the lower back. And if you ate a doughnut, the results were visible before you had digested it. The new outfits – two-piece for the men, one-piece for the women – were made of 'breathable' wool gabardine and cost three thousand dollars each, so initially only the featured cast got to wear them. In time they would be phased in for everyone above ensign rank.)

In 'The Defector' (3.10) a Romulan clerk escapes across the neutral zone with important information about a possible Romulan military advance. Is he for real? Is he telling the truth? 'The Offspring' (3.16) sees Data build another android, his 'child', whom he names Lal. Once again a Starfleet busybody wants to take her off and dissect her, but Hallie Todd gives such a sweet and nuanced performance as Lal that we're willing to forget that we saw essentially the same episode only twelve months before.[*]

'Sins of the Father' (3.17), meanwhile, is the start of something big. For the first time we go back to the Klingon homeworld, Qo'noS,[†] which turns out to be cloudy and not very well lit. Worf's father, long dead, has been accused of collaborating with the Romulans at the Khitomer massacre a quarter of a century before. We meet Worf's long-lost younger brother Kurn, played with enormous teeth and gallons of extra saliva by Tony Todd, and before we know it we are in the midst of another courtroom drama, with Captain Picard acting as Worf's attorney, or Cha'Dich.

'I am Worf, son of Mogh. I have come to challenge the lies that have been spoken of my father!'

But realpolitik intervenes, and for the future of the Klingon Empire it becomes necessary for Worf to withdraw his

---

[*] This was Jonathan Frakes's first directorial assignment on the show. Having nagged Rick Berman to let him have a go, he was sent away to learn the job, and reckoned he had spent 'three hundred hours' in edit suites, on dubbing stages and in casting sessions, as well as shadowing other directors and reading everything there was to be read on the subject. He was the first of more than a dozen *Star Trek* cast members to direct episodes. LeVar Burton ended up as the most prolific of them, with twenty-eight credits, spanning *The Next Generation*, *Deep Space Nine*, *Voyager* and *Enterprise*.

[†] Pronounced 'Kronos', as in the San Franciscan string quartet, of which remarkably few Klingons seem to have heard.

challenge, and thus admit his father's guilt. The episode ends
with his fellow Klingons turning their back on the big man,
thus branding him an outcast. It's dramatic, and clearly not the
end of the story. Worf, we know, will return to clear his father's
besmirched reputation.

And what a pleasure it was to know this. Until now, *Star
Trek* hadn't done loose ends. Every story had been finished,
tied up and sent out into the world to fend for itself. 'Sins
of the Father' suggested the possibility of longer, more
expansive narrative arcs. Co-writer Ronald D. Moore,
another of the young writers brought in by Piller, called
it 'pivotal'. 'As soon as Worf walks out the door with his
dishonour, it demands a follow-up . . . All the Worf stories spring from that moment.' Michael Dorn said that he
played Worf 'in a different light' after that episode. 'Hey,
it's [the writers'] fault. They wrote it. So now, I'm going
to carry on with it.'

And yet, perfectionist that I am, I still give 'Sins of the
Father' only four stars. It's fascinating and revelatory, and
it won Emmys for production designer Richard James and
set director Jim Mees. But only the rarest, most glorious
episode merits the full five stars, and one such is 'Yesterday's
Enterprise' (3.15). Ambling through space in its usual way,
the *Enterprise* encounters a temporal rift, through which
flies another starship, and WHOOSH! everything instantly
changes. Our familiar *Enterprise*, light and airy, is now a
claustrophobic warship. There are no children, Troi and Worf
are gone, but there, at the tactical console, is Tasha Yar, who
wasn't killed by a psychotic oil slick two years before. For this
is an alternate timeline, one where the Federation and the
Klingons did not sign a peace treaty and are still at war. All
this has happened as a result of the arrival of the other ship,
which by uncanny coincidence is a previous version of the
Enterprise, NCC-1701-C, an Ambassador-class ship thought

lost at the battle of Khitomer, twenty-five years before.* The *Enterprise-C* had answered a distress call from a Klingon outpost under attack from the Romulans, and its courageous performance on that day had led to long-lasting peace between the Federation and the Klingon Empire. Except that now it hadn't. On the *Enterprise-D*, only Guinan notices that things are not as they should be. On no more than a hunch, she has to persuade Picard that the *Enterprise-C* has to go back through the rift to its own time to do what it was supposed to have done and prevent the war, even if it means Almost Certain Death. Even Captain Picard, who has seen a thing or two, finds this one a bit of a stretch.

'Who is to say that this history is any less proper than the other?' he says, gruffly. (He is very gruff in this timeline.)

'I suppose I am,' says Guinan.

'Not good enough, damn it!' says Picard. 'Not good enough! I will not ask them to die!'

'We've known each other a long time,' says Guinan. 'You have never known me to impose myself on anyone or take a stance based on trivial or whimsical perceptions. This timeline must not be allowed to continue. Now, I've told you what I must do. You have only your trust in me to help you to decide to do it.'

Or as Michael Piller put it, Picard must send five hundred people back to their deaths 'on the word of a bartender'.

What gives the episode real resonance, though, is the Tasha Yar subplot. For Guinan also remembers that she doesn't know Tasha in the other timeline, that Tasha isn't there, that she has died. The *Enterprise-C* could use another skilful officer, and Tasha has conveniently fallen in love with their dashing second-in-command. If she goes back through the time rift with

---

* The same Khitomer where Worf's father was supposed to have betrayed the Klingons to the Romulans but obviously didn't. Do try to keep up.

them, it's her only chance of survival. Paradox alert! And if the *Enterprise-C* does go back and correct history, no one will remember any of this, except Guinan, and no one will believe her then either.

Here's Jonathan Frakes in interview several years later: 'To this day I do not understand "Yesterday's Enterprise". I do not know what the fuck happened in the episode. I'm still trying to understand it. But I liked the look.'

Remarkably, it works. Even the little teaser scene at the beginning is inspired. Worf is in Ten-Forward (before the temporal rift has been encountered) and Guinan brings him a drink to try. He has a sip and, to his surprise, loves it. Guinan says it's an old Earth drink, prune juice.

'A warrior's drink,' says Worf.

'Yesterday's Enterprise' had its genesis in two story ideas suggested nearly a year earlier, but there wasn't actually a script when the show was pushed up in the production schedule to accommodate the availability of Whoopi Goldberg and Denise Crosby. The staff writers had three days over Thanksgiving weekend to knock something together. Ira Steven Behr, Manning/Beimler and Ronald D. Moore each took an act, with Piller doing an overall polish at the end. Watching the show for about the tenth time recently, I will admit that at times I thought the dialogue creaked a little. Still, you can see the writers enjoying the rare opportunity to make the show tougher and darker, and the episode is full of delicious details. Picard calls Riker 'Commander' rather than 'Number One' to show that they are not quite as friendly in this timeline. Captain's log is now 'military log'. Stardate is 'combat date'. Picard's command chair is more of a throne, and everyone carries phasers as a matter of routine. In the battle scene at the end, before the original timeline reasserts itself, Riker is killed, which perversely is the moment you know for certain that everything will be OK. Sadly, further blood-shed in the episode was prevented by time constraints. In Moore's original draft, Data was electrocuted and Wesley had his head blown off.

Slowly, by tiny increments, *The Next Generation*'s universe has started to expand. Transporter Chief O'Brien, played by the knobbly-faced Irish actor Colm Meaney, makes another thirteen appearances in this season, after seventeen in season two. Mostly he has little to do other than beam someone in or beam someone out. Is he standing there all day? Maybe he's busy realigning the pattern buffers. But he is already a reassuring presence, unlikely ever to make a mistake and always good for a wry raised eyebrow when the situation demands it. As the years go by, and the writers discover what a warm and able actor Meaney is, situations will demand ever more of O'Brien, until he ends up appearing in more episodes of *Star Trek* than anyone other than Worf.

One of the knottiest problems the show still had to resolve was how to acknowledge its own past. Although 138-year-old Bones had paid the new *Enterprise* a brief visit in episode one, Roddenberry had promised that the new show would look forward and not back. New situations, new stories, new villains. Then they put a Klingon on the bridge, did a rerun of 'The Naked Time' and resurrected the Romulans. No one objected. Nostalgia for the original series remained strong. Some fans still refused to watch the new series because Kirk and Spock weren't in it. So an episode like 'Sarek' (3.23) did a lot of good work. Vulcans live to more than 200 of our flimsy Earth years, so Spock's father, middle-aged in 'Journey to Babel', is now getting on a bit. Still an Ambassador – and still played by Mark Lenard – Sarek comes onto the *Enterprise* to negotiate a vital peace treaty with Some Aliens We Will Never Hear

Of Again. Listening to a string quartet playing Mozart's String Quartet No. 19 in C Major (The 'Dissonant'), he is seen to weep quietly, which for a Vulcan is about as disturbing as if he had leapt up and zapped the players with random bursts of phaser fire. For the great man has Bendii syndrome, a type of Vulcan dementia that erodes emotional control. Can he complete his mission? Only by mind-melding with Picard, who is thus exposed to a lifetime of Sarek's repressed emotions. It's another huge emotional scene, and director Les Landau came close to admitting that he just pointed the camera at Stewart and let him get on with it. Piller said later that the episode 'reflected what was going on with the show at the time'. Roddenberry, the Great Bird of the Galaxy, was not the man he had been. 'We all respected him so much, and he had been such an important, strong leader of the franchise and everything it stood for. But here is this great man going into decline . . . If you go back and look at "Sarek" closely, what that character is, is Gene Roddenberry.'*

And so to the season finale, the first true cliffhanger in the show's history, another five-star episode, and some people's all-time favourite. 'The Best of Both Worlds' (3.26) often has 'Part I' added to its title, but you don't know it's going to be one of two until its very last moment. The Borg, unseen for more than a year, have finally made inroads into Federation space. Starfleet sends along its best tactician – another one – to decide how to deal with the threat. Commander Shelby, as played by Elizabeth Dennehy, is young, small, blonde and as tough as a saddle. She tells Riker she wants his job. Riker, meanwhile, has been offered the captaincy of the USS *Melbourne*, and can't decide whether to take it or not. (How

---

* The irony being that if Roddenberry had still been in control, he would never have countenanced producing an episode that looked back as fondly as did 'Sarek'.

can you captain a starship if you can't make up your mind whether you want to captain a starship?) All this occupies a lot of time, as we perch on the edge of our seats waiting for the Borg cube to show up. Finally it does. 'We have engaged the Borg,' says Picard, with a solemnity that sends shivers down the spine. The Borg announce that they want Picard personally. LaForge and his team start working on a new weapon using the main deflector dish, but before they have time to finish it the Borg beam in, kidnap the captain and beam out again. The cube turns round and heads straight for Earth.

'Captain Jean-Luc Picard, you lead the strongest ship of the Federation fleet,' say the Borg. 'You speak for your people.'

'I have nothing to say to you!' yells Picard. 'And I will resist you with my last ounce of strength!'

'Strength is irrelevant. Resistance is futile. We wish to improve ourselves. We will add your biological and technological distinctiveness to our own. Your culture will adapt to service ours.'

'Impossible! My culture is based on freedom and self-determination!'

'Freedom is irrelevant. Self-determination is irrelevant. You must comply.'

'We would rather die!'

'Death is irrelevant.'

The Borg have all the answers. Or maybe they just have the one answer, and repeat it ad infinitum.

In this instance they have decided that they need a human voice to speak to the Federation on their behalf. When the away team come to rescue him, they find that Picard has had Borg implants installed and is now one of them. Back on the *Enterprise*, the new weapon is finally ready to be used. The Borg hail the ship. On screen come the Borgified features of their former leader. Everyone on the bridge gulps.

'I am Locutus of Borg. Resistance is futile. Your life, as it has been, is over. From this time forward, you will service . . . us.'

(It's impossible to overstate the menace imbued in this final monosyllable.)

Close-up on Riker.

'Mr Worf . . . Fire.'

Fade to black. Caption: 'TO BE CONTINUED'.

CHAPTER 13

JUST A BIT OF A HEADACHE

Even as they were shooting 'The Best of Both Worlds', the writing team had no idea how the story would end. After the show went out, rumours abounded that Patrick Stewart was renegotiating his contract with Paramount, and might be leaving the show. Would Riker become captain? Would Shelby become his Number One? As the Borg would say, rumours are irrelevant. Contracts are irrelevant.

Interesting, though, that the Borg should speak Latin. They must have picked it up when they assimilated Picard. 'Qui locutus est' is Latin for 'he who has spoken'.

Assistant director Chip Chalmers remembers the moment Stewart first came on set in his Borg costume. 'We got every-one settled down and did one rehearsal. All he had to do was walk up to the camera. He did so and towered over everyone.

It was just so creepy and so spooky, and he said, "I am Locutus of Borg. Have you considered buying a Pontiac?"'

'The Best of Both Worlds' went out on US television in June 1990, and in Ronald D. Moore's words, 'all hell broke loose'. If there had been any doubt before that *The Next Generation* was a worthy enterprise in its own right, or that Patrick Stewart was a worthy captain of the flagship, there was none now. 'The Best of Both Worlds' episodes humanised Picard (even as they mechanised him), and season four would continue that process. In the meantime, viewers had three long, warm, agonising summer months to wait for Part II.

Behind the scenes, the show was in flux. Michael Piller had only signed a one-year contract, and had always planned to leave when it lapsed. His year in charge had not lacked its dramas – indeed, all the staff writers bar Moore left at season's end – but the show had improved beyond measure and Roddenberry and Berman wanted him to stay. Riker's dilemma – take the captaincy of the USS *Melbourne* and fly off to adventures unimagined, or stay where he was happy and settled – mirrored Piller's dilemma, and they came to the same decision. Only after Piller had signed his new contract did he start thinking about 'The Best of Both Worlds, Part II'. 'I'm a very instinctive writer,' he told Gross and Altman, 'and the people I don't work with are the people who need all the answers laid out before they start writing. I find the discovery process is what the life of scripts is about.' In this case, the solution came to him only two days before filming was due to start.*

'Mr Worf ... fire,' but the deflector-dish weapon doesn't work. Locutus tells them that all Picard's knowledge and experience have been added to the Borg's, so they know exactly

---

* One of the new writers, Brannon Braga, met Piller on his first day in the job. 'He introduced himself and said, "I'm trying to figure out how to beat the Borg. I have no idea how to do it."'

what the *Enterprise* might do in any situation. 'Your resistance is hopeless ... Number One.' Which sort of suggests, as the Borg cube heads for Earth, that a little of the old Picard is still in there somewhere. The Borg continue the assimilation process, adding more pipes and tubes to the former captain than really seem necessary, and we see a single tear trickle down his grey, Borgified cheek. Near Wolf 359 – a real star, just over seven-and-a-half light years from our solar system – a Federation fleet stands ready to take on the Borg cube. The fleet is ripped apart. Riker and his crew can only look on from afar, as the wounded *Enterprise* is patched up.*

What to do? Inspired by Guinan (wearing her purple cardinal's hat today), Riker develops an ingenious plan to kidnap Locutus/Picard. They bring him back to the ship, but can't quite decide what to do with him. Like all Borg, Locutus will insist on trying to assimilate everything. They can't be much fun at parties.

'Red wine or white wine?'

'Wine is irrelevant. Canapés are is futile.'

It is Dr Crusher who sees that the Borg's strength, their interdependence, may also be their weakness. Picard fights through his Borg programming to say one word: 'Sleep'. Data implants a command in his software that spreads through the Borg, and causes the cube to power down and activate its regenerative cycle. In short, the entire race falls asleep. The Borg cube conveniently explodes, Dr Crusher removes all the implants from Picard's body, and he resumes the captaincy of the *Enterprise*.

'How do you feel?' asks Troi.

'Almost human,' says Picard. 'With just a bit of a headache.'

But he knows, as we do, that nothing will ever be the same again.

---

* To have shown the battle itself would have cost far too much money, so we just see the wreckage afterwards. One of thirty-nine starships destroyed is the one whose command Riker had been offered, the *Melbourne*.

'The Best of Both Worlds, Part II' was not a patch on 'Part I'. Piller had set himself an insoluble problem, and you needed a leap of faith or two to accept his resolution. And it ended very suddenly. 'We ran out of time,' said director Cliff Bole. 'We only shoot forty-two minutes [an episode]. God, the old hours we used to shoot were like fifty-one or fifty-two minutes . . . It was just a real quick ending for such a big show.'*

But it did the job, just about, and reinforced the show's new focus on characters and consequences. Just as Worf was changed by the events of 'Sins of the Father', so Captain Perfect would need a while to come to terms with his assimilation by the Borg. In 'Family' (4.2) the *Enterprise* has returned to Earth for repairs, and all the regulars have some time off. Worf's human foster parents come on board to see their boy. He finds them hugely embarrassing, as well as about a foot shorter than him. Beverly Crusher shows Wesley a holotape his father made just before he died. (You can imagine the direction. 'Wesley! Serious face!') But the main story is of Picard, who goes home to France for the first time in twenty years to see his brother and his family. This is of course 'France' rather than France (those vineyards are palpably Californian), and British actors play the 'French' family: gurning, oyster-eyed Jeremy Kemp as furious brother Robert, and Samantha Eggar as peacemaking sister-in-law Marie. Even if the brothers can't stand each other, home is where the heart is, or at least where the plot is.

'You don't know, Robert,' says Jean-Luc. 'They took everything I was. They used me to kill and destroy, and I couldn't stop them! I should have been able to stop them! I tried, I tried so hard. But I wasn't strong enough. I wasn't good enough. I should have been able to stop them. I should, I should.'

---

* He exaggerates slightly. In the late 1960s, most episodes of 'hour-long' drama on US television were forty-eight or forty-nine minutes long without ads.

'So, my brother is a human being after all,' says Robert. 'This is going to be with you a long time, Jean-Luc. A long time.'

One could ask, where's the science fiction in this? This episode had the lowest viewing figures of the season, so *TNG*'s core following may have asked themselves the same question. But 'Family' was boldly going where the show had not gone before. Its entire purpose was to enrich character-isation and backstory. We even learned Chief O'Brien's first names, Miles Edward, a mere three years after he joined the show.

And it set the tone for a season in which several relatives, friends and enemies from past episodes would make return visits. It's a huge galaxy, vast beyond our imagination, but if you fly around it for long enough, it's amazing how often you bump into the same old faces. Data's evil brother Lore, the mys-terious Traveller (who told us early in season one that Wesley was a genius, the Mozart of the warp field), Worf's ex-girl-friend K'Ehleyr, Lwaxana Troi and silly old Q all find their way onto the ship. We also meet Tasha Yar's younger sister, Worf's son, Data's creator and loads and loads of Klingons. If season three had been the breakthrough year, this was the year of consolidation. It may lack the Himalayan peaks of 'Yesterday's Enterprise' and 'The Best of Both Worlds', but I think the fourth is the most consistently satisfying of *The Next Generation*'s seven seasons.

'Reunion' (4.7) was, effectively, episode two in the Klingon saga. It brought back K'Ehleyr and then, shamefully, killed her off (for sound and sensible story reasons, but it was disappointing nonetheless). It also introduced Robert Reilly's pop-eyed Gowron, who after the usual intrigue will become the new leader of the Klingon Empire and turn up semi-regularly, always overacting without fear of the consequences. Are there any quiet, thoughtful Klingons?

'Remember Me' (4.5) and 'Future Imperfect' (4.8) were the first two in an occasional series of what-on-earth-is-going-on-here episodes, in which one of the crew wakes up and everything is different and wrong. In the first, Dr Crusher's crewmates keep disappearing until she is left alone on the *Enterprise*, convinced she is going mad. In the second, Riker has missed sixteen years, he's now captain of the *Enterprise* and Admiral Picard has an inadvisable goatee beard. (Data is first officer and there's a Ferengi at the con.) Glimpses into the future are even more fun than forays into the past, even if, as in this case, none of it turns out to be real.*

Confident, positive and unrestrained by studio or network interference, Michael Piller and Rick Berman were now able to say to their writers, 'OK, amaze me, show me something I haven't seen before.' (As the years went by, this would slowly mutate into 'OK, show me something I've seen quite a lot of times before.') Take 'Data's Day' (4.11), which doesn't so much break the rules as simply disregard them. It's a day in the life of the *Enterprise*, told by the only member of its crew who never sleeps. The A-story is supplied by Chief O'Brien's forthcoming wedding to Keiko Ishikawa, ship's botanist, played by Rosalind Chao. Data introduced them and is to be Miles's best man. The day will also include four birthdays, two transfers, four promotions, two chess tournaments, a secondary school play and a celebration of the Hindu Festival of Lights. The texture of the episode is also the substance of it. We meet Data's cat for the first time, although it will be a while before we discover that it's a she, and she is called Spot. We see the arboretum, where Keiko works, and the barber shop, where the Bolian chatterbox V'Sal

---

* 'Real', that is, within the context of a series in which spaceships travel at many times the speed of light, people transport to other locations by being turned into energy and then back into matter again at the other end, and dust, the common cold and decent medium-priced red wine have vanished as though they never existed.

presides. (His skin is a becoming shade of lilac.) Wedding guests go 'shopping' for presents at the replication centre. Worf announces that he won't be attending the ceremony – 'Human bonding rituals often involve a great deal of talking and dancing and . . . crying.'

Dr Crusher gives Data a dancing lesson. (An inspired choice, given Gates McFadden's parallel career as a dancer and chore-ographer.) And when the wedding finally takes place, Captain Picard's speech is, almost word for word, the same one given by Captain Kirk in 'Balance of Terror', all those years ago.*

A few weeks earlier, 'Final Mission' (4.9) had seen the end of Wesley Crusher, at least as a regular character. Wil Wheaton had asked to leave so he could take advantage of film offers that were coming this way, thus confirming one of the first rules of series television: that the young rarely stay for long. (On daily soaps, the older actors often stick around for ever, delighted with the regular work, while the young ones come and go as frequently as first season *Next Generation* writers.) Wheaton may also have become weary of the endless teas-ing he received for playing the boy genius who always saved the ship from imminent destruction in act three.† After the perfunctory slaying of Tasha Yar in season one, however, the writers were determined to give him a decent send-off. Wesley is therefore shipped off to Starfleet Academy for a few years, with an option to return when he has learned a few more facial expressions. Before he goes, he saves not the ship but the cap-tain, injured in a cave on a baking hot planet, with a supply of fresh water hidden behind an impenetrable force field. Guest

---

* Data's Day, according to the Memory Alpha website, seems likely to be 24 October 2367, if you are willing to ignore various chronological inconsistencies in the screenplay, which I'm afraid we are.

† 'He directly saved the ship only one and a half times,' Wheaton told an interviewer shortly after his departure, 'and had a hand in contributing to the solution of the problem two times! That's it!'

star here, as a crusty old pilot, is Nick Tate, the Australian actor
who played crusty young pilot Alan Carter in *Space: 1999* in the
mid-1970s, in one of those knowing little nods that producers
of science-fiction TV series can never resist. They're fans too,
these people, like the rest of us.

After Michael Piller joined the show, he insisted that every
story had to be 'about' one of the regular characters. 'Sins of the
Father' was obviously a Worf story; 'The Best of Both Worlds'
was, rather less obviously, a Riker story; and 'The Measure of
a Man' looked like a Data story but was in fact a Picard story.
'Yesterday's Enterprise' was a rare exception in that it was a
Tasha story, the first and only one she ever had; and 'Data's
Day' was an *Enterprise* story. 'The Wounded' (4.12), deftly
scripted by new supervising producer Jeri Taylor, provided
another first, an O'Brien story, as well as introducing some
new adversaries, the Cardassians. Humanoid, sallow, effort-
lessly sinister, with jet-black hair and prominent facial ridges,
Cardassians were mainly recognisable by their massively thick
necks. No other heads in the quadrant can have been so solidly
supported. They would make a fine addition to the pantheon
of *Star Trek* villainy, and give a lot of work to actors with sharp,
angular faces and a certain theatrical manner.

Again, though, it's the episodes that break the rules that
make the strongest impression. 'First Contact' (4.15), as the
title broadly hints, is about the Federation making first contact
with an alien species, but this time it's told from the point of
view of the alien species. We're with the Malcorians all the way
as one of their number, bearing a remarkable resemblance to
Commander Riker, is injured and taken to a hospital, where he
turns out to be not quite as Malcorian as he should be. Picard
must beam down and reveal himself to the Malcorian leader,
as he did in 'Who Watches the Watchers?' Some Malcorians
are welcoming to the newcomers, while others are profoundly
suspicious. In short, this is *Star Trek*'s version of the 1951 SF film

The Day the Earth Stood Still, only in this case we are the visiting aliens. We know we are peaceful and mean no harm, but
they don't, and why should they trust us? It's a clever episode,
although the shifted point of view only just conceals that it's a
variation on an increasingly familiar theme.

Raise people's expectations, though, and you give yourself
a new problem: how to satisfy those raised expectations. After
'The Best of Both Worlds', every *Star Trek* season would now
have to end with a cliffhanger, even if none of them quite lived
up to the first. 'Redemption' (4.26) returns us to the Klingon
home world for Gowron's accession to the throne. The sisters
of Duras (whose father was the real traitor at Khitomer) oppose
him, and there's an awful lot of shouting and posturing as the
dry ice swirls.* Treachery, we quickly establish, runs in the
family. The Duras family is backed by the Romulans, one of
whom is the spitting image of Tasha Yar, even down to the
blonde hair.

'We should not discount Jean-Luc Picard yet,' she says,
knowingly. 'He is human, and humans have a way of showing
up when you least expect them.'†

This was the first properly false note of the Piller era. As
'Redemption, Part II' would explain three months later, the
alternate-timeline Tasha Yar, who had gone back in time in
'Yesterday's Enterprise', had somehow survived the battle,
been captured by Romulans, had a relationship with one of her
captors and given birth to a daughter who looked and sounded
exactly like her, except for the pointy ears. It was Crosby's
idea. On first hearing it, Ron Moore rolled his eyes. 'But as we

---

* B'Etor and Lursa, the sisters of Duras, wear remarkable upholstered costumes that show
their embonpoints to their full advantage. This led to the coining of the now widely used
phrase 'Klingon kleavage'.

† 'Redemption' was the one hundredth episode of *The Next Generation* to be produced.
During the shoot, former President Ronald Reagan paid a visit to the set. Introduced to
various Klingons, he was asked what he thought of them. 'I like them,' he said. 'They
remind me of Congress.'

started to get into the story, I needed some sort of Romulan thing to actually happen . . . It just seemed natural. It fit and we did it.' But it was silly, and felt like a misjudgement.

Denise Crosby's return to the show would be brief. Commander Sela, her new character, would appear only twice more in the series. It may not have been her fault. The writers may have been running out of things for the Romulans to do. One problem was the awful uniforms they had to wear: silvery and stiff, with enormous padded shoulders, like Joan Collins in *Dynasty*. If you knocked one over, would he be able to get up again? You could conquer Romulus by seeding a small planet-wide earthquake, enough to make everyone fall on the floor. You can see them now, in their billions, waving their legs in the air like upended beetles. Abandon all your territorial claims to the neutral zone, says Picard, or we won't help you up.

The relentless turnover of a TV series shows up the more gentle rhythms of the feature-film business. *Star Trek IV* came out a year before *The Next Generation* first appeared on TV screens; *Star Trek V* appeared in the summer break between seasons two and three; and *Star Trek VI: The Undiscovered Country*, the last film with the original cast, would emerge halfway through season five. The first four films had had the benefit of an acute and almost painful *Star Trek* shortage. Audiences fell upon them with the ravening hunger of the starved. But with new adventures for Captain Picard and his crew on TV most weeks, the hunger had been assuaged. Indeed, Harve Bennett blamed the relative failure of *The Final Frontier* on the success of the new show, and not on the fact that it was a feeble film with next to no redeeming features that had nearly killed off the series single-handedly.

Fortunately, Bennett had a plan. The next film, he proposed, would be *Starfleet Academy*, which would join Kirk, Scott, McCoy et al. at the very beginning of their careers, as bright young shavers with full heads of hair and tight, washboard stomachs. Encouraged by Paramount, Bennett and David Loughery spent more than a year developing this script, which would not only renew the film series in an unexpected direction but also save the now considerable fees of the old cast. We would meet young Kirk in Iowa, anxiously waiting to hear whether he has been accepted for the Academy, and in Shatner's words, 'copping feels off the local females and buzzing airplanes through haystacks in an effort to vent some of his restless energy'. Spock would have left Vulcan against his father's wishes, while Bones, a few years older than either, would have spent the past few years looking after his terminally ill father. At the Academy they would be taught by a gifted young professor of engineering, Montgomery Scott. Kirk and Spock would start as rivals but become friends when Kirk stood up for Spock in the face of nasty racial prejudice. At the end of the film the cadets would be thrown into some life-or-death battle of an only-you-can-save-us variety, and the team would thus be formed, oven-ready for future adventures.*

What could go wrong? Paramount had had a bad year, bankrolling a number of big films that had failed (most notably *The Godfather Part III*). Executives had left, to be replaced by new executives who liked Bennett's idea less than the old executives had. They were also browbeaten by Roddenberry, who liked the idea even less and intended to do all he could to stop it.

In fact, Bennett did not discover until later that in all the time he had spent working on *Starfleet Academy* – they had gone as far as scouting for locations – no one had mentioned

---

* All of which may sound familiar to anyone who has been to the cinema more recently.

the idea to Martin Davis, the new CEO of Paramount's parent company, Gulf + Western. Now, at last, someone did. Davis blew his top. Don't want that, he said. Want another adventure with the old crew. And that was that. Bennett was instructed to mothball his great notion and get on with *Star Trek VI* like a good little producer.

Bennett was 'stunned, feeling as low as I ever had. It was the bottom of a pit of despair.' Feeling that he had been personally betrayed, he resigned, and thereafter endured a long dark night of the soul. (This appears to be mandatory for anyone who has had a close connection with *Star Trek* and had the drug removed.)*

This was in August 1990. The next film was due in cinemas in the autumn of 1991, to coincide with the show's twenty-fifth anniversary. The studio rang Leonard Nimoy and asked if he fancied writing the next film, producing, directing, anything. Nimoy said he didn't want to direct another, but knew a man who might. He rang Nick Meyer, who was on holiday with his family in Cape Cod.

'We want to make another *Star Trek* movie. Can I come talk to you?'

'Sure! Come on out.'

They went for a walk on the beach.

'I want to do a movie about the Berlin Wall coming down in space.'

'Perfect!' said Nick Meyer, and in Nimoy's words, 'We were off.'

They worked out the main beats of the story that afternoon. There has been a Chernobyl-like disaster somewhere

---

* As Nick Meyer wrote, 'Someone has observed that the chief problem in Hollywood is behaviour. Paramount's treatment of the man who had saved the franchise for them, making who knows how much money for the studio in the process, seemed graceless at best.' Lauded for three successes, Bennett had been punished for one failure. That's showbusiness.

in the Klingon Empire. Overarmed, ecologically doomed, the Klingons reach out to the Federation for help, but their Gorbachev figure is assassinated. Kirk, who has been chosen as Starfleet's 'olive branch', mainly because he hates the Klingons so much, is framed for the murder, along with Dr McCoy, and the pair of them are shipped off to a Klingon penal colony. They must escape while Spock and the others unravel the conspiracy and prove their friends' innocence.

In *I Am Spock*, Nimoy admits he had to pinch himself to make sure it was true. 'After all, it really didn't seem all that long ago that I had been a struggling actor, driving a cab at nights trying to make ends meet, grateful to get even the smallest bit part. And here I was, being handed the reins of a major motion picture and told, "Whatever you want to do is fine with us!"'

When it came out, I remember *Star Trek VI: The Undiscovered Country* as a slightly underwhelming experience: good and enjoyable, but not life-changing, as *The Wrath of Khan* and *The Voyage Home* had been. Maybe my hunger too had been sated by Captain Picard and the *Enterprise-D*, for the latest adventures of this creaky old crew, notably bewigged in two cases and disturbingly combed over in one other, didn't seem as *valuable* somehow. We are so fickle, we fans. Watching the film again a quarter of a century later – a quarter of a century! – I loved it, and was moved by it, and admonished my younger self for his frivolity and complacency.

What I didn't see at the time is that there are still things for these characters to do. Kirk and Spock each have unfamiliar problems to grapple with, beyond the vagaries of the plot. And that's even before we see that the USS *Excelsior*, the one with the transwarp drive that didn't work, is now under the command of Captain Hikaru Sulu. Indeed, they have spent the three years since the last film charting gaseous anomalies in the Beta Quadrant. It has only taken twenty-five years, but finally Mr Sulu has a first name.*

The film gains a lot of its energy, though, from two new characters. Kim Cattrall, later of *Sex and the City*, plays Lieutenant Valeris, a young Vulcan with a severe haircut who has just graduated from the Academy at the top of her year. (She has a rather high youthful voice, unlike Cattrall's more familiar sexy rasp.) Nicholas Meyer had wanted to bring back Saavik, but Kirstie Alley was at the peak of her *Cheers* fame and far too expensive, and Robin Curtis's portrayal was felt not to have cut the mustard. So, new character, new actress, although Cattrall had actually auditioned for Saavik all those years ago. What would the films have been like if she had got the role? (Despite her youth – she was nineteen years younger than anyone else in the cast – her intelligence and quick wit made her a remarkably neat fit into the ensemble.)

The other casting coup was Christopher Plummer as the Klingon warrior General Chang. If there can be such a thing as playful evil, Plummer embodies it in this film. Kirk invites a Klingon delegation over to the *Enterprise* for dinner, an extended feast of mutual distrust and wondrous embarrassment.

'I offer a toast,' says Chancellor Gorkon, the Gorbachev figure played by David Warner. 'The undiscovered country . . . the future.'

Hamlet, Act III, Scene I, says Spock approvingly.

'You have not experienced Shakespeare,' says Gorkon, 'until you have read him in the original Klingon.'

In fact, it's Plummer's General Chang who picks this up and

---

* He also has Christian Slater, then a big teen star, as the *Excelsior*'s communications officer. Slater was a *Star Trek* fan from childhood, and the casting director on *The Undiscovered Country* was his mother. By all accounts, he was incredibly keen to be involved. Said Takei, 'I have a new puppy and it's the cutest thing. Its tail wags, it just bounces up and down.'

runs with it. 'taH pagh, taH be,' he says, with a chuckle. (That is the question.) Thereafter, much of his dialogue consists of direct quotations from Shakespeare. Nick Meyer wrote the role for him, and then had to hope that he would do it. Plummer acceded, but didn't want to wear as many prosthetics as other Klingons. He is as worthy an adversary for Kirk as we have ever seen.*

Meyer likes to lard his scripts with literary allusions, and this one, co-written with Denny Martin Flinn, is full of artful little references for the sharp-eared to spot. During the show trial, as Kirk and McCoy hold translation devices to their ears, Chang asks a question of them and follows it up with 'Don't wait for the translation! Answer me now!', which were the words Adlai Stevenson said to the USSR's Valerian Zorin at the United Nations during the 1962 Cuban Missile Crisis. Seventeen political historians will have chuckled sagely in the audience when they heard that.

'An ancestor of mine,' says Spock a little later, 'maintained that if you eliminate the impossible, whatever remains, however improbable, must be the solution.' Nimoy (and indeed Christopher Plummer) had previously played Sherlock Holmes on stage and screen, and Nick Meyer had written two pastiche novels based on the character.

The Kirk we see at the beginning of the film is a sadder, more defeated Kirk than we have seen before. 'I've never trusted Klingons and I never will,' he tells his personal log. 'I can never forgive them for the death of my boy.' (He has a framed photo in his quarters of his son, as played by Merritt Butrick, who had himself died, of an Aids-related illness, two years earlier.) The old warrior seems ground down by the burden of his hatred.

---

* Plummer and Shatner went way back. Indeed, Plummer had played Henry V at Stratford, Ontario in the late 1950s, and Shatner had been his understudy. One day Plummer was indisposed, Shatner took the role and Plummer watched. 'He did everything different from me,' Plummer told Nick Meyer, 'and that's when I knew he would be a star.'

Only when he and McCoy are interned on the ice planet of Rura Penthe, from which it is impossible to escape, does Kirk wake up and become the dynamic, odds-defying sprite of old.

For Spock, the challenge comes when he discovers that the traitor on the *Enterprise* is his protégée Lieutenant Valeris. For the first time in twenty-five years we see him truly angry. When Valeris will not reveal the names of her fellow conspirators, Spock uses a mind-meld to interrogate her. We have seen nothing like this before, and the shock on her face shows that it is a form of assault, far beyond what is acceptable. The needs of the many outweigh the needs of the few, or the one. But you certainly feel relieved that Spock didn't lose his temper any earlier in his Starfleet career.

The Undiscovered Country was written at speed and produced on the cheap, and occasionally it shows. Kirk and McCoy escape from the unescapable with the help of a cigar-chomping shapeshifter played by the model Iman. Nimoy, who seems to have been an unusually rigorous and demanding executive producer (at least as far as his writers were concerned), felt this was a gimmick and a missed opportunity, and a better idea would have been to have a Klingon help them escape, who might persuade Kirk that not every Klingon was a bad Klingon. Meyer disagreed. (The pair of them disagreed on rather a lot during the making of this film, and weren't quite as good friends at the end as they had been at the beginning.)*

The one editorial misjudgement, though, is the casual racism shown by members of the *Enterprise* crew towards the Klingons. Gene Roddenberry took exception to this, and I think he was right to.

'Did you see the way they ate?' says Uhura after the dinner party.

---

* For a more bathetic sign of the film's cost-paring, take a look at the seating at the grand inter-species conference at Camp Khitomer. Cheap office furniture imported directly from the twentieth century, I surmise.

'Terrible table manners,' says Chekov.

It's not funny, it's just ... uncomfortable. Nichelle Nichols had problems with several lines she had to say, and refused outright to say one or two of them.* Brock Peters, the distinguished black actor who had starred in *To Kill a Mockingbird*, had a speech that was so inflammatory that he found it impossible to learn, and Meyer had to shoot it line by line.

In the main, though, the film rattles along like a much loved and well maintained old vehicle on its last long trip. It ends on the bridge, where all the principals (bar Captain Sulu) are gathered.

'Course heading, Captain?' asks Chekov.

'Second star to the right,' says Kirk. 'And straight on till morning.'

(*Peter Pan*. Subtext aplenty there.)

Meyer says that everyone was irritable that day, and the scene never quite gelled. But it was the last scene of the film to be shot, and therefore the last scene of these performers' careers on the *Enterprise*. This time it really was all over. As Spock had said to Kirk a little earlier, 'Is it possible that we two, you and I, have grown so old and so inflexible that we have outlived our usefulness?' This wasn't just Spock to Kirk: this was Nimoy to Shatner. And Shatner didn't know the answer any more than Kirk did.

---

* Chekov's wry little 'Guess who's coming to dinner', for instance, was originally Uhura's.

CHAPTER 14

COMFORTABLE CHAIR

During *The Next Generation*'s first, hectic, crazy year, Denise Crosby went to the producers and asked for more to do. They said they couldn't guarantee it. 'The series was about Picard, Riker and Data. The other characters – the rest of the regular crew, the aliens-of-the-week, the special guest stars – were there to fill the gaps.'*

In four years, the show had travelled a long way at high warp. Now we had a true ensemble. After his years at the RSC, frequently working on several plays at once, Patrick Stewart found the grind of episodic television less irksome than he had feared. It helped that this group of actors liked each other, and that Stewart's talents inspired rather than

---

* Reported in Block and Erdmann.

intimidated his fellows. Everyone raised their game on this set.

The tone is set by the star. William Shatner was notorious for counting his lines, for bigging up his role and making sure he was at the centre of everything, and the ill-feeling this generated with his fellow cast members resonated down the decades. George Takei remembers Dorothy Fontana, when she was story editor, showing him or Jimmy Doohan or Nichelle Nichols early drafts of scripts, 'which might contain a wonderful scene for our respective characters or even a fun line or two of dialogue . . . But when the final shooting script was delivered, the eagerly awaited scene or line would now be in someone else's mouth, and invariably, it was Bill's.'[*]

Stewart was never a line-counter. All the other actors had the space to be as good as they could be. In the case of LeVar Burton as Geordi, or Gates McFadden as Dr Crusher, or Brent Spiner as Data, their talents were clear from the beginning. Burton, despite having to hide his eyes behind a plastic hair-slide, was a wonderfully instinctive and likeable performer. McFadden had a stillness, a dancer's poise, that the show took a while to learn how to use. Spiner, who sometimes went over the top in other roles, reined it all in as Data, and created such a rich and multi-faceted character you can see why all the writers wanted to write Data episodes.

But Jonathan Frakes had also risen to the challenge. Although still shouty when riled, Riker had moved beyond the action-adventure hero archetype and gained a certain bearded authority. In season one he felt like the weak link; by season five you couldn't imagine anyone else in that seat. The vulnerability Frakes couldn't hide became, perversely, Riker's strength. When he says 'Mr Worf, fire!' it's all there on his face.

---

[*] Leonard Nimoy was always more sensitive towards the idea of the ensemble. It can be no coincidence that the two films he directed were the ones that gave the second-string characters most to do.

He knows what he is doing, and he knows what it means, on every level.

Marina Sirtis, while still too often underemployed as Deanna Troi, had also become a crucial member of the group: the empath, the conscience, her intellect in service to her emotions rather than the other way round. Only Wesley Crusher, saddled with Eugene Wesley Roddenberry's hopes and dreams (not to mention the burden of being the Mozart of the warp field), had struggled to grow beyond his original bounds.

Arguably, though, the character who had come the furthest was Michael Dorn's Worf. He didn't always have the most lines, but often he had the best. In 'The Emissary' (2.20), Worf must pretend to be the captain of the *Enterprise* to call some much madder Klingons to heel. It's a bravura performance, enjoyed by everyone on the bridge.

'How did you like command?' asks Riker, afterwards.

'Comfortable chair,' says Worf.

In 'Déjà Q' (3.13), Q arrives on the *Enterprise* claiming to have lost all his powers, but no one believes him.

'What do I have to do to convince you that I'm human?' he asks in despair.

'Die,' says Worf.

'Oh very good, Worf,' says Q. 'Eat any good books lately?'

(It's not a bad line, but Worf's was better.)

In 'Qpid' (4.20), Q throws the bridge crew into a simulation of Sherwood Forest, with Picard as Robin Hood and Q as the Sheriff of Nottingham. (This was shameless coat-tail chasing, as the Kevin Costner film was about to be released.) Worf discovers that he is Will Scarlett.

'Sir, I protest! I am *not* a merry man!'

Throughout the series, in an echo of Bones's 'I'm a doctor, not a ...' catchphrase, Worf helps us build up a picture of Klingon cultural life in its infinite variety:

'Klingons appreciate strong women.' ('Angel One')

'Klingons never bluff.' ('The Emissary')

'Klingons do not surrender.' ('The Emissary')

'I did not faint. Klingons do not faint.' ('Up the Long Ladder')

'Klingons do not laugh.' ('Redemption')

'Klingons do not pursue relationships. They conquer that which they desire.' ('In Theory')

'Klingons do not allow themselves to be ... probed.' ('Violations')

Riker: 'If I didn't know you better I'd say you were procrastinating.'

Worf: 'Klingons do not procrastinate. It is a ... tactical delay.' ('Liaisons')*

Any dramatic series that reaches season five has done what it set out to do. With the fourth-season cliffhanger 'Redemption', *The Next Generation* notched up its hundredth episode, which meant it could play in syndication until the end of time. In the fifth season, then, we began to see the first small signs of decay. Several of the best episodes were still to come, but consistency was becoming tougher to achieve. Maybe the limitations of the format were simply too powerful. You have to tell a single stand-alone tale in forty-two minutes or so. While some back-story is allowed, new viewers need to be able to switch on and work out what is going on without their heads exploding like Remmick's in 'Conspiracy'. One can only imagine the intense pressure of having to produce twenty-six of these between June and April every year, and make them all bright, shiny, intelligent, different. The process, as we have seen, chews up ideas and people. Once you have set up your situation and your

---

* Vulcans never bluff, either ('The Doomsday Machine'). Although, as has been sug-gested, to claim that Vulcans never bluff could itself be a bluff.

characters, there is only a certain number of things you can do with them. The Doctor in *Doctor Who* keeps bumping into the Daleks. Each time he meets them, they are on the verge of destroying a planet and/or enslaving humanity, and somehow he manages to foil them. Every time. For fifty years. They never win. They can never win.

Edward Gross and Mark Altman interviewed everyone and his dog for their book. Some of their interviewees were almost too candid. Of an episode called 'The Masterpiece Society' (5.13), Ron Moore had this to say: 'This is another example of a show that doesn't really work too well. We sort of show up at a genetically perfect colony – which in and of itself is starting to bore me – and when we get there, it's "Gee, Troi falls in love with one of the people." You can't wait to get up and get a beer.'

Perfectly put. Grant Rosenberg was a writer/producer under contract at Paramount and well known to the *Star Trek* team: 'Rick Berman called me and said, "We need a *Star Trek*: would you like to write one?" and I said, "I'd love to." They said do not come in with ideas. The chance of you coming in with a fresh idea that we haven't heard or rejected or done is slim. So they gave me an idea which had been developed by a writing team which never went from idea to script, and they handed me a story and we stripped it down to the bare bones.'

Which says it all, really. Every idea they could have had, they had already had. And there were still two and a half years of the show to go.

Meanwhile, Paramount boss Frank Mancuso had had an idea. With *The Undiscovered Country* in post-production and nearly ready to go, why not link the two franchises by offering Leonard Nimoy a guest slot on the new series? *The Next Generation* would

never be able to afford his fee in normal circumstances, but as
the film's executive producer, Nimoy might be persuaded to
scale down his salary requirements as a Vulcan gesture of good
will. Thus it came to pass. Like 'Sarek', the 'Unification' two-
parter (5.7 and 5.8) owed its existence to the long lives of Vulcans.
Good grief, Spock had barely aged a year. Poor old Bones, hobbling around with his stick, would have been furious.*

The news reaches Picard that Sarek is on his deathbed, and
the *Enterprise* drops whatever it's doing and heads for Vulcan.
At the same time, a rumour is abroad that Ambassador Spock
(the mere mention of whose name makes everyone invol-
untarily gasp in awe) has been seen on the planet Romulus,
having apparently defected to the Romulan empire. Lawks!
Sarek doesn't know for sure – he and his son have again been
estranged for years – but he thinks Spock may be working
towards the reunification of the Vulcan and Romulan peoples,
whose paths had diverged thousands of years before. Picard
and Data grab a lift on a cloaked Klingon ship, have themselves
disguised as Romulans and sneak down to Romulus to find out
what's going on, i.e. interfere and get in the way.

On Romulus, Picard and Data look for Spock everywhere.
He's not here, nor is he there. It's a big planet. There are people
with pointy ears walking through every street, but not the
ears we yearn to see. In fact, after a brief glimpse early in the
episode, the man once addressed by his captain as 'Spocko'
doesn't make his entrance until the very last scene. He *is* the
cliffhanger.

'I have come on an urgent mission from the Federation,'
Picard tells an intermediary. 'I'm looking for Ambassador
Spock.'

---

* Speaking to *Star Trek: The Official Fan Club Magazine* in 1994, Nimoy said it had been all
his idea. 'It just seemed to me that it made sense for me to make an appearance at that
point. So I went to Rick Berman and Michael Piller and said, "How about it?"' Block and
Erdmann suggest that he came up with the episode's basic storyline as well.

'Indeed,' says Spock, walking out of the shadows. 'You have found him, Captain Picard.'

Fade to black. 'TO BE CONTINUED'.

Tune in next week! Please!

'Unification II', happily, more than makes up for the Spock shortfall in 'Unification I', and there's even a mind-meld between Spock and Picard, to help the son gain access to those of his father's memories that were previously stored in the captain's head. Nimoy is as splendid as ever, more the wry, playful Spock of the films than the more contained Spock of the original series. There's just one small problem with these episodes. They are a bit dull.

For as well as bringing back Spock, 'Unification' echoed *The Undiscovered Country* by employing its own up-to-the-moment socio-political metaphor. The Berlin Wall had recently fallen, Nelson Mandela was out of prison and for about five minutes, peace was in the air. If West and East Germany could be unified, why not Vulcan and Romulus? And why not fans of the original series and fans of the new? The logic was unarguable, as more people tuned into the 'Unification' episodes than to any *Next Generation* episode since its pilot. It's just unfortunate that they witnessed the new show at its most leaden. The political plot, weighed down by its own significance, never takes off. There's one last lip-curling contribution from Commander Sela, whose future in pantomime seems assured. At least 'Sarek' had something to say about ageing and illness, but 'Unification' doesn't have anything to say other than 'Hey look! It's Spock!' And it takes two long episodes to say it.

By eerie coincidence, 'Unification I' was the first episode to air after the death of Gene Roddenberry. Ill for more years than he had acknowledged, and confined to a wheelchair for some months, he had succumbed to a series of strokes. Two days before he died he was given an early viewing of *The Undiscovered Country*. Having told everyone there it was 'a fine film', he went off and wrote a furious memo insisting on vast numbers of changes. He died before the memo could be sent. 'Unification I' carried the title card 'Gene Roddenberry 1921–1991'.

The next generation were now fully in charge of *The Next Generation*. 'Ensign Ro' (5.3) introduced a spiky young Bajoran bridge officer played by Michelle Forbes. The Bajorans, we learn, were displaced from their homeworld by the thick-necked Cardassians forty years ago. Tiny little ridges between their eyebrows make them look chronically irritated. Ro has been brought in to spark things up on the squeaky-clean conflict-free *Enterprise*. She will find it hard going. She has been created to find it hard going.

In 'Darmok' (5.2), Picard makes contact with the Children of Tama, a peaceable and sophisticated race whose language is incomprehensible to everyone else. The universal translator is helpless to interpret what sound like endless descriptive phrases of people and places. Nor does our more prosaic language mean anything to them. Picard and the Tamarian captain stare blankly into their viewscreens, wondering what on earth the other is talking about. Suddenly the Tamarian has an idea. 'Darmok and Jalad at Tanagra!' he says to his first officer, and immediately Picard finds himself beamed down to a planet, with the Tamarian captain, where they must work together to defeat a huge and malevolent electromagnetic monster. It's a little like 'Arena' from the original series, except flipped round, for the two captains are collaborating rather than trying to bash each other's brains out. What we and Picard slowly work out is that the Tamarians communicate only in metaphor, referring only to past events in their history. 'Darmok and Jalad at Tanagra' means to fight a common enemy. 'Shaka, when the walls fell' means a failure, and so on. Slowly, the two races work out how to talk to each other. It's a wonderful premise, and another new staffer, Joe Menosky, produced the sort of script that wins awards, if *Star Trek* ever won awards, which it didn't. Paul Winfield, who had had a creature put in his ear in *The Wrath of Khan*, played the Tamarian captain, and his scenes with Patrick Stewart fizzed and crackled. Once they have begun to understand one another, Picard tells him the myth of Gilgamesh and Enkidu, which itself is a metaphor for the situation the two of them find themselves in. The Tamarian's eyes are ablaze. 'Darmok' is a story about the telling of stories, and about all the stories layered in our own lives, told in a medium, science-fiction television, that prizes story above all else. Linguistics teachers have used the episode as a study aid to show their students how languages work and evolve.*

'Cause and Effect' (5.18) has one of the best pre-credits teasers you could hope to see. The crew are playing poker, and Dr Crusher has a maddening sense of déjà vu. She knew Riker was bluffing, and she knew she was going to win that hand. The *Enterprise* is charting a huge area of empty space called the Typhon Expanse, when suddenly there's a distortion in the space-time continuum just outside the ship. Another ship emerges from the distortion. It's on a collision course and helm isn't responding. Data advises using the tractor beam to change the other ship's trajectory. It doesn't work. The ships collide, the starboard nacelle goes boom, there's a warp-core breach and the *Enterprise* explodes.

The opening credits roll.

We are at the poker game again. Riker bluffs, Dr Crusher wins the hand, and this time everyone notices the déjà vu. The whole story is played out again, with slightly different camera angles. The other ship appears out of the distortion, Data suggests the tractor beam, boom!

Back to the poker game again . . .

---

* Russell T. Davies, the writer-producer behind the rebooted *Doctor Who*, liked the description of this episode so much that he deliberately didn't watch it. 'I love the idea so much, I'd rather think about it. For ever.'

On the very slight possibility that you have not seen this episode, which is quite brilliantly constructed, I shall not give away the ending. In truth, though, it makes for exhilarating viewing however many times you have seen it.

'The First Duty' (5.19) takes us somewhere else we have always wanted to go, Starfleet Academy, back on Earth. A member of Wesley Crusher's five-person flight squadron has been killed in an accident, and there's an inquiry to find out what happened. We meet Boothby (played by ancient hoofer Ray Walston), the gardener who was Captain Picard's mentor all those years ago. Someone even wiser than Jean-Luc! Cue any number of overdone gardening metaphors. Wesley and his chums are covering up the truth out of misplaced loyalty. Should he come clean? Lots of Serious Face in this one.

The greatest *Star Treks* often combine a high concept – something that makes your brain throb with pleasure and pain – with sound character work. We are getting to know these people now. 'Cause and Effect' is, oddly, all about team-work: between the seven or eight main characters, they solve the puzzle. 'The First Duty' is about growing up, and 'The Inner Light' (5.25), one of the best of them all, is about the simple dignity of a life well lived. The *Enterprise* encounters a probe, which transmits a beam that locks onto the captain, who passes out. He wakes up on a drought-stricken planet, where no one has ever heard of Starfleet or the Federation. He is Kamin, an iron weaver, and he is married to Eline. Back on the ship, Dr Crusher tries to revive the captain, who is in a deep coma, but 'undergoing tremendous neurological activity'. On the planet, however, five years have passed. Picard has accepted his new life as 'Kamin', and he and Eline start to talk about having children. We learn that the planet is dying, that its sun will go supernova, that nothing tangible of this society will survive. Picard lives thirty years on this planet, becomes a father, finds peace. 'I always believed that

I didn't need children to complete my life. Now, I couldn't imagine life without them.' But on the *Enterprise*, only half an hour has passed. We learn that the inhabitants of this planet, long since destroyed, sent out the probe so that someone like Picard could learn their story and tell others about them. Picard awakes and, for the second time in two years, has to readjust to normal life in a couple of minutes before the final credits.

How much punishment can a man take?

Writers, as we know, are sadists. Actors like to be stretched. On an AOL chat in 1997, Ron Moore commented as follows: 'I've always felt that the experience in "Inner Light" would've been the most profound experience in Picard's life and changed him irrevocably. However, that wasn't our intention when we were creating the episode. We were after a good hour of TV, and the larger implications of how this would really screw somebody up didn't hit home with us until later.'

Next week, Picard will be back to normal as though nothing has happened. And if you didn't watch 'The Inner Light' the previous week, nothing *has* happened. But then Captain Kirk seemed to get over Joan Collins pretty damn swiftly. Indeed, he never mentioned her again. Deep space does this to you. Deep space, overworked writers and starships called *Enterprise.**

Season five ended with a better cliffhanger, 'Time's Arrow' (5.26), in which Data's disembodied head is found in an archaeological dig in San Francisco, where it has apparently lain for several hundred years. His shipmates are rather more upset by

---

* The episode ends with Picard playing his Ressikan flute, which this long-dead civilisation has left him as a memento. In 2006 Christie's offered the flute prop for sale at auction. Its estimated value was $300. It sold for $40,000.

this than Data himself, but the trail leads to a time rift in a cave on a distant planet, and Data finds himself back on Earth in the nineteenth century, hobnobbing with Mark Twain and a young Guinan (who looks remarkably like the older Guinan). In Part II, the rest of the *Enterprise* crew follow him through the time vortex to foil the villainous plans of some mysterious aliens, who eat human life energy for breakfast. It's all fantastically complicated, and resolved with so much chat the eyes begin to water, for once again the writing team had not worked out how they were going to resolve the cliffhanger before they went off on their holidays. New showrunner Jeri Taylor promised that this would never happen again. Far too stressful.

Taylor, a fifty-something woman corralling a roomful of twenty-something male writers, had been promoted because Michael Piller had begun work on a spin-off series. *Star Trek: Deep Space Nine* would launch in early 1993, halfway through *The Next Generation*'s sixth year. To split the entire production team in two and double production from twenty-six to fifty-two episodes a year was to take creative risks that, some might say, didn't need to be taken, but the older series bore up well under the strain. Absolute solidity characterises the sixth season, even if the show's most adventurous days are now behind it. 'Relics' (6.4) miraculously brings back Scotty, who has been trapped in a transporter beam for seventy-five years until Geordi LaForge finds a way of rematerialising him. You can see Jimmy Doohan struggling a little with the techno-babble that now constitutes most *Next Generation* engineering talk, but there's a lovely sequence in which Picard takes the old fellow onto a holodeck recreation of the original *Enterprise* bridge. To have built this anew would have cost a fortune, although the production team were grievously tempted. In the end they rebuilt the turbolift alcove and Scotty's old engineering station, and superimposed that on a few frames, suitably computer-enhanced, of an empty bridge taken from the original series episode 'This Side of Paradise'. It's all a bit soppy and sentimental, but then so are we.*

'Rascals' (6.7) transforms four crew members, Picard, Keiko O'Brien, Guinan and the new Bajoran strop-queen Ensign Ro, into ten-year-old children, who must recapture the ship from marauding Ferengi. 'Ship in the Bottle' (6.12) sees the return of Daniel Davis's splendid holodeck villain Professor Moriarty, who couldn't be used before for legal reasons unconnected with the show. In this one Moriarty somehow manages to take over the ship, despite Roddenberry's promise in season one that people wouldn't be trying to take over the ship every week. 'Starship Mine' (6.18) is *Die Hard*-style action-adventure, in which Picard zips round an almost deserted *Enterprise* knocking off a band of guerrillas who have, er, taken over the ship. It's well done, though, and Patrick Stewart gets a break from his usual standing and talking scenes. Not a single cup of Earl Grey is consumed in the episode.

The two-part 'Chain of Command' (6.10 and 6.11) does take us somewhere new. In Part I, Picard, Dr Crusher and Worf are sent on a secret mission while the *Enterprise* is placed under the command of Captain Edward Jellico, a no-frills martinet played without the hint of a smile by Ronny Cox. To see the familiar cast suddenly having to hop to it after the comfortable years of Picard's rule is just what the show needs, and it's a shame that Jellico only appeared in these two episodes. The secret mission is behind Cardassian lines, and is really only an excuse for Picard to be captured and interrogated by David Warner's Gul Madred. Part II is fierce stuff, as interrogation descends into torture and a ferocious battle of wills between the two

* One useful prop was a perfect replica of the captain's chair, which fan Steve Horch had built for use at conventions, along with Chekov and Sulu's console. When Ron Moore sat in the chair, he was moved to tears. 'It was like I was touching a piece of my childhood. Bob Justman came down, and Majel Barrett came down. People who had some relationship with the original series kept materialising to see the bridge we had recreated. It was a very special episode.'

men. As Michael Piller said, 'There's just nothing better than putting Patrick Stewart alone in a room with one other good actor and really letting him go for an hour.' Piller took out a full-page ad in *Variety* as a broad-ish hint to the Emmy nominations committee. They weren't watching. Stewart remained unnominated. 'It is not possible that there are five better male actors in this town than Patrick Stewart!' said Jeri Taylor. But the five who were nominated were not acting in SF series.[*]

'Chain of Command, Part II' was pure theatre (more darkened studio than proscenium arch) and a five-star episode if ever I saw one. Not far behind was Ron Moore's ingenious 'Tapestry' (6.16), a what-if story extrapolated from a couple of lines in a second-year episode, when Picard told young Wesley about his artificial heart and how he came to acquire it. As a fresh-faced ensign, he had got into a fight in a bar with some Nausicaans and been stabbed through his own, very human heart. Now Q, in a rerun of 'A Christmas Carol', shows him what would have happened if he hadn't picked that fight, if he had done the sensible thing and avoided confrontation. Suddenly Picard finds that he is a junior lieutenant on the *Enterprise*, and Riker and Troi tell him he plays it too safe ever to have a chance at command. It's a strange thing, but as a junior lieutenant Picard looks physically slighter than he does as a captain. Maybe authority confers a couple of inches on everyone.

Season six ends disappointingly with a cliffhanger of uncharacteristic cheesiness. In 'Descent, Part I', Data's evil brother Lore returns, heading up a small army of Borgs, and we feel that the series has started to eat itself. *The Next Generation* cast had signed up for six seasons, as is the norm in US TV drama,

---

[*] One of Captain Jellico's more inspired commands was that the ship's counsellor should henceforth wear Starfleet uniform like everyone else. Marina Sirtis was delighted. 'It covered up my cleavage, and, consequently, I got all my brains back. Because when you have cleavage, you can't have brains in Hollywood. So I got all my brains back, and I was allowed to do things that I hadn't been allowed to do for five or six years. I went on away teams, I was in charge of staff, I had phasers.'

but after months of fan speculation and some fervid negoti-
ations behind the scenes, executive producer Rick Berman
formally announced in April 1993 that there would be a seventh season, followed soon after by a feature film starring the
new cast. Berman said they were working on two possible
screenplays, one by former head writer Maurice Hurley, and
another by incumbent whizzkids Brannon Braga and Ron
Moore. Both scripts, he said, could be structured to include at
least some of the original series' cast.

Season seven, then, was an extended farewell, a victory
parade to celebrate *Star Trek*'s unebbing popularity. Ratings
were still buoyant, and in 1994 Paramount announced that
aggregate sales of official merchandise had reached $650
million, very nearly enough to start a war. Why go out now?
Why not give it an eighth season, and a ninth? For the same
reason that a studio does anything: money. Just as the original
cast's fees had pushed up the budgets of the later films – both
Shatner and Nimoy were on seven figures by the end – so this
maturing cast would now cost more with every succeeding
year. Creatively, too, some seventh-season shows suggested
that it might be time to start thinking about other stories,
other characters, other crews. We had seen Troi's mother often
enough; now let's see her dead father! LaForge's parents! Worf's
foster brother! Data's mother! (Well, Data's creator's ex-wife.)
The wheels weren't falling off, exactly, but the nuts were a little
loose and there was a nasty grinding sound in the gears.

A few episodes, though, were still memorable for the right
reasons. In 'Phantasms' (7.6), Data has disturbing dreams, and
imagines Troi's body as a gelatinous sponge cake. In 'Parallels'
(7.11), Worf keeps sliding between alternate universes, in one of
which he is married to Troi. 'Lower Decks' (7.15) is a wonderful
show, told from the point of view of four junior crew members
on the *Enterprise*: the 'little people' we only ever see walking
through corridors, or occasionally running if it's a red alert.

One of them we know already: Patti Yatsutake's Nurse Ogawa, who has been working in sickbay for some time now.* Another, Shannon Fill's Ensign Sito, was one of Wesley Crusher's Academy flight team in 'The First Duty', found guilty of covering up for their dead friend. These are sympathetic and pleasing young characters, and the rumour spread that one or two of them might return in the imminent *Star Trek: Voyager* series. They didn't, but if they had, they would surely have done better than one or two cast members chosen in their place.

The appropriately titled final episode, 'All Good Things' (7.25), was a double-lengther that put Picard through the psychological mill once again. The man is made for suffering. Only a few weeks after Worf hopped between parallel universes, the captain starts leaping between three distinct time zones: the familiar present; seven years ago, just after he took command of the *Enterprise*; and twenty-five years in the future, when everyone is old and grizzled and scattered to the winds by happenstance. It's all down to Q, as it should be, for this episode is about symmetry, squaring the circle, giving shape to the series and also to the universe in which the series exists. It's also about giving us, the viewers, a really good time, a reward for seven years' close attention. For all we want to know when a much-loved series ends is: what happened next? Drama needs a climax, but life goes on, and 'All Good Things' shows us one possible future among many. *Star Trek* fans had their own possible future to consider: the forthcoming *Star Trek Generations*, the seventh feature film of the series, and the first with an honestly bald captain in the big chair.†

---

* And had been introduced after George Takei noted the lack of Asian-American characters in the show.

† For Stewart, the series' end came at a good time. 'The last two years have found me feeling an intense restlessness. I needed to go on to something else. This is the toughest job I've ever done, except maybe when I worked on a building site, unloading cement blocks. That was marginally tougher.'

CHAPTER 15

SPIN-OFFS, TAKE-OFFS AND TURN-OFFS

There were eleven more years of *Star Trek* on television after *The Next Generation* ceased trading, some great, some good, and one or two not strictly necessary. This survey now speeds up, to acknowledge the incontrovertible fact that the wider audience had started to tune out. In some ways *Star Trek: Deep Space Nine*, which first aired in January 1993, was a more ambitious show than its immediate predecessor, but it didn't capture the public imagination in the same way. I loved it, and watched it hungrily to the end, feeling lonelier in my madness with each successive season.

Deep Space Nine is set on Deep Space Nine, a space station built by the Cardassians (thick necks, military tendencies) not far from the planet Bajor, on the edge of Cardassian space. Forty years ago the Cardassians invaded the planet and took over, but they have left as a result of the new treaty with the Federation. This station, therefore, is run by the Federation and the Bajorans (single dangly earring, spiritual bent), an uncomfortable arrangement constantly made more uncomfortable by heavy-duty plotting. The man in charge is Commander Benjamin Sisko, played by Avery Brooks, the first African-American to take the lead in a *Star Trek* series. His deputy might have been Ensign Ro from *The Next Generation*, but Michelle Forbes said no, so the part was recast and became the equally cantankerous Major Kira, played by Nana Visitor. The other regulars are drawn from a variety of alien races and make-up schemes. René Auberjonois is Odo, a shapeshifting alien of unknown provenance, who works as the station 'constable', in charge of law and order; Armin Shimerman is Quark, the Ferengi bartender; and Terry Farrell is Lieutenant Jadzia Dax, a member of the Trill species, who look human enough on the outside but have a huge hyper-intelligent slug lodged within them: a symbiont. Other humans on the station are Cirroc Lofton as Sisko's teenage son Jake (for the youth demographic); cuddly old Colm Meaney as Chief Miles Edward O'Brien from *The Next Generation*; and the Sudanese-born Siddig El Fadil playing the chief medical officer Dr Julian Bashir with wide eyes and a cut-glass British accent. And that's just the beginning of it.

The western analogy remained apposite. If *Star Trek* and *The Next Generation* were both 'Wagon Train to the Stars', *Deep Space Nine* was the outer space western set in the frontier town: *Gunsmoke*, maybe. It's wild out there, and anything can happen. Instead of Injuns there are Cardassians, and instead of bank robbers dodgy Ferengi. Sisko is the US marshal and Odo the sheriff. To enhance plotting potentialities yet further, up the road is the first-ever stable wormhole, which takes you untold millions of light years to another part of the galaxy (we're calling it 'the Gamma Quadrant') in a matter of minutes. *Deep*

Space Nine is therefore on a multi-dimensional crossroads of routes. It's like living next to Spaghetti Junction. A quiet life is not an option.

This was a complicated set-up, to say the least, and like *The Next Generation*, the show took a while to find its way. One thing was immediately clear, though. One of the fundamental tenets of *Star Trek* – the boldly-going-where-no-one-had-gone-before – had been abandoned. We weren't going anywhere. People were boldly coming to us. The dynamic had shifted. More precisely, it had slowed down and come to a stop. The dynamic was now a static. The writers, I believe, realised what they had rather faster than the audience did, but with *The Next Gen* so well established and clear in its intent, *Deep Space Nine* did initially look unsure and underpowered. Many viewers jumped ship, never to return.

Another weakness was the lead character. Kirk always led from the front. Picard's natural authority was unquestioned. But Sisko is an administrator. He drives a desk rather than a ship.* The writers had to find ingenious ways of enhancing his role. In the very first episode he is discovered to be 'the emissary' long predicted in Bajoran religious texts, with powers as yet undisclosed. Later on, more as a panic measure than because the underlying narrative demands it, Sisko will be given his own ship to captain, the USS *Defiant*. At around the same time, Avery Brooks toughened up his image by shaving his head and growing a don't-mess-with-me beard. He also grew more mannered in his performance, with a staccato delivery that sounded a bit like someone spitting melon pips at you. But for reasons beyond his control, this was the first *Star Trek* series in which the lead actor wasn't the centre of attention, just one character of many.

---

* It's particularly odd because Brooks had been so convincingly hard-boiled in his previous role, as Hawk in the detective show *Spenser: For Hire*.

In season three, Michael Piller left to develop *Voyager*, and Ira Steven Behr took over as showrunner. Under his care, *Deep Space Nine* became richer, deeper and more operatic, embracing long narrative arcs and an ever-broadening cast of recurring characters. Andrew Robinson's Cardassian tailor-cum-spy Garak, written as a one-off, became a cornerstone of the show, as did J. G. Hertzler's one-eyed Klingon General Martok, the great and glorious Louise Fletcher as the machiavellian Bajoran high priestess Kai Winn, and many others. By the end of the seventh and final season, Behr reckoned that he and his writers were servicing thirty distinct characters, each of whom needed his or her own send-off as their interlocking stories were brought to a conclusion. They managed it rather deftly, as it happens, finishing with a nine-episode arc that amply rewarded those of us who had stuck with the show the whole way through.*

One small masterstroke had been the arrival, also in season four, of Michael Dorn as the newly promoted Lieutenant Commander Worf, shamelessly imported as viewer bait. He added a modest heft to proceedings, filling a Worf-shaped hole we hadn't known was there. The *Next Generation* veteran who really made *Deep Space Nine* his own, though, was Colm Meaney's Chief O'Brien, who took over from Picard as the character the writers most enjoyed torturing. This was a compliment to the actor as well as to the resilience of the character. At one point, O'Brien spent twenty-five years serving time in a mental prison for a crime he hadn't committed, while only hours passed on the space station. And still he could realign the EM manifolds in the magnetic flux resonator in less time than you or I could make a cup of tea.

---

* Unlike previous *Star Trek* incarnations, *Deep Space Nine* relied on a relatively small group of writers, which included Behr himself, writing first with Robert Hewitt Wolfe and later with Hans Beimler, as well as Ronald D. Moore and the new young partnership of Bradley Thompson and David Weddle.

Television production is an industrial process, and by 1994 the *Star Trek* factory was operating at full capacity. After *The Next Generation* went offline, the next shiny new product off the conveyor belt was the robot-tooled *Generations* feature film. Were we allowed to call it *Star Trek VII*? We were not, even if that's what it was. If it had been the seventh film with the original cast, William Shatner could have insisted that it was his turn to direct. That's why it wasn't the seventh film with the original cast.

On television, *Deep Space Nine* was able to take a risk or two. With a $35 million budget, *Generations* was obliged to play safer. It did so by fashioning a storyline in which old captain Shatner and new captain Stewart met and worked together in nearly perfect harmony. It might have been more fun, if less lucrative, if they had hated each other.

We begin, then, in the year 2293, a little while after the events of *The Undiscovered Country*. Kirk, Scotty and Chekov, all safely retired, are invited to attend the launch of the new *Enterprise-B*. But on its maiden voyage, just up the road and back in time for tea, the ship runs into a strange energy ribbon, the sort of thing that, if Spock had been there, he would have said was unlike anything he had seen before. The ribbon packs a mighty punch, the hull is breached, and Kirk is sucked out into space, presumed dead. Although presumed by whom? Not by anyone who has seen an episode of *Star Trek* before.

Seventy-eight years later, the *Enterprise-D* finds the same energy ribbon, which Guinan tells Picard is called 'the Nexus'. This is an extradimensional realm in which you can live for ever, experiencing your past all over again, in a state of permanent blissed-out happiness. Another *Star Trek* paradise, in short. Guinan has been there, and rather liked it. So too has Malcolm McDowell's mad scientist, Dr Tolian Soran, who will do anything to get back there, including destroying stars and planets with six billion inhabitants. Picard must stop him, but first he must enter the Nexus himself. And there he finds the family he never had, all wearing Victorian fancy dress as they celebrate Christmas Day in Downton Abbey. None of it is real, he realises, several minutes after the audience. So he heads off to find his fellow *Enterprise* captain, who is in ersatz Iowa, chopping wood, riding horses and making breakfast for his girlfriend Antonia.

'You say history considers me dead,' says Kirk. 'Who am I to argue with history?'

'You are a Starfleet officer,' says Picard. 'You have a duty.'

'I don't need to be lectured by you,' says Kirk. 'I was out saving the galaxy when your grandfather was in diapers. Besides which, I think the galaxy owes me one.'

Needless to say, they do go off together and foil Soran, but in the process Kirk is mortally injured, and so like Spock in *The Wrath of Khan*, gets to die twice in the same film. (Remember the favoured nations clauses in their contracts.)

'Did we do it? Did we ... make a difference?" asks Kirk, about to croak.

'Oh yes, we made a difference. Thank you,' says Picard, who was very well brought up. It's all a little underwhelming, to be honest. We have seen Kirk cheat death so often that when death finally gets its own back, we don't quite believe it. And the 'chemistry' between the two skippers is notional, at best. Brannon Braga and Ronald D. Moore, clever writers who have overcome challenges greater than this, were for once defeated by the dullness of the premise. As if to compensate, they packed their script full of little nods and winks, show-ing us the film for fans concealed within the film they had to make for non-fans and *Trek* agnostics. Possibly their boldest move – even now, I'm not sure it works – was in giving Data the emotion chip for which he had long yearned. Data thus

mutates into a semi-comic character, weeping with happiness when he rescues his cat Spot from a tight corner, and saying 'Ohhhhh, shit!' when the *Enterprise*'s saucer section crash-lands on the planet. But we miss the old, unemotional Data, who was more complex than this, and more interesting. 'The *Star Trek* saga has always had a weakness for getting distracted by itself,' wrote Roger Ebert. *Generations*, he said was 'undone by its narcissism'. The film still made a pile of money: $118 million on a budget of $35 million.*

Early work had started on *Star Trek: Voyager* in 1993, as Paramount re-explored the idea of launching its own dedicated TV network. As in 1977, a new *Star Trek* show would be the main draw, and this forward planning allowed elements of its back-story to be seeded in episodes of *The Next Generation* and *Deep Space Nine*. The Maquis, named after the French Second World War resistance movement, were a most un-Roddenberry-like group of rebels who had left the Federation's warm embrace after the planets they had colonised were handed over to the dastardly Cardassians. At last, conflict! Our straight-up-and-down Starfleeters couldn't deal with these scruffy renegades and their underhand methods. When this series begins, the USS *Voyager* is pursuing a Maquis ship into an area of space known as the Badlands, but a mysterious energy wave – there is never any other type – sweeps up both ships and deposits them seventy thousand light years away, in the unexplored Delta Quadrant of the galaxy. It'll take them seventy-five years

---

* William Shatner was as reluctant to 'die' in character as Leonard Nimoy had been, but a reported $6 million fee may have been some compensation. 'Captain Kirk lived pretty much the way I wanted him to live,' he said afterwards. 'He was a distillation of all that I would like to be: heroic and romantic, forceful in battle and gentle in love, wise and profound.'

to get home. The Maquis ship is damaged beyond repair, and both ships have lost several crew. Sworn enemies must throw differences aside and work together if they are to survive the long and perilous journey back to civilisation.

The USS *Voyager* is commanded by Captain Kathryn Janeway, played by the gravel-voiced Kate Mulgrew. The part had originally gone to the French-Canadian actress Genevieve Bujold, but after a few days' filming she decided she had made a terrible mistake, and the part was hurriedly recast. (Unedited footage featuring Bujold can be found on YouTube, and suggests that her decision was a sound one.) Mulgrew thus became the first female lead of a *Star Trek* series, and the first without any hair issues at all, although she does occasionally shift from short to long and back again without obvious reason. (She is very decisive on other matters. But anyone can have a bad hair episode, even in the twenty-fourth century.)

The rest of the crew encompasses more races than a Benetton ad. There's a black Vulcan, Tuvok (Tim Russ); a Native American first officer, Chakotay, played by a Mexican-American actor, Robert Beltran; a mixed-race, quarter-Klingon chief engineer, B'Elanna Torres (Roxann Dawson); and fresh-faced Chinese-American Ensign Harry Kim (Garrett Wang). The whiteness and blondeness of helmsman Tom Paris (Robert Duncan McNeill) almost seem out of place in this line-up: had the series been made now, he would surely have had only one leg. The ship also offers refuge to a couple of spare aliens, the unfeasibly jolly Neelix (Ethan Phillips), who is a Talaxian with 'mottled temple ridges' and a blonde 'hair tube' stuck on top of his head, and his girlfriend Kes (Jennifer Lien), an Ocampan with pixie ears. Some of these characters are more interesting than others; some actors are more adept than others. But all the lovely potential for argument and drama between these characters will come to very little, and the crew become nearly as close-knit and wearily professional as the *Enterprise-D*'s.

Two characters stand out. 'The Doctor', as played by Robert Picardo, is an Emergency Medical Hologram, called into action because all the real medical staff have been rendered dead. Bald, grumpy and possessed of impeccable comic timing, the Doctor achieves sentience of his own and is quickly given all the best lines. Then there is Jeri Ryan's Seven of Nine, a Borg woman liberated from the collective, who joins the crew in season four and freshens up the show no end. Captain Janeway, a worthier leader than poor old Sisko at *Deep Space Nine*, has good, strong relationships with these characters, and they feature more and more prominently as *Voyager* whooshes across the galaxy, pursued by the local nasties in every successive 'neighbourhood'. Get past the Kazon (a very dull race indeed) and the body-part-harvesting Vidiians, and some lizardy nomadic hunters called the Hirogen will be waiting for you, and after that there's the Borg, whose backyard this turns out to be. Every so often there's a useful short cut that cuts years off the journey, and it will give nothing away to say that it takes seven of your Earth years, and 172 of your Earth episodes, for *Voyager* to get all the way home.

So why doesn't *Voyager* quite work? Four different executive producers acted as showrunner: Michael Piller for seasons one and two, Jeri Taylor for three and four, Brannon Braga for five and six, and Kenneth Biller (who had been part of the writing team since the beginning) for season seven. Talented people all, and between them they produced some stunning episodes, but there were several reasons the show never quite took flight. One was, yet again, a perilously slow start. The aliens for season one were dreary. They talked too much under too much make-up. You started to wish for some displaced Romulans just to warm things up.

The second problem was the cast. We long ago realised that there was only one William Shatner, and he was lucky enough to have the only known Leonard Nimoy and the absolutely unique DeForest Kelley by his side. Would *The Next Generation* have flourished without Patrick Stewart? *Deep Space Nine* had a magnificent supporting cast and the ability to expand on it at whim. Mulgrew's Captain Janeway is brave and admirable, but there's an oddly monochrome quality to this racially diverse cast. It's only a tinge of dullness, but it's a tinge too far.

The third problem with the show was identified by Ronald D. Moore, who worked there for a season and found it a frustrating experience. He had liked the original premise, as he told Anna Kaplan of fandom.com:

> Get them away from all the familiar *Star Trek* aliens, throw them out into a whole new section of space where anything can happen ... Before it aired, I was at a convention in Pasadena, and Rick Sternbach and Michael Okuda* were on stage, and they were answering questions from the audience about the new ship. And they were talking about the fact that in the premise the ship was going to have problems. It wasn't going to have unlimited sources of energy. It wasn't going to have all the doodads of the *Enterprise*. It was going to be rougher, fending for themselves more, having to trade to get supplies that they want. That didn't happen. It doesn't happen at all, and that's a lie to the audience. I think the audience intuitively knows when something is true and something is not true. *Voyager* is not true. If it were true, the ship would not look spick-and-span every week, after all these battles it goes through. How many times has the bridge been destroyed? How many shuttlecrafts have vanished, and another one just comes out of the oven? That kind of bullshitting the audience, I think, takes its toll.

That's the best analysis of the show I have heard. What

---

* Long-serving scenic illustrators and technical consultants, who defined the look and feel of these shows as much as anyone.

seems to have happened was a fundamental disagreement between Rick Berman and Michael Piller. Berman, as he would be the first to admit, was dedicated to preserving Gene Roddenberry's vision. 'Gene had very, very strong ideals about what he wanted *Star Trek* to be,' he said in 2006. 'And he wasn't going to let anybody mess with that. And I never messed with it. Or let me rephrase that: I *rarely* messed with it.'

And according to Ron Moore, Berman thought that Roddenberry wouldn't have approved of the whole Maquis storyline. Whereas Piller was all for it. 'He was always arguing for something more complex, more nuanced, more character-based, more sociologically interesting,' said Moore.* 'The initial idea for *Voyager* was that the Maquis who joined the crew would not put on the Starfleet uniforms. Michael lost that fight.' Moore has described a fractious atmosphere behind the scenes, in contrast to the more mutually supportive group of writers who had worked on *Deep Space Nine*. He was also dismayed by the reliance on technobabble, a problem that had begun to blight *The Next Generation* in its later seasons, but achieved its apogee in *Voyager*, where writing about tachyon discharges in the starboard nacelle was always easier than writing about people, because the people weren't that exciting.

Ron Moore went on to develop and executive-produce the rebooted *Battlestar Galactica*, which ran for four seasons between 2003 and 2009, and was his version of what *Voyager* should have been. It's an infinitely superior show: more cannily cast, better written, with narrative arc at the centre of everything and the constant, claustrophobic sense that everything is at stake. Life for the human survivors on *Galactica* is fragile and may not last long. And which of them is actually human and which of them is not? As Robert Bianco wrote in *USA Today*, 'Driven by violence and rage, *Galactica*

---

* Interviewed by Block and Erdmann.

is perhaps the darkest space opera American TV has ever produced. In *Galactica's* future, humans are on the run, and if external enemies don't get us, internal divisions will . . . You'll understand [the characters], their conflicts and their desires, because they're recognisable humans in all their glorious complexity. And that's what makes *Galactica* a great TV series.' It was the lack of these that made *Voyager* less than great.

Before *Voyager*, Braga and Moore had co-written the second and best of the *Next Generation* feature films, *Star Trek: First Contact* (1996). The cast's own Jonathan Frakes directed, apparently after two better-known directors said no.* Rick Berman, again producing, wanted a time-travel story, while Braga and Moore wanted something about the Borg. Why not do both? The Borg had not been featured in *The Next Generation* in full war-cry since 'The Best of Both Worlds', partly because of cost and partly because the writers always struggled to find things for them to do. (They destroy. They assimilate. They say 'Resistance is futile.' It's a limited repertoire.) But as Moore told Larry Nemecek, 'The Borg were really liked by the fans, and we liked them. They were fearsome. They were *unstoppable*. Perfect foils for a feature story.'

The Borg are heading straight for Earth once more and the *Enterprise* follows. But just above the Earth's atmosphere, the familiar cube issues forth a smaller and even deadlier Borg sphere, a time-travelling device trailing 'chronometric particles'. It zips back in time and, again, the *Enterprise* follows. But just before the present blanks out, they see that the Earth has changed. It now has a toxic atmosphere and is populated

---

* Ingmar Bergman? Michelangelo Antonioni? According to Frakes himself, it was Ridley Scott and John McTiernan, director of *Die Hard*.

by nine billion Borg drones. The Borg have gone back in time and assimilated humanity before it was strong enough to resist.

Plan A, as Braga and Moore were writing early drafts, was to go back to Renaissance Italy. (Their working title was *Star Trek: Renaissance*. I would pay good money, and maybe bad money too, to see a film with that title.) The crew of the *Enterprise* would have tracked the Borg back to their castle dungeon. Data would have become Leonardo da Vinci's apprentice. Swordfights would have featured alongside phaser battles. But while this sounds like an excellent (even a typical) episode of late-period *Doctor Who*, it sounded a bit campy for a $45 million *Star Trek* film. In addition, informal research suggested that the core audience knew nothing and cared less about Europe in the fifteenth century. And Patrick Stewart didn't want to wear tights.

The setting of the film therefore moved to twenty-first-century Montana, where, according to original series legend, Zefram Cochrane invented the warp drive and made first contact with some passing Vulcans. The Borg wish to assimilate Earth before this happens, which will save a lot of trouble later. The *Enterprise* destroys the sphere (almost too easily), but Borg drones beam onto the beloved flagship and start assimilating that instead. Picard, in action-adventure mode as never before, leads the resistance, which he deems not to be futile.

'I will not sacrifice the *Enterprise*,' he whispers cinematically. 'We've made too many compromises already. Too many retreats. They invade our space and we fall back. They assimilate entire worlds and we fall back. Not again. The line must be drawn here. This far, no further. And I will make them pay for what they've done!'

Meanwhile in Montana, Riker's away team must help Cochrane achieve what he was going to achieve anyway, and change the timeline back to the way it should have been. The writers wanted to show us something we hadn't seen before, the de facto birth of the Federation. 'The one image I brought to the table was the image of the Vulcans coming out of the ship,' said Brannon Braga. 'That, to me, was what made the time-travel story fresh. We get to see what happened when humans shook hands with their first aliens.'

We also get to see a leader of the Borg for the first time, for reasons of drama rather than consistency. (The faceless hive mind, while terrifying, makes a dull conversationalist.) Alice Krige plays the Borg Queen with glistening lips and icy menace, and as much dignity as you can muster when what remains of the top half of your humanoid body is being lowered onto the robotic arms-and-legs bit.* She attempts to seduce Data, who still has his emotion chip, but is much less irritating this time around. James Cromwell plays Zefram Cochrane as a real, flawed human being, and not the 'saint and visionary' of Starfleet myth; Alfre Woodard is his assistant Lily Sloane, with whom Picard forms something of a bond; and there are cameos by a host of familiar faces, including Robert Picardo as yet another Emergency Medical Hologram. Asked to defend Sick Bay from a horde of rampaging Borg drones trying to bash their way in, he responds, 'I'm a doctor, not a door-stop.'

By some way the most action-packed of the series, *First Contact* did what only *The Voyage Home* had really done before: it delighted audiences who knew nothing about *Star Trek* as well as audiences who knew far too much. There's little of the wit of the later original-series films, and very little time for reflection, but the show's spirit and flavour are untainted, and Patrick Stewart becomes the action-adventure hero part of him had always wanted to be. Even before they had finished

---

* Roger Ebert wrote that she 'looks like no notion of sexy I have ever heard of, but inspires me to keep an open mind'.

filming, the production team knew it would be a hit. How many ways there are for films to go wrong, and how very few there seem to be for films to go right.

One should add, though, that the film incorporates a few familiar themes. For the third film out of eight, *Moby-Dick* is directly referenced, this time by Lily Sloane, who spots that Picard is Ahab and the Borg his whale. But at least there are no Klingons quoting Shakespeare. Timed to coincide with *Star Trek*'s thirtieth anniversary in autumn 1996, the film opened on the day that Mark 'Sarek' Lenard died, aged seventy-two. It would eventually gross $146 million, which disappointed no one.

Golden geese are well known for their poor life expectancy. For years there was not enough *Star Trek*; then there was as much as we needed; then, one day, there was too much. *Star Trek: Insurrection*, the ninth feature, followed in November 1998, and felt like an extended episode of *The Next Generation*, with yet another planetary paradise under threat from yet another predatory alien species. Michael Piller wrote the screenplay and Jonathan Frakes again directed, but they couldn't solve the underlying problem: the inexorable passing of time. What was there left for these characters to do? Where else could they go? Worried that he was growing too old and saggy to play an unageing android, Brent Spiner actually asked for Data to be killed off. His copy of the script arrived with a note from the producers, saying, 'Sorry, kill you later.'

Insurrection fulfilled all the promise of *Star Trek* films not divisible by two, and its greatest achievement may have been to make just enough money for *Star Trek: Nemesis* to be made four years later. But in between, a *Star Trek* film far better than either was released, a film in which *Star Trek*

wasn't even mentioned but whose provenance was so obvious you were amazed Paramount didn't sue. *Galaxy Quest*
was about the cast of a once-popular, long-cancelled TV
show called *Galaxy Quest*. Tim Allen played Jason Nesmith,
once Commander Peter Quincy Taggart of the spaceship
Protector, and now a very slightly washed-up middle-aged
actor with not quite enough work but a long queue of fans
lining up at a convention in a shopping mall car park to get
a signed photo of him and the rest of the cast. Sigourney
Weaver was Gwen DeMarco, who had played Lieutenant
Tawny Madison, the *Protector*'s computer officer. Her job,
as the show's sex symbol, was essentially to repeat whatever
the computer had just told her, while looking gorgeous.
Most sublime of all, Alan Rickman played Sir Alexander
Dane, the classically trained British actor who has found
himself miserably typecast as Dr Lazarus, a Mak'tar from
the planet Tev'Meck. His character had the catchphrase
'By Grabthar's hammer, by the suns of Warvan, you *shall*
be avenged!' Small children asked him to repeat this every
day of his life.

So we have a troupe of bitter, underemployed actors who,
one day, are kidnapped by a real alien race, the Thermians,
octopoidal creatures with a device that makes them look and
seem nearly human. The Thermians have been watching
Galaxy Quest reruns on syndication but they do not realise that
it's a drama series; they think it's all for real. Gwen DeMarco
tries to explain TV to them.

'They're not all "historical documents". Surely you don't
think *Gilligan's Island* is a . . .'

The Thermians wail in despair.

Up in real outer space, though, they have their own battle
to fight against some evil alien predators, and they need help
because they are peaceable octopoidal creatures who wouldn't
say 'Boo!' to a multi-dimensional goose. So they have built a

real working version of the *Protector*, and now they ask Jason
Nesmith and his crew to fly it and defend them from their
enemies. But the crew are actors. They don't know about
anything.

'You're just going to have to figure out what it wants,' says Sir
Alexander Dane, when they encounter a rock monster. 'What's
its motivation?'

'It's a rock monster,' says Jason Nesmith. 'It doesn't have
motivation.'

'See, that's your problem, Jason,' says Sir Alexander. 'You
were never serious about the craft.'

The actors are all at sea, not even knowing which buttons to
press on the consoles. But someone remembers the fans, who
know everything there is to know about the *Predator*, so they
contact one of them, who helps them defeat the nasties and
save the day. As the real *Protector* crash-lands in another shopping mall car park, you hardly know whether to laugh or cheer.

Galaxy Quest speaks our language. Jason Nesmith (catchphrase: 'Never give up, never surrender') takes his shirt off at
any opportunity and is widely disliked by his fellow cast members. 'All right, let's settle down. If we're going to get through
this we're going to need self-control.'

'Self-control?' says Gwen DeMarco. 'That's funny coming
from the guy that slept with every Terrakian slave girl and
Moon Princess on the show.'

Sir Alexander Dane is never seen in public without his prosthetic forehead, and indeed, even has it on in his hotel room.

Sam Rockwell plays Guy Fleegman, who played a redshirt
killed in episode 81. He is convinced throughout the film that
he is going to be killed and there's nothing he can do about it.

'Let's get out of here before one of those things kills Guy,'
says Gwen DeMarco.

The *Protector* has the registration number NTE-3120. 'NTE'
stands for 'Not The *Enterprise*'.

'I had originally not wanted to see *Galaxy Quest* because I heard that it was making fun of *Star Trek*,' said Patrick Stewart. 'And then Jonathan Frakes rang me up and said, "You must not miss this movie! See it on a Saturday night in a full theatre." And I did, and of course I found it was brilliant. Brilliant. No one laughed louder or longer in the cinema than I did.'

'I think it's a chillingly realistic documentary,' said George Takei. 'Tim Allen had that Shatner-esque swagger down pat. And I roared when the shirt came off, and Sigourney rolls her eyes and says, "There goes that shirt again." How often did we hear that on the set?'

At a convention in Las Vegas in 2013, fans voted for their favourite *Star Trek* feature films. *Galaxy Quest* came seventh.

When the pastiche outpaces the original, you know the game is up. *Star Trek: Nemesis* was the tenth film and thus favoured by numerical precedent. But the most expensive of the series ($60 million) was also the least seen ($67 million) and the soonest forgotten. A very young Tom Hardy, in his first major film role, plays the Romulan warlord Shinzon, who turns out to be a crafty clone of Picard, even though he looks and sounds nothing like him. In the ensuing mêlée, Data gets the death Brent Spiner wanted, and Spiner gets another Data-like android to continue the story, if required. But I think we all knew, sitting in the cinema, that this was the last train out of this particular station. Disappointingly, several character-rich scenes were scripted and filmed but cut in favour of action sequences, which no one saw anyway. Jonathan Frakes, director of the previous films, had not been asked back. But if he had been, he thinks the film would have made more money.

When *Voyager* ended in spring 2001, it was swiftly succeeded by *Star Trek: Enterprise*, a prequel series that sought to fill one of the few gaps in the timeline that had not been mined to exhaustion. It's set in the year 2151, ninety years after Zefram Cochrane's first warp flight, and 115 years before the events of the original *Star Trek* series. Humanity has developed its first spaceship capable of warp five, and this makes interstellar exploration possible for the first time. The ship is of course the *Enterprise*, its designation NX-01, and it's a far smaller, pokier and more functional vessel than we are accustomed to. Its captain is Jonathan Archer, played by Scott Bakula, well known to science fiction audiences after five seasons on *Quantum Leap*. He has the now usual crew of misfits and oddities, including a female Vulcan science officer and a Denobulan chief medical officer, Dr Phlox, played with great gusto by John Billingsley. Had we not seen it all before, we might have relished these characters and their adventures rather more. But we had seen it all before, many times.

Created by Rick Berman (the great survivor) and Brannon Braga, *Enterprise* tried hard to distinguish itself from its numerous parent series. For one thing there was no 'Star Trek' in its title (until belatedly introduced in season three, when viewing figures were faltering). It had a vocal theme tune, a Diane Warren song sung by Russell Watson, which wasn't just revolting in itself, but had actually been used before (with a different title) for the unspeakable Robin Williams film *Patch Adams*. But you can't blame them for trying. *Enterprise* had to be different, to justify its existence; but it also had to be the same, because it alone was carrying the *Star Trek* flame.

Enterprise had the best captain since Picard, some good political wranglings with the Vulcans (who since first contact had kept humanity on a technological leash, fearing their irrationality and impulsiveness if they were allowed to venture too far from their own world), and in the first two seasons, a ferociously complex time-travel-based narrative arc, which occasionally made sense. But the tone of the show, and its plotlines, were more *Next Generation* and *Voyager* than they were original *Star Trek*. It felt like a show out of its natural time, whatever that might have been. Changes were made in season three (some new villains) and season four, which focused again on the prequel concept, which had been slightly put to one side. But viewers were bored. Season four was the last. Add them all up, and you have twenty-eight seasons of *Star Trek* on TV, and if you include the films, 726 episodes. I myself watched, with absolute dedication, until the end of the second season of *Enterprise*, and fitfully thereafter. It has been very nearly a lifetime's enthusiasm, rekindled, I'm happy to say, by the writing of this book. But by spring 2005, when *Enterprise* was quietly discontinued, it seemed that the franchise had run its course. There were no more stories to be told, no more deep-space anomalies to be charted, no more warp-core breaches to be prevented, no more, no more, no more.

CHAPTER 18

REBOOT

In 1995, the Student Union Building at McGill University in Montreal was renamed the Shatner Centre in honour of its best-known graduate. 'He's the only McGill graduate ever to command a starship within fifteen years of graduating,' said one of the students who organised the campaign.

In June 1999, DeForest Kelley, that 'sweet, humble man' in Leonard Nimoy's words, died of stomach cancer aged seventy-nine. In an interview in the late 1990s, he had said that one of his biggest fears was that the words etched on his gravestone would be 'He's dead, Jim.' They weren't.

In April 2000, aged eighty, Jimmy Doohan became a father for the seventh time when his third wife Wende gave birth to a little girl, Sarah. The couple had married in 1974 when the groom was fifty-four and the bride eighteen.

William Campbell, the Squire of Gothos, had served as best man.

In 2003, a BBC viewers poll voted William Shatner's 'Lucy in the Sky with Diamonds' (to be found on his gravity-warping 1968 album *The Transformed Man*) the worst Beatles cover version of all time. In the same year George Clooney, appearing on the BBC radio show *Desert Island Discs*, chose Shatner's version as one of his eight records. 'You need a reason to get off the island,' he explained, 'and if you play William Shatner singing "Lucy in the Sky with Diamonds" then you will hollow out your own leg and make a canoe out of it to get off this island.'*

In 2005 the British ufologist Dr David Clarke, leafing through old police files, discovered that detectives from Scotland Yard had kept dossiers on *The X-Files* and *Star Trek*, 'fearing that the television series could cause riots and mass suicide'.

In July 2005 Jimmy Doohan died, aged eighty-five. Some of his ashes were launched in a Falcon 1 rocket in 2008, and some more went up in a Falcon 9 rocket in 2012.

In October 2005, George Takei announced that he was gay and had been in a committed relationship with his partner, Brad Altman, for eighteen years. He said, 'It's not really coming out, which suggests opening a door and stepping through. It's more like a long, long walk through what began as a narrow corridor that starts to widen.' In 2008, George and Brad became the first same-sex couple to apply for a marriage licence in West Hollywood, and tied the knot a month later.

---

* Leonard Nimoy also recorded regularly in the late 1960s and early 1970s. *Two Sides of Leonard Nimoy* (1969) is an album of original poems set to music. *The New World of Leonard Nimoy* (1970) has been described by Robert Schnakenberg as 'yet another album of pop classics disemboweled by the master'. Nichelle Nichols's *Uhura Sings* (1986) includes a song called 'Ode to the Space Shuttle'. And Brent Spiner's 1991 album of Thirties and Forties standards, *Ol' Yellow Eyes Is Back*, includes vocal renderings by a backing band called 'the Sunspots', comprising Messrs Dorn, Burton, Frakes and Stewart.

In November 2005 Michael Piller, who had run *The Next Generation* writers' room in its best years and subsequently helped create *Deep Space Nine* and *Voyager*, died of cancer aged fifty-seven. 'He was a man of principle and character,' said his fellow producer Jeri Taylor, 'a good and decent person who always tried to do what was right.'

In January 2006, William Shatner sold a kidney stone he had passed to the online casino website GoldenPalace.com for $25,000. They originally offered him $15,000 but he said he had *Star Trek* tunics that had sold for more than that. When they increased their offer, he gave in. 'I retain visitation rights,' he explained.

In January 2007 George Takei joined the cast of the NBC series *Heroes*, as Kaito Nakamura, a successful Japanese businessman and father to one of the main characters. The licence plate of the limousine he arrived in was NCC 1701.

In 2007, Leonard Nimoy published a collection of photographs he titled *The Full Body Project*. All the photos are in black and white, and feature groups of women smiling and laughing, dancing or embracing, sometimes staring into the camera. They are all naked, and they are all fat. 'In these pictures,' said Nimoy, 'these women are proudly wearing their own skin. They respect themselves and I hope that my images convey that to others.' They do indeed. It's a fantastic and beautiful collection.

In May 2008 Bob Justman, *Star Trek*'s line producer in seasons one and two, and cruelly passed over for the top job in favour of the ridiculous Freiberger in season three, died aged eighty-one. Rick Berman said he was 'like a mentor and a father' to him. Alexander Courage, composer of the theme tune, died in the same month, aged eighty-eight, as did Joseph Pevney, who had directed more episodes than anyone else, aged ninety-six.

In 2010, in the New Year's Honours List, Patrick Stewart was knighted for services to drama. In 2012 he carried the Olympic torch as part of the official relay for the London Olympics. He said it was an experience he would never forget.

Disasters don't end a story like *Star Trek*'s. Damp squibs are far more effective. *Nemesis* and *Enterprise* didn't make a bad impression, exactly; they just made no impression at all. By 2005, when *Enterprise* shuffled to a close, the franchise had worn out all but its most tireless followers. There seemed to be no way back.

Imagine, though, that you were trying to build something like *Star Trek* today from scratch. A TV show that would eventually generate a long and (mostly) profitable series of feature films, four spin-off TV series, hundreds of dedicated novels, a multi-billion-dollar merchandising industry and enough conventions around the world to keep its typecast former cast members in regular funds? Over fifty years? Good luck with that.

There are excellent reasons why the entertainment industry endlessly returns to old formats and ideas, and remakes them for a new generation. It's easier than having new ideas. It's cheaper, because people know about them already. And every new generation, we have discovered, wants its own Spiderman or Batman, so will happily see the same old film remade with new young actors and more spectacular special effects. Why remake *Total Recall* or *Robocop*? Why not?

Sooner or later, someone would cast an eye on *Star Trek* and think, hmm, there's a bit more to be squeezed out of that. The surprise was that it happened so quickly. In 2005 the franchise was dead. J. J. Abrams's film started shooting in late 2007. In reality, the franchise had been dead for about as long as Spock had been.

Harve Bennett, long retired (he died in early 2015, aged

eighty-four), must have felt vindicated by Abrams's choice of storyline – either that or very angry indeed. For what was *Star Trek* (as the film was called) but a glossed-up, mega-high-budget retooling of his own *Starfleet Academy* idea? Abrams introduces Kirk, Spock, Bones and the rest as young men and women (or at least younger, in the case of Scotty), entering Starfleet Academy, getting into trouble and out of it again, and gradually coalescing as the crew of the starship *Enterprise*. The narrative trick that enables Abrams and his writers Roberto Orci and Alex Kurtzman to make substantial changes and forge their own very different *Star Trek* is time travel. A Romulan ship emerges from the future, kills Kirk's father just before young James T. is born, and alters the timeline for ever. Which means that whatever happened in 'classic' *Star Trek* now won't happen, even though the aged Ambassador Spock also returns from the future, and he remembers it all very clearly. It's not just the series that has been rebooted. It's the entire twenty-third century.

Abrams casts well. The younger actors are not impersonating the originals (although Karl Urban as McCoy comes close), more reinterpreting. Chris Pine as Kirk is even more brash and impulsive than Shatner was, but we understand that, without his father, he has had a more troubled childhood and adolescence than Shatner's Kirk had. Zachary Quinto as Spock seems young in a way that Leonard Nimoy never did. Simon Pegg's Scotty is more of a comic turn than Jimmy Doohan ever was, but that's allowed. The character whose role has expanded most is Zoe Saldana's Uhura, who gets a love affair with Spock and more to do in a single film than Nichelle Nichols managed in decades.

Everything is bigger, brighter, flashier. The *Enterprise* bridge is gigantic. The special effects take the breath away. It's *Star Trek*, but not as we know it. I went to see it on the first Saturday it was out, with my old friends David and Stephen:

three hopelessly excited men in their late forties (as we then were), in the Empire Leicester Square surrounded by people dressed as Klingons. We all loved the film, particularly the space-jump-onto-the-drilling-platform sequence. And when the original theme tune was played in the end credits, each of us wiped away a manly tear.

My feeling afterwards was slightly more muted: it's great but it's not necessarily for me. This was the first *Star Trek* episode or film I had seen that did not seem to have been made with me in mind. There was less character work than we were used to, and what there was seemed blunter, more a means to an end. There was far less talk. There was an astonishing amount of destruction. Not only is Romulus destroyed, far in the future, but so is the planet Vulcan, mainly out of spite. This means too much to old *Star Trek* viewers, and probably not enough to the newer ones. And certainly not enough to the people making the film.

Abrams and his collaborators were interviewed in a 2009 documentary, 'A New Vision', and gave the game away:

'Damon [Lindelof, producer] and I were kind of the *Trek* guys, and actually it was Alex and J. J. who said, what can we learn from *Star Wars* here?' (Roberto Orci)

'As sacrilegious as it is to even bring that up in relation to *Trek*, but I think the key is, you know, a modern audience is going to be already attuned to a much faster-paced movie.' (Alex Kurtzman)

'I didn't want to impose a *Star Wars* tone on *Star Trek*. But there was a certain kind of pace that *Star Wars* and *Empire Strikes Back* and *Return of the Jedi* had that I thought, that was the pace that I loved.' (J. J. Abrams)

'I always think of it as, *Star Trek* as beautiful classical music and *Star Wars* as rock 'n' roll. And it felt like, *Star Trek* needed a bit more rock 'n' roll to connect to a modern audience.' (Alex Kurtzman)

In other words, they didn't want to be making a *Star Trek*

film at all. Abrams's film was a boundlessly expensive audition tape for the space opera franchise he really wanted to be in charge of.

With hindsight, I can see that the film did show a degree of respect to the source material. Its script is full of quotes and references and artful nods to the past. 'Are you out of your Vulcan mind?' says McCoy. 'I don't believe in no-win scenarios,' says Kirk. 'I am and always shall be your friend,' says the most reassuring presence of all, Leonard Nimoy, making a brief appearance as the elderly Ambassador Spock, or 'Spock Prime' as the credits call him. At the film's end, young Spock meets old Spock, and they have a chat, which you can barely hear for the weeping of older fans in the audience.

'Since my customary farewell would appear oddly self-serving, I shall simply say ... good luck,' says old Spock, now positively avuncular.

(When Zachary Quinto first met Nimoy in real life, they were just about to appear together in front of six thousand people. Older man looked at younger and said, 'You have no idea what you're in for.')

If Abrams's first film was understandably cautious with the sensibilities of the older fans, its box office success allowed him to do exactly what he liked with film number two. *Star Trek: Into Darkness* (2013) is a travesty. Heavy metal where the first one was rock 'n' roll, it retells the Khan legend in a way that makes less than no sense, from action-packed beginning through action-packed middle to an explosive, action-packed climax. Benedict Cumberbatch plays Khan, although for reasons unknown he conceals his true identity early on, while he is firing phasers at the conference room at Starfleet Command and then appearing moodily backlit on a distant planet, glowering significantly at Klingons. *Into Darkness* seeks to echo and reshape *The Wrath of Khan*, but unlike the earlier film, it has no 'Space Seed' to bounce off. This is the first time Kirk and Khan have met. In *The Wrath of Khan* they hate each other because of what has gone before, but if nothing has gone before, what's the problem exactly? The film is all present because there hasn't been time yet for any past. At the end of the film there is a replay of Spock's 'death' in *The Wrath of Khan*, with much of the same dialogue, only this time it's Kirk's 'death'. (And it doesn't take an entire extra film to reverse, but about five minutes of screen-time.) We have the same great declarations of undying friendship, which actually meant something when these two men had served with each other for fifteen years. But this Kirk and Spock only met each other five minutes ago. IT MAKES NO SENSE.

It's worse than that, though. Abrams and his writers play fast and loose with characters, with storylines and with the very heart of *Star Trek*. Not only do they not understand the show, but you get the impression they don't even like it. Next to this, *Star Trek V: The Final Frontier* was a work of towering integrity, and I'm never watching that again for as long as I live.

In *The Wrath of Khan*, Kirk and Khan in their respective ships play an entertaining cat-and-mouse game in a nebula where sensors do not work. 'He is intelligent, but not experienced,' says Spock. 'His pattern indicates two-dimensional thinking.' A quarter of a century later, much the same could be said of J. J. Abrams and his team. Both the villains in their films wear black and are incredibly villainous. You could never mistake either of them for anyone who wasn't a villain. But here's the real two-dimensional thinking: they both have INCREDIBLY HUGE spaceships with lots of ENORMOUS GUNS pointing at the *Enterprise*, which looks small and weedy by comparison. This is the sumo wrestling theory of space battles: the really fat guy will always win. On this theory there can never be a spaceship too large. If you've got half a dozen massive phasers, strap on another half-dozen and point them all at the little ship down there. Better still, let's just stamp on it. The lack of subtlety – what one might call the Mark of Abrams – is bad enough, but repeating exactly the same idea in the second film that looked silly enough in the first? That suggests a lack of imagination, the one thing in science fiction that is truly unforgivable.

After *Into Darkness* came out, a writer and fan called David Hooks wrote a piece on the website whatculture.com that, for me, summed the problem up perfectly. He called it 'Ten Ways *Star Trek* Just Isn't *Star Trek* Any More'.

> There are those, even among the biggest fans of the original series and the various spin-offs, who will absolutely love both of the new films. They are fun blockbusters with high production values, good actors and impressive CGI. Glossy, entertaining and full of all the plot points you would expect from a modern sci-fi film.
>
> Except it's just not *Star Trek*.

The characters, he went on, show certain similarities to their original incarnations but the world they inhabit is not the one Gene Roddenberry had in mind. The peaceful, utopian future has vanished and even Starfleet is shown to be rotten to the core.

Kirk, for example. The original, for all his strut and priapism, was a man of authority, a leader, with fourteen years in the field before we first met him. This new one, says Hooks, is a 'rebel without a clue'. He is arrogant, cocky and insolent. 'He violates the Prime Directive without even caring, ignores orders with no good reason, makes dangerous decisions and seems to be devoid of the tactical awareness and dedication that made the original Kirk the man he was.'

Spock, meanwhile, doesn't conceal his emotions so much as delight in them. In *Into Darkness* he loses his temper, argues with an admiral, bickers with his girlfriend and, when he thinks Kirk is dead, loses his rag completely and swears undying revenge. This is not Spock.

We could go on, and Hooks does. 'You canna change the laws of physics,' as Scotty might have said once or twice, but Abrams can't be bothered with anything like that. Thanks to 'trans-warp beaming', his characters beam from Earth to the Klingon homeworld Quo'nos, eighty light years away, just because they need to for the storyline to work. Why travel anywhere in a starship when you can do that? Where is the internal consistency? Where is that wonderful TV show we used to like?

Hooks quotes John D. F. Black, the first-season story editor who wrote 'The Naked Time', thus: 'The primary thing as a science fiction writer, never ask your audience to believe more than one extraordinary thing.' Abrams and his team throw this tenet aside as they throw aside everything else they don't think matters. It's the arrogance of their approach I find hard to stomach. They would say they were 'updating' the franchise for a new, younger audience, and box office figures would suggest they are doing the right thing. But better no films than these films, frankly.

Ronald D. Moore, long-time *Trek* writer and still, miraculously, a fan, had a more diplomatic response. 'I think that *Star Trek*, in its DNA, is a television show,' he told StarTrek.com.

> The features are very big action-adventure movies, lots of spectacle, run and jump, shoot-em-up and blowing things up . . . But *Star Trek*, as originally conceived, was really a morality play every week, and it was about an ensemble of players. They were exploring science fiction ideas, sociological ideas and moral ideas. The movies are just pitched in a different way at a different audience.

The TV series will do a story where the captain is split in

two by a transporter accident and one half is evil and one half is good and the whole story is about, where does the nature of a man's strength come from? What makes a man a man? Is it his good side? His bad side? Or how the two come together to make something greater than the sum of its parts?

The movies will never do that . . . They'll never do all the things that all of us who are fans fell in love with this franchise for. So I think, at some point, *Star Trek* will return to television, and that would be great. I'd love to watch the weekly adventures again.

So would I. Live long and prosper.*

---

* Just as we were preparing this book for publication, CBS Television announced a new *Star Trek* TV series, to premiere in January 2017. It'll be run by Alex Kurtzman, who co-wrote and produced the first two reboot films. So we wait with hope, expectation, no little excitement and that familiar sense of creeping dread . . .

APPENDIX: OUTRAGEOUSLY SUBJECTIVE FIVE-STAR RATINGS

As mentioned occasionally in the text, these are my entirely personal ratings, out of five, for all the episodes of *Star Trek* (the original series) and *Star Trek: The Next Generation*. Five stars denote a work of deathless genius, while one star means I would have to be paid handsomely ever to watch it again. There are no half-stars, because I have a life to lead.

These episodes are in order of original transmission, rather than production order.

STAR TREK: SEASON ONE (1966–7)

The Man Trap	★★★
Charlie X	★★★
Where No Man Has Gone Before	★★
The Naked Time	★★★
The Enemy Within	★★★
Mudd's Women	★★
What Are Little Girls Made Of?	★★★
Miri	★★★
Dagger of the Mind	★★★
The Corbomite Maneuver	★★★★
The Menagerie, Part I	★★★★
The Menagerie, Part II	★★★
The Conscience of the King	★★★★
Balance of Terror	★★★★★
Shore Leave	★★
The Galileo Seven	★★★★★
The Squire of Gothos	★★
Arena	★★★★
Tomorrow Is Yesterday	★★★
Court Martial	★★★
The Return of the Archons	★★★
Space Seed	★★★★
A Taste of Armageddon	★★★
This Side of Paradise	★★★★
The Devil in the Dark	★★★★★
Errand of Mercy	★★★
The Alternative Factor	★★
The City on the Edge of Forever	★★★★★
Operation – Annihilate!	★★★★

STAR TREK: SEASON TWO (1967–8)

Amok Time	★★★★★
Who Mourns for Adonais?	★
The Changeling	★★★
Mirror, Mirror	★★★★
The Apple	★
The Doomsday Machine	★★★★★
Catspaw	★★
I, Mudd	★★
Metamorphosis	★★★★
Journey to Babel	★★★★★
Friday's Child	★★
The Deadly Years	★★★
Obsession	★★★
Wolf in the Fold	★★
The Trouble with Tribbles	★★★★
The Gamesters of Triskelion	★★
A Piece of the Action	★★
The Immunity Syndrome	★★★
A Private Little War	★★
Return to Tomorrow	★★★
Patterns of Force	★★★
By Any Other Name	★★
The Omega Glory	★
The Ultimate Computer	★★★
Bread and Circuses	★★★
Assignment: Earth	★★

STAR TREK: SEASON THREE (1968–9)

Spock's Brain	★★★
The Enterprise Incident	★★★★
The Paradise Syndrome	★★★
And the Children Shall Lead	★★
Is There in Truth No Beauty?	★★★
Spectre of the Gun	★★★
Day of the Dove	★★
For the World Is Hollow and I Have Touched the Sky	★★
The Tholian Web	★★★★
Plato's Stepchildren	★
Wink of an Eye	★★★
The Empath	★★
Elaan of Troyius	★★
Whom Gods Destroy	★
Let That Be Your Last Battlefield	★★★
The Mark of Gideon	★★
That Which Survives	★★
The Lights of Zetar	★★
Requiem for Methuselah	★★
The Way to Eden	★★
The Cloud Minders	★
The Savage Curtain	★
All Our Yesterdays	★★
Turnabout Intruder	★

Whether an episode gets two, three or four stars sometimes turns on the smallest thing. 'Wolf in the Fold' isn't far away from three stars, but fails on account of a toe-curling opening scene, in which Scotty, McCoy and Kirk sit like a trio of old pervs watching a girl belly-dancing. And 'Let That Be Your Last Battlefield', a two-star show if ever there was one, gains an extra for an excellently handled scene in which Kirk begins the *Enterprise*'s self-destruct sequence, and halts it at the last possible moment.

THE NEXT GENERATION: SEASON ONE (1987–8)

Encounter at Farpoint	★★★
The Naked Now	★★
Code of Honour	★★
The Last Outpost	★★
Where No One Has Gone Before	★★★
Lonely Among Us	★★
Justice	★★
The Battle	★★
Hide and Q	★★
Haven	★★
The Big Goodbye	★★★
Datalore	★★
Angel One	★★
11001001	★★★
Too Short a Season	★
When the Bough Breaks	★★
Home Soil	★★★
Coming of Age	★★★
Heart of Glory	★★
The Arsenal of Freedom	★★
Symbiosis	★★★
Skin of Evil	★★
We'll Always Have Paris	★★
Conspiracy	★★★★
The Neutral Zone	★★★

THE NEXT GENERATION: SEASON TWO (1988–9)

The Child	★★★
Where Silence Has Lease	★★
Elementary, Dear Data	★★★
The Outrageous Okona	★
Loud as a Whisper	★★★
The Schizoid Man	★★★
Unnatural Selection	★★★
A Matter of Honor	★★★
The Measure of a Man	★★★★★
The Dauphin	★★
Contagion	★★
The Royale	★
Time Squared	★★★
The Icarus Factor	★★
Pen Pals	★★★★
Q Who?	★★★★
Samaritan Snare	★★
Up the Long Ladder	★★
Manhunt	★★
The Emissary	★★★
Peak Performance	★★★
Shades of Grey	* (and that's generous)

THE NEXT GENERATION: SEASON THREE (1989–90)

Evolution	★★★
The Ensigns of Command	★★★★
The Survivors	★★★★
Who Watches the Watchers?	★★★★
The Bonding	★★★
Booby Trap	★★★
The Enemy	★★★
The Price	★★★
The Vengeance Factor	★★
The Defector	★★★★
The Hunted	★★★
The High Ground	★★
Déjà Q	★★★
A Matter of Perspective	★★
Yesterday's Enterprise	★★★★★
The Offspring	★★★★
Sins of the Father	★★★★
Allegiance	★★
Captain's Holiday	★★
Tin Man	★★★★
Hollow Pursuits	★★★
The Most Toys	★★★
Sarek	★★★★
Ménage à Troi	★★
Transfigurations	★★
The Best of Both Worlds	★★★★★

THE NEXT GENERATION: SEASON FOUR (1990–1)

The Best of Both Worlds, Part II	★★★★
Family	★★★★
Brothers	★★★
Suddenly Human	★★★
Remember Me	★★★
Legacy	★★★
Reunion	★★★★
Future Imperfect	★★★
Final Mission	★★★
The Loss	★★★★
Data's Day	★★★★
The Wounded	★★★
Devil's Due	★★★
Clues	★★★
First Contact	★★★★
Galaxy's Child	★★
Night Terrors	★★★
Identity Crisis	★★★
The Nth Degree	★★★
Qpid	★★★
The Drumhead	★★★
Half a Life	★★★
The Host	★★
The Mind's Eye	★★★★
In Theory	★★
Redemption	★★★

THE NEXT GENERATION: SEASON FIVE (1991–2)

Redemption II	★★★
Darmok	★★★★★
Ensign Ro	★★★
Silicon Avatar	★★★
Disaster	★★★★
The Game	★★★
Unification	★★★
Unification II	★★
A Matter of Time	★★★
New Ground	★★
Hero Worship	★★
Violations	★★★
The Masterpiece Society	★★★
Conundrum	★★★★
Power Play	★★★
Ethics	★★★
The Outcast	★★★
Cause and Effect	★★★★
The First Duty	★★★
Cost of Living	★★
The Perfect Mate	★★★★
Imaginary Friend	★★
I, Borg	★★★
The Next Phase	★★★
The Inner Light	★★★★★
Time's Arrow, Part I	★★★★

THE NEXT GENERATION: SEASON SIX (1992-3)

Time's Arrow, Part II	★★★
Realm of Fear	★★★
Man of the People	★★★
Relics	★★★
Schisms	★★★
True Q	★★★
Rascals	★★
A Fistful of Datas	★★★
The Quality of Life	★★★
Chain of Command, Part I	★★★★
Chain of Command, Part II	★★★★★
Ship in a Bottle	★★★★
Aquiel	★★
Face of the Enemy	★★★
Tapestry	★★★★
Birthright, Part I	★★★
Birthright, Part II	★★
Starship Mine	★★★
Lessons	★★★
The Chase	★★★
Frame of Mind	★★★
Suspicions	★★
Rightful Heir	★★★
Second Chances	★★★
Timescape	★★★
Descent, Part I	★★

THE NEXT GENERATION: SEASON SEVEN (1993–4)

Descent, Part II	★★
Liaisons	★★★
Interface	★★★
Gambit, Part I	★★★
Gambit, Part II	★★★
Phantasms	★★★★
Dark Page	★★★
Attached	★★★
Force of Nature	★★★
Inheritance	★★★
Parallels	★★★★
The Pegasus	★★★★
Homeward	★★★
Sub Rosa	★★
Lower Decks	★★★★★
Thine Own Self	★★★
Masks	★★★
Eye of the Beholder	★★★
Genesis	★★★
Journey's End	★★★
Firstborn	★★★
Bloodlines	★★★
Emergence	★★★
Pre-emptive Strike	★★
All Good Things	★★★★

(Didn't the titles get boring? Was this intentional, or just careless?)

On playboy.com, the indefatigable trekologist Jordan Hoffman put all 700-odd episodes of *Star Trek* in order of excellence, just because he could. Although just the idea of doing this gives me a headache and makes me take to my bed, his top ten are worth repeating here. These, then, are Hoffman's ten best episodes across all *Trek* series, even the animated ones:

1. The City on the Edge of Forever (original series, season 1)
2. The Inner Light (*The Next Generation*, season 5)
3. Mirror, Mirror (original series, season 2)
4. Yesterday's Enterprise (*The Next Generation*, season 3)
5. Darmok (*The Next Generation*, season 5)
6. Arena (original series, season 1)
7. By Inferno's Light (*Deep Space Nine*, season 5)
8. The Best of Both Worlds, Parts I and II (*The Next Generation*, seasons 3–4)
9. Chain of Command, Parts I and II (*The Next Generation*, season 6)
10. Amok Time (original series, season 2)

ACKNOWLEDGEMENTS

The most ferocious insult in the Klingon language is 'Hab Sosl'I Qu'ch!', which means 'Your mother has a smooth forehead.' My thanks, therefore, to my friend and publisher Richard Beswick, who rejected this as a title for this book and several others that were nearly as good; to my friend and agent Patrick Walsh, who knew this was a good idea before anyone; and to the many friends and family members who gave me ideas or encouragement or their own quintessential Trektastic insights: Stephen Arkell, James Berkmann, Martha Berkmann, Jean Berkmann-Barwis, Paula Bingham, Thomas Coops, Richard Corden, Sam Craft, Amanda Craig, Sally Ann Fitt, Sarah Hesketh, Ian Hislop, Tom Holland, 'Big Dave' Jackson at the Prince of Wales, Sarah Jackson, David Jaques, Bob Jones, Aalia Khan, Deborah Levy, Nicholas Lezard, Howard McMinn, Mark Mason, Nick Newman, Simon O'Hagan, Julian Parker, Chris Pollikett, Lucy Reese, Padraig Reidy, Andy Robson, Simon Rose, Terence Russoff, Joanna Ryan, Kate Saunders, Paul Simpson, Mitchell Symons, Russell Taylor, Jane Thynne, Hilary Todd, Nathalie Webb, Robin Welch, Alan White, Helen White and Ceili Williams.

A PARTIAL BIBLIOGRAPHY

Allan Asherman • *The Star Trek Companion* (Titan Books, 1987, third edition 1993)

Paula M. Block (with Terry J. Erdmann) • *Star Trek: The Original Series 365* (Abrams, 2010)

Paula M. Block and Terry J. Erdmann • *Star Trek The Next Generation 365* (Abrams, 2012)

James Doohan (with Peter David) • *Beam Me Up, Scotty* (Pocket Books, 1996)

Harlan Ellison • *The City On the Edge of Forever* (Open Road, 1995, revised 1996)

Joel Engel • *Gene Roddenberry: The Myth and the Man Behind Star Trek* (Virgin Books, 1994)

Terry J. Erdmann (with Paula M. Block) • *Star Trek Deep Space Nine Companion* (Pocket Books, 2000)

David Gerrold • *The World of Star Trek* (Ballantine, 1973)

Edward Gross and Mark A. Altman • *Captain's Logs: The Complete Trek Voyages* (Boxtree, 1993)

Tim Heald • *The Making of Space: 1999* (Ballantine, 1976)

Lawrence M. Krauss • *The Physics of Star Trek* (Flamingo, 1995)

Nicholas Meyer • *The View from the Bridge* (Plume, 2009)

Larry Nemecek • *The Star Trek: The Next Generation Companion* (Pocket Books, 1992, revised 1995)

Nichelle Nichols • *Beyond Uhura* (Boxtree, 1994)

Leonard Nimoy • *I Am Spock* (Century, 1995)

Michael Okuda and Denise Okuda • *Star Trek Chronology: The History of the Future* (Pocket Books, 1993)

Robert Schnakenberg • *The Encyclopedia Shatnerica* (Quirk, 2008)

William Shatner and Chris Kreski • *Star Trek Memories* (HarperCollins, 1993)

William Shatner and Chris Kreski • *Star Trek Movie Memories* (HarperCollins, 1994)

William Shatner (with David Fisher) • *Up Till Now: The Autobiography* (Sidgwick & Jackson, 2008)

Herbert F. Solow and Robert Justman • *Inside Star Trek: The Real Story* (Pocket Books, 1996)

George Takei • *To the Stars* (Pocket Books, 1994)

Stephen E. Whitfield and Gene Roddenberry • *The Making of Star Trek* (Ballantine, 1968)

Grace Lee Whitney • *The Longest Trek: My Tour of the Galaxy* (Quill Driver, 1998)

NOTES

CHAPTER 1: WHERE NO MAN HAS GONE BEFORE

11   *'I've got another series idea . . .'*: Engel, *Gene Roddenberry*, p. 38.
    'I don't think Gene . . .': Ibid., p. 43.

12   *'Duplicating a page . . .'*: Rodenberry's original synopsis, quoted in ibid., p. 50.
    'Archon is anything but a paradise . . .': Ibid., p. 46
    'It's pleasant, isn't it? . . .': Ibid., p. 50.

14   *'I looked at him . . .'*: Gross and Altman, *Captain's Logs*, p. 12.
    'Once I was there . . .': Engel, p. 68.

15   *'This is not the kind of show . . .'*: Solow and Justman, *Inside Star Trek*, p. 63.
    'but that's what pilots are for . . .': Ibid., p. 59.
    'I must tell you something, Herb . . .': Ibid.

16–17 *'Gene seemed both upset and relieved . . .'*: Ibid., p. 61.

18   *'it is an indisputable fact . . .'*: Engel, p. 63.
    'Jack takes his name too seriously': Ibid., p. 67.
    'the team did not really master . . .': Toño del Barrio, 'Esperanto and Cinema', November 2003, <http://www.delbarrio.eu/cinema.htm>.

19   *'tempered by a touch of doubting Hamlet'*: Engel, p. 67.
    'Bill's Captain Kirk . . .': Nimoy, *I Am Spock*, p. 34.

20   *'You should have killed me . . .'*: From 'Where No Man Has Gone Before' (1966), written by Samuel A. Peeples.
    'Well, if he's going to be an engineer . . .': Solow and Justman, p. 78.

21   *'The most arresting thing . . .'*: Takei, *To the Stars*, p. 230.
    'Neutralise warp . . .': From 'Where No Man Has Gone Before'.

CHAPTER 2: GENE AND GENE

23 '*his contributions were minimal*': 'Stephen Edward Poe', <http://en.memory-alpha.wikia.com/wiki/Stephen_Edward_Poe>.

24 '*tall unkempt person . . .*': Solow and Justman, *Inside Star Trek*, p. 15.
    '*a pleasant man . . .*': Nimoy, *I Am Spock*, p. 23.
    '*became overly protective . . .*': Solow and Justman, p. 21.
    '*I cautioned Gene . . .*': Ibid.
    '*A new side of Gene . . .*': Ibid.
    '*Immature poets imitate . . .*': T. S. Eliot, 'Philip Massinger', *The Sacred Wood* (London: Methuen, 1920).

25 '*intended to construct . . .*': Engel, *Gene Roddenberry*, p. 87.

26 '*We've got phaser weapons . . .*': From 'The Corbomite Maneuver' (1966), written by Jerry Sohl.
    '*We therefore grant you . . .*': Ibid.
    '*Not chess, Mr Spock. Poker*': Ibid.

27 '*I miss company, conversation . . .*': Ibid.
    '*Beats me what makes it go . . .*': Ibid.

28 '*a very calm, gentle soul . . .*': Nimoy, pp. 39–40.
    '*What am I, a doctor or a . . .*': From 'The Corbomite Maneuver'.

29 '*When I first rehearsed it . . .*': Engel, p. 70.

30 '*He's dead, Jim*': From 'The Enemy Within' (1966), written by Richard Matheson.
    '*The impostor had . . .*': Ibid.
    '*I can't imagine any more . . .*': Whitney, *The Longest Trek*, p. 95.

31 '*If this doesn't work . . .*': From 'The Enemy Within'.
    '*My mother . . .*': From 'The Naked Time' (1966), written by John D. F. Black.

33* '*How are you, friend? . . .*': Translation from 'The Man Trap (episode)', <http://en.memory-alpha.wikia.com/wiki/The_Man_Trap_(episode)>.

34 '*I can't change the laws of physics . . .*': From 'The Naked Time'.
    '*Oh, please, don't let them take me . . .*': From 'Charlie X' (1966), written by George Clayton Johnson.

35 '*the distant reaches of our galaxy*': From 'Miri' (1966), written by Adrian Spies.
    '*It seems impossible, but there it is*': Ibid.

36 '*Leave any bigotry in your quarters . . .*': From 'Balance of Terror' (1966), written by Paul Schneider.
    '*I regret that we meet in this way . . .*': Ibid.
    '*Since the days of the first wooden vessels . . .*': Ibid.

37 '*It never makes any sense . . .*': Ibid.

38 '*it's a hidden, personal thing . . .*': From 'Dagger of the Mind' (1966), written by S. Bar-David.

CHAPTER 3: STEADY AS SHE GOES, MR SULU

41   *'the cold, cruel banker...'*: Shatner and Kreski, *Star Trek Memories*, p. 157.
'Then, when I first saw ...': Ibid.
'My friend is obviously ...': From 'The City on the Edge of Forever' (1967), written by Harlan Ellison.

42   *'After very careful consideration ...'*: Quoted in 'Miri (episode)', <http://en.memory-alpha.wikia.com/wiki/Miri_(episode)>.

43   *'And this ship...'*: From 'The Conscience of the King' (1966), written by Barry Trivers.

44   *'Mr Spock ...'*: From 'The Galileo Seven' (1967), story by Oliver Crawford, teleplay by Oliver Crawford and S. Bar-David.

45   *'All of my old friends look like doctors...'*: From 'Court Martial' (1967), story by Don M. Mankiewicz, teleplay by Don M. Mankiewicz and Steven W. Carabatsos.
'She's a very good lawyer...': Ibid.

46   *'The brain is what life is all about ...'*: From 'The Menagerie' (1966), written by Gene Roddenberry.

47   *'it's viewscreens all the way down'*: Eugene Myers and Torie Atkinson, *'Star Trek* Re-Watch: "The Menagerie" Part I', <http://www.theviewscreen.com/the-menagerie-part-i/>, 12 May 2009.

48   *'Bill's hairpiece was being applied ...'*: Solow and Justman, *Inside Star Trek*, p. 236.
'I wasn't proud of these feelings ...': Shatner and Kreski, pp. 195–6.

48*   *'I don't wear a hairpiece...'*: Quoted in Schnakenberg, *The Encylopedia Shatnerica*, p. 231.

49   *'represents the ultimate ...'*: Ibid, p. 262.

49–50   *'Don't peek ...'*: From 'Shore Leave' (1966), written by Theodore Sturgeon.

50   *'Does your logic find this fascinating...'*: From 'The Squire of Gothos' (1967), written by Paul Schneider.

51   *'We never did tell him ...'*: Solow and Justman, p. 207.
'It's a matter of policy ...': From 'Arena' (1967), story by Frederic Brown, teleplay by Gene L. Coon.

52   *'Very good, Captain ...'*: Ibid.

53*   *'had they continued ...'*: Stephen Hawking, introduction to Krauss, *The Physics of Star Trek*, p. xii.

54   *'What is that? Is that a uniform ...'*: From 'Tomorrow Is Yesterday' (1967), written by D. C. Fontana.

55   *'joy peace and tranquility ...'*: From 'The Return of the Archons' (1967), story by Gene Roddenberry, teleplay by Boris Sobelman.
'The plug must be pulled': Ibid.

'*That refers to a living, growing culture*': Ibid.

56 '*Death, destruction, disease, horror . . .*': From 'A Taste of Armageddon' (1967), story by Robert Hamner and Gene L. Coon, story by Robert Hamner.

'*Diplomacy, gentlemen . . .*': Ibid.

'*Sir, there's a multi-legged creature . . .*': Ibid.

CHAPTER 4: I'M A DOCTOR, NOT A BRICKLAYER

58 '*The scientists overlooked one fact . . .*': From 'Space Seed' (1967), story by Carey Wilber, teleplay by Gene L. Coon and Carey Wilber.

59 '*I've been reading up on starships . . .*': Ibid.

'*Captain, although your abilities intrigue me . . .*': Ibid.

'*habitable, although a bit savage . . .*': Ibid.

'*it might even be interesting to check things out . . .*': Eugene Myers and Torie Atkinson, '*Star Trek* Re-Watch: "Space Seed"', <http://www.theviewscreen.com/space-seed/>, 18 June 2009.

59* '*I signed aboard this ship to practise medicine . . .*': From 'Space Seed'.

60 '*I said to myself . . .*': Quoted in Shatner and Kreski, *Star Trek Memories*, p. 192.

61 '*You belong in a circus, Spock . . .*': From 'This Side of Paradise' (1967), story by Nathan Butler and D. C. Fontana, teleplay by D. C. Fontana.

61–2 '*I have a little to say about it . . .*': Ibid.

62 '*That's great. What is it? . . .*': 'The Devil in the Dark (episode)', <http://en.memory-alpha.wikia.com/wiki/The_Devil_in_the_Dark_(episode)>.

62* '*If you put Dorothy's scripts together . . .*': Nimoy, *I Am Spock*, p. 118.

63 '*You can't be serious . . .*': From 'The Devil in the Dark' (1967), written by Gene L. Coon.

'*it impressed me because it presented the idea . . .*': Arthur C. Clarke, 'Foreword: Reflections on the Final Frontier', *TV Guide Collector's Edition – Star Trek: Four Generations of Stars, Stories, and Strange New Worlds*, spring 1995.

'*By golly, Jim! . . .*': From 'The Devil in the Dark'.

64 '*Sold-out sponsorship? Barely . . .*': Solow and Justman, *Inside Star Trek*, p. 305.

65 '*It's a mind-sifter or mind-ripper . . .*': From 'Errand of Mercy' (1967), written by Gene L. Coon.

'*This is a laboratory specimen . . .*': Ibid.

'*To us, violence is unthinkable*': Ibid.

65* '*Star Trek was renewed because it was good . . .*': Solow and Justman, p. 307.

66 'Well, Commander . . .': From 'Errand of Mercy'.
'In the future, you and the Klingons . . .': Ibid.
'I should say the Organians . . .': Ibid.

66–7 'What would you say the odds . . .': Ibid.

67 'What is it? . . .': From 'The City on the Edge of Forever' (1967), written by Harlan Ellison.
'Strangely compelling, isn't it? . . .': Ibid.

68 'He has passed into... what was': Ibid.
'You deliberately stopped me, Jim! . . .': Ibid.

69 'Where would you estimate we belong . . .': Ibid.
'Let's get the hell out of here': Ibid.
'Don't ever tell Harlan . . .': Quoted in Solow and Justman, p. 276.

70 'Harlan's script was brilliant . . .': Ellison, The City on the Edge of Forever, p. 283.
'This place is dead, empty . . .': Ibid., pp. 140–1.

70–1 'temper burned at such a low firing point . . .': Ibid., p. 284.

71 'I tried to build the relationship of love . . .': Ibid., p. 285.

72 'The award for the most outstanding script . . .': Solow and Justman, p. 288.
'That was Gene. Couldn't write for sour owl poop . . .': Ellison, p. 38.

72* 'it was sort of dull . . .': Solow and Justman, p. 288.

73 'Harlan had the last word . . .': Ellison, p. 286.
'It is not life as we know or understand it': From 'Operation – Annihilate!' (1967), written by Steven W. Carabatsos.
'I am free of it and the pain . . .': Ibid.

74 'My first sight was the face of Dr McCoy . . .': Ibid.

CHAPTER 5: LIVE LONG AND PROSPER

78 'Have you ever wondered why . . .': Block with Erdmann, Star Trek: The Original Series 365, p. 195.

81 'All right, I'll admit it . . .': Takei, To The Stars, p. 255.

81* 'I never felt Star Trek was silly . . .': Shatner and Kreski, Star Trek Memories, p. 224.
'a man damned by his sensitivity and his intelligence': Takei, p. 258.

82 'If we weren't missing two officers . . .': From 'Catspaw' (1967), written by Robert Bloch.

83 'It is undignified for a woman . . .': From 'Amok Time' (1967), written by Theodore Sturgeon.
'How do Vulcans choose their mates? . . .': Ibid.

84 'He never told us his family was this important': Ibid.
'Proceed . . .': Ibid.

85 'Live long and prosper . . .': Ibid.

'*Excellent script* . . .': Interview for 'To Boldly Go: Season 2', special feature on *Star Trek: The Original Series – Season Two* DVD (2004).

86 '*planet killer . . . miles long . . .*': From 'The Doomsday Machine' (1967), written by Norman Spinrad.

'*Matt, where's your crew?* . . .': Ibid.

88 '*This is one of your units, creator?* . . .': From 'The Changeling' (1967), written by John Meredyth Lucas.

89 '*What is love?* . . .': From 'The Apple' (1967), story by Max Ehrlich, teleplay by Max Ehrlich and Gene L. Coon.

90* '*The goddamned smog* . . .': Solow and Justman, *Inside Star Trek*, pp. 428–9.

91 '*So you die, Captain* . . .': From 'Mirror, Mirror' (1967), written by Jerome Bixby.

'*Has the whole galaxy gone crazy?* . . .': Ibid.

91–2 '*brutal, savage, unprincipled* . . .': Ibid.

93 '*Do you know what you get* . . .': From 'The Trouble with Tribbles' (1967), written by David Gerrold.

'*A most curious creature* . . .': Ibid.

CHAPTER 6: THE ENGINES CANNA TAKE IT

96 '*a heavily industrialised 20th-century-type planet* . . .': From 'Bread and Circuses' (1968), written by Gene Roddenberry and Gene L. Coon.

'*You bring this network's ratings down* . . .': Ibid.

'*Shatner came round the corner* . . .': Solow and Justman, *Inside Star Trek*, p. 354.

96–7 '*The scenes in the arena* . . .': 'Star Trek: Bread and Circuses', <http://senensky.com/bread-and-circuses/>.

97 '*My mother was a schoolteacher* . . .': From 'This Side of Paradise' (1967), story by Nathan Butler and D. C. Fontana, teleplay by D. C. Fontana.

97–8 '*You don't understand the Vulcan way* . . .': From 'Journey to Babel' (1967), written by D. C. Fontana.

98 '*do not argue for reasons* . . .': Ibid.

'*They were just wonderful* . . .': 'Journey to Babel (episode)', <http://en.memory-alpha.wikia.com/wiki/Journey_to_Babel_(episode)>.

99 '*Spock, I've always suspected* . . .': From 'Journey to Babel'.

100 '*a deep penetration into Kirk's psyche* . . .': 'Star Trek: Obsession', <http://senensky.com/obsession/>

101 '*What was it you sensed?* . . .': From 'The Immunity Syndrome' (1968), written by Robert Sabaraoff.

'*We do not colonise* . . .': From 'By Any Other Name' (1968), story by Jerome Bixby, teleplay by D. C. Fontana and Jerome Bixby.

105   '*There are no constraints or absolutes* . . .': Quoted in Solow and Just-man, p. 143.

106   '*If anyone was let go* . . .': Nichols, *Beyond Uhura*, p. 161.
     '*Nichelle, there is someone* . . .': Ibid., p. 164.
     '*You cannot* . . .': Ibid., pp. 164–5.

107   '*It makes me homesick* . . .': From 'The Apple' (1967), story by Max Ehrlich, teleplay by Max Ehrlich and Gene L. Coon.
     '*Scotch?* . . .': From 'The Trouble with Tribbles' (1967), written by David Gerrold.
     '*He disappeared again* . . .': From 'Who Mourns for Adonais' (1967), written by Gilbert Ralston.

108   '*All very tough, strong, short-sounding names* . . .': Nimoy, *I Am Spock*, p. 74.
     '*one of the best designed science fiction sets* . . .': Gerrold, *The World of Star Trek*, p. 35.

109   '*Why don't you put seat belts on the chairs?* . . .': Quoted in ibid., p. 36.
     '*Your captain has an excellent body* . . .': From 'Return to Tomorrow' (1968), written by John Kingsbridge.
     '*Shatner is a very athletic actor* . . .': Gerrold, p. 70.

110   '*William Shatner is too much of a professional* . . .': Ibid., p. 71.
     '*We watched the actors do their stuff* . . .': 'Bjo Trimble: The Woman Who Saved Star Trek – Part 1', <http://www.startrek.com/article/bjo-trim-ble-the-woman-who-saved-star-trek-part-1>, 31 August 2011.

112   '*Why?* . . .': Gerrold, p. 167.

CHAPTER 7: HE'S DEAD, JIM

114   '*the adrenaline once again* . . .': Shatner and Kreski, *Star Trek Memories*, p. 256.
     '*Gene baby!* . . .': Interview with Majel Barrett in ibid., p. 257.

115* '*Gene was a wonderful friend* . . .': Engel, *Gene Roddenberry*, p 132.

116   '*I thought I could never have* . . .': Quoted in Solow and Justman, *Inside Star Trek*, p.395.

118   '*Solomon, Alexander, Lazarus* . . .': From 'Requiem for Methuselah' (1969), written by Jerome Bixby.

119   '*I walk in, Freddy Freiberger is looking at me* . . .': Gross and Altman, *Captain's Logs*, p. 97.

120   '*Fred was looking for all-action pieces* . . .': Ibid., p. 66.
     '*literally breaking up*': From 'The Tholian Web' (1968), written by Judy Burns and Chet Richards.

122   '*I'll kill you, you filthy traitor* . . .': From 'The Enterprise Incident' (1968), written by D. C. Fontana.

123   *'There is a well-known saying ...'*: Ibid.

       'raining kisses ...': 'The Enterprise Incident (episode)', <http://en.memory-alpha.wikia.com/wiki/The_Enterprise_Incident>.

123*   *'Scripts like this ...'*: Nimoy, *I Am Spock*, p. 118.

124–5   *'It's the greatest technical job ...'*: From 'Spock's Brain' (1968), written by Lee Cronin.

125   *'In this whole galaxy ...'*: Ibid.

       'We mean you no harm ...': Ibid.

126   *'late lamented'*: Interview for *Star Trek: The Original Series – Season 3* DVD (2004).

128   *'the first kiss between ...'*: 'Plato's Stepchildren (episode)', <http://en.memory-alpha.wikia.com/wiki/Plato's_Stepchildren_(episode)>.

129   *'If anyone's gonna get to kiss Nichelle ...'*: Nichols, *Beyond Uhura*, p. 194.

       'It was bullshit! ...': Shatner and Kreski, p. 286.

       'We received one of the largest ...': Nichols, p. 196.

       'I'm a white Southern gentleman ...': Quoted in ibid., p. 197.

130   *'I felt we were really on a downhill slide ...'*: Shatner and Kreski, p. 295.

CHAPTER 8: HE'S STILL DEAD, JIM

131   *'It was a favour to Gene ...'*: Engel, *Gene Roddenberry*, p. 139.

132   *'never smiling, never telling a joke ...'*: Shatner and Kreski, *Star Trek Memories*, p. 279.

       'I was, in a way, in deep isolation ...': Ibid.

133   *'I should think you'd get bored ...'*: Reprinted in Charles M. Schulz, *The Complete Peanuts 1971–1972* (Edinburgh: Canongate, 2012), p. 174.

133*   *'early warning signs of a Trekkie ...'*: '20 Questions: William Shatner', *Playboy*, 7-89 (July 1989).

135   *'Whatever else one might say ...'*: Gerrold, *The World of Star Trek*, p. 206.

       'All of your production problems ...': Quoted in ibid., p. 207.

       'one or two individuals caught in a trying situation': Ibid., p. 216.

135–6   *'the slightest error will magnify ...'*: Ibid., p. 218.

136   *'it's adventure all right, but it isn't real drama'*: Ibid., p. 221.

137   *'If Star Trek had been a truly dramatic series ...'*: Ibid., p. 232.

137–8   *'The shows that are mentioned ...'*: Ibid., p. 91.

138   *'For the world is hollow ...'*: From 'For The World Is Hollow And I Have Touched The Sky' (1968), written by Rik Vollaerts.

139   *'Television demands ...'*: Gerrold, p. 206.

142   *'a captain, whether he be the captain ...'*: Ibid., p. 240.

143   *'Just as Vulcans have a problem with emotions ...'*: Gene Roddenberry, *Star Trek: Phase II* bible, quoted in Asherman, *The Star Trek Companion*, p. 153.

       'returned in high honour to Vulcan ...': Ibid., p. 152.

CHAPTER 9: HE PUT CREATURES IN OUR BODIES

145   'Hollywood has such a type-casting mentality . . .': Doohan with David, *Beam Me Up, Scotty*, p. 166.

146*   'an enormous mistake . . .': Nimoy, *I Am Spock*, p. 6.

147   'I noticed he either drank a lot . . .': Engel, *Gene Roddenberry*, p. 181.
'unanimously considered inept by the production staff': Ibid., p. 182.
'Why did you do this? . . .': Shatner and Kreski, *Star Trek Movie Memories*, p. 58.

148   'He wanted what he thought . . .': Engel, p. 182.
'What's this? . . .': Shatner and Kreski, p. 66.

148–9   'I met with him the following morning . . .': Ibid., pp. 73–4.

149   'What is this shit?': Ibid., p. 74.
'Gene, you wouldn't know a good story . . .': Ibid., p. 84.
'On a scale of one to ten . . .': Engel, p. 193.

150   'Never in the history of motion pictures . . .': Ibid., p. 203.

151   'Your answer lies elsewhere': *Star Trek: The Motion Picture* (1979), story by Alan Dean Foster, screenplay by Harold Livingston.
'My oath of celibacy is on record, captain.': Ibid.
'Your revered Admiral Nogura invoked . . .': Ibid.

153   'Jim, I want this . . .': Ibid.
'Heading, sir? . . .': Ibid.
'the beast that is eating the entire corporation': Engel, p. 204.

154   'Gene simply didn't have the skills . . .': Ibid., p. 203.

154–5   'Sit down . . .': Ibid., p. 205.

156   'I can't send it to you . . .': Meyer, *The View from the Bridge*, pp. 76–7.
'bits and pieces of interest . . .': Ibid., p. 78.

156–7   'And the script? . . .': Ibid., pp. 81–2.

158   'I am, and always shall be, your friend': From *Star Trek II: The Wrath of Khan* (1982), story by Harve Bennett and Jack B. Sowards, screenplay by Jack B. Sowards.

159   'I suppose it could be some pre-animate . . .': Ibid.
'Botany Bay? . . . Botany Bay! Oh no!': Ibid.
'Admiral! . . .': Ibid.

159*   'I never forget a face': Ibid.

160   'When the news leaked . . .': Shatner and Kreski, pp. 120–1.
'If Spock dies, you die': Meyer, p. 119.

161   'He caught me completely by surprise . . .': Gross and Altman, *Captain's Logs*, p. 113.
'Aren't you dead?': From *Star Trek II: The Wrath of Khan*.
'Our characters seemed alive again . . .': Shatner and Kreski, p. 135.
'From hell's heart . . .': From *Star Trek II: The Wrath of Khan*.

'*It was as if the years between* . . .': Gross and Altman, p. 117.

161* '*It's all in this book*': Meyer, p. 100.

'*They've captured the essence* . . .': Gross and Altman, p. 118.

161–2 '*I think that if you can point* . . .': Ibid.

162 '*I have never driven a Lamborghini* . . .': Meyer, p. 110.

'*He put creatures in our bodies* . . .': From *Star Trek II: The Wrath of Khan*.

'*I've done far worse than kill you* . . .': Ibid.

'*No! You'll flood the whole compartment!* . . .': Ibid.

163 '*I thought they were very lucky* . . .': Gross and Altman, p. 118.

CHAPTER 10: THERE BE WHALES HERE!

165 '*All is well* . . .': From *Star Trek II: The Wrath of Khan* (1982), story by Harve Bennett and Jack B. Sowards, screenplay by Jack B. Sowards.

'*By now the test audience* . . .': Shatner and Kreski, *Star Trek Movie Memories*, p. 147.

'*Space, the final frontier* . . .': From *Star Trek II: The Wrath of Khan*.

'*virtually danced back onto the bridge*': Shatner and Kreski, p. 152.

166 '*It was an entirely spur-of-the-moment idea*': Ibid., p. 153.

'*Oh I think that's terrific* . . .': Ibid.

'*Absolutely not* . . .': Ibid., p. 154.

'*What a great hook!* . . .': Ibid., p. 154.

166–7 '*Are you prepared to let this ship* . . .': Meyer, *The View from the Bridge*, p. 157.

167 '*The green-blooded son of a bitch!* . . .': From *Star Trek III: The Search for Spock* (1984), written by Harve Bennett.

168 '*My God, Bones, what have I done?* . . .': Ibid.

169 '*I wanted the emotions to be very large* . . .': From commentary for *Star Trek III: The Search For Spock* DVD (2009).

170 '*The idea is to do something nice*': Meyer, p. 160.

170–1 '*I wanted people to* . . .': Shatner and Kreski, p. 189.

172 '*I rarely get ideas myself* . . .': Meyer, p. 160.

'*When are we?* . . .': From *Star Trek IV: The Voyage Home* (1986), story by Harve Bennett and Leonard Nimoy, screenplay by Steve Meerson, Peter Krikes, Nicholas Meyer and Harve Bennett.

172–3 '*Does the species exist on any other planet?* . . .': Ibid.

173 '*Admiral! There be whales here!*': Ibid.

'*Excuse me, sir* . . .': Ibid.

173* '*Everybody remember where we parked*': Ibid.

174 '*I could have cried* . . .': Shatner and Kreski, p. 214.

'*Don't tell me* . . .': From *Star Trek IV: The Voyage Home*.

175 '*We are better off not explaining it* . . .': Shatner and Kreski, p. 215.

'In art, questions are always more interesting . . .': Meyer, p. 164.

'I was furious, furious!': Shatner and Kreski, p. 215.

175* 'Like too many other people . . .': Nichols, *Beyond Uhura*, p. 249.

176 'Twenty years ago . . .': Quoted in Nemecek, *The Star Trek: The Next Generation Companion*, p. 1.

'I'm not at all sure . . .': Ibid., p. 2.

177 'I need many followers . . .': Gross and Altman, *Captain's Logs*, p. 129.

177* 'Oh my God! What are we going to do?': Schnakenberg, *The Encyclopedia Shatnerica*, p. 212.

178 'the real problem with V . . .': Quoted in ibid.

'I found that very, very hard to do . . .': Doohan with David, *Beam Me Up, Scotty*, pp. 197–8.

CHAPTER 11: MAKE IT SO

182 'Most 25th-century [sic] humans believe . . .': *Star Trek: The Next Generation* bible, quoted in Nemecek, *The Star Trek: The Next Generation Companion*, p. 5.

182* 'four-breasted, oversexed hermaphrodite': Quoted in Engel, *Gene Roddenberry*, p. 226.

183 'We saw some rather good actors . . .': Justman BBC interview, Available at <http://bbc.adactio.com/cult/st/interviews/justman/page6.shtmlpicard/>.

'Every time anyone mentioned . . .': Ibid.

'We figured they would not go for a bald man . . .': Ibid.

186 'I did not wear make-up . . .': Nemecek, p. 20.

187 'I'm not a family man, Riker . . .': From 'Encounter at Farpoint' (1987), written by D. C. Fontana and Gene Roddenberry.

'You are still a dangerous, savage child race': Ibid..

188 'We have no fear . . .': Ibid.

'A feeling of great joy and gratitude!': Ibid.

189 'I don't see no points on your ears, boy . . .': Ibid.

190 'Pygmy cretins': From 'The Last Outpost' (1987), story by Richard Krzmeien, teleplay by Herbert Wright.

191 'When you look . . .': All quotes from *William Shatner Presents: Chaos on the Bridge* (2014).

192 'Every time I sit down at the typewriter . . .': Engel, p. 224.

'What we saw in the first season . . .': Takei, *To The Stars*, p. 380.

192* 'the steamroller of lies': Quoted in Ellison, *The City on the Edge of Forever*, p. 288.

193 'What's a knockout like you . . .': From '11001001' (1988), written by Maurice Hurley and Robert Lewin.

195   *'uncustomary reshuffling of personnel ...'*: From 'Conspiracy' (1988), story by Robert Sabaroff, teleplay by Tracy Tormé.
'Patience is one of our virtues ...': Ibid.
'You don't understand! ...': Ibid.

196   *'an unexplored sector of our galaxy ...'*: Ibid.

197   *'I'm not sure how much he drank ...'*: Engel, p. 238.

CHAPTER 12: RESISTANCE IS FUTILE

199   *'There were those who believed ...'*: Nemecek, *The Star Trek: The Next Generation Companion*, p. 64.
'She was adored. And suddenly she was gone.': From *William Shatner Presents: Chaos on the Bridge* (2014).

200   *'Come quick, come quick ...'*: Quoted in 'Star Trek's Uhura Reflects on MLK Encounter', NPR, 17 January 2011. Transcript available at <http://www.npr.org/2011/01/17/132942461/Star-Treks-Uhura-Reflects-On-MLK-Encounter>.

201   *'The Borg are the ultimate user ...'*: From 'Q Who' (1989), written by Maurice Hurley.

202   *'Worf, we're alone now ...'*: From 'The Emissary' (1989), story by Richard Manning, Hans Beimler and Thomas H. Calder, teleplay by Richard Manning and Hans Beimler.
'Tea, Earl Grey, hot': From 'Contagion' (1989), written by Steve Gerber and Beth Woods.

203   *'It was our opinion ...'*: Nemecek, p. 99.

204   *'I saw her broken body ...'*: From 'The Survivors' (1989), written by Michael Wagner.

205   *'send them back ...'*: From 'Who Watches the Watchers?' (1989), written by Richard Manning and Hans Beimler.

206   *'I am Worf, son of Mogh ...'*: From 'Sins of the Father' (1990), story by Drew Deighan, teleplay by Ronald D. Moore and W. Reed Moran.

207   *'As soon as Worf walks out the door ...'*: From 'Chronicles From The Final Frontier', special feature on *Star Trek: The Next Generation – Season Four* DVD (2002).
'Hey, it's [the writers'] fault ...': Gross and Altman, *Captain's Logs*, pp. 193–4.

208   *'Who is to say that this history ...'*: From 'Yesterday's Enterprise' (1990), story by Trent Christopher Ganino and Eric A. Stilwell, teleplay by Ira Steven Behr, Richard Manning, Hans Beimler and Ronald D. Moore.
'on the word of a bartender': Gross and Altman, p. 192.

209   *'To this day I do not understand ...'*: Ibid.
'A warrior's drink': From 'Yesterday's Enterprise'.

211   'reflected what was going on . . .': From Judith and Garfield Reeves-Stevens, *Star Trek: The Next Generation – The Continuing Mission* (New York: Pocket Books, 1997), quoted at <http://en.memory-alpha.wikia.com/wiki/Sarek_(episode)>.

212   'We have engaged the Borg': From 'The Best of Both Worlds' (1990), written by Michael Piller.
       'Captain Jean-Luc Picard . . .': Ibid.

213   'I am Locutus of Borg. Resistance is futile . . .': Ibid.

CHAPTER 13: JUST A BIT OF A HEADACHE

214–15   'We got everyone settled down . . .': Gross and Altman, *Captain's Logs*, p. 200.

215   'I'm a very instinctive writer . . .': Ibid., p. 199.

215*   'He introduced himself . . .': From Dale Kutzera, 'All Our Yesterdays', *Cinefantastique*, 25:6/26:1 (1994), p. 86.

216   'Your resistance is hopeless . . . Number One': From 'The Best of Both Worlds, Part II' (1990), written by Michael Piller.
       'How do you feel? . . .': Ibid.

217   'We ran out of time . . .': Gross and Altman, p. 207.

217–18   'You don't know, Robert . . .': From 'Family' (1990), written by Ronald D. Moore.

220   'Human bonding rituals often involve . . .': From 'Data's Day' (1991), story by Harold Apter, teleplay by Harold Apter and Ronald D. Moore.

220†   'He directly saved the ship . . .': Interview for *Star Trek: The Official Fan Club Magazine*, 77 (December 1990/January 1991), p. 3.

222   'We should not discount . . .': From 'Redemption' (1991), written by Ronald D. Moore.

222*   'I like them . . .': Quoted in 'Redemption (episode)', <http://en.memory-alpha.wikia.com/wiki/Redemption>.

222–3   'But as we started . . .': Gross and Altman, p. 227.

224   'copping feels off the local females . . .': Shatner and Kreski, *Star Trek Movie Memories*, p. 271.

225   'stunned, feeling as low as I ever had . . .': Ibid., pp. 275–6.
       'We want to make another . . .': Nimoy, *I Am Spock*, pp. 314–15.

225*   'Someone has observed that the chief problem . . .': Meyer, *The View from the Bridge*, p. 199.

226   'After all, it really didn't seem all that long ago . . .': Ibid., p. 35.

227   'I offer a toast . . .': From *Star Trek VI: The Undiscovered Country* (1991), written by Nicholas Meyer and Denny Martin Flinn.

227*   'I have a new puppy . . .': Gross and Altman, p. 142.

228 *'Don't wait for the translation! Answer me now!'*: From *Star Trek VI: The Undiscovered Country*.

'An ancestor of mine . . .': Ibid.

'I've never trusted Klingons . . .': Ibid.

228* *'He did everything different . . .'*: Meyer, n.p.

229–30 *'Did you see the way they ate? . . .'*: From *Star Trek VI: The Undiscovered Country*.

230 *'Course heading, Ceptain? . . .'*: Ibid.

'Is it possible that we two . . .': Ibid.

230* *'Guess who's coming to dinner'*: Ibid.

CHAPTER 14: COMFORTABLE CHAIR

231 *'The series was about Picard, Riker and Data . . .'*: Block and Erdmann, *Star Trek: The Next Generation 365*, p. 59.

232 *'which might contain a wonderful scene . . .'*: Takei, *To The Stars*, p. 259.

233 *'How did you like command? . . .'*: From 'The Emissary' (1989), story by Richard Manning, Hans Beimler and Thomas H. Calder, teleplay by Richard Manning and Hans Beimler.

'What do I have to do . . .': From 'Déjà Q' (1990), written by Richard Danus.

'Sir, I protest! I am not a merry man!': From 'Qpid' (1991), story by Randee Russell and Ira Steven Behr, teleplay by Ira Steven Behr.

'Klingons appreciate strong women': From 'Angel One' (1988), written by Patrick Barry.

234 *'Klingons never bluff'*: From 'The Emissary'.

'Klingons do not surrender': Ibid.

'I did not faint. Klingons do not faint': From 'Up The Long Ladder' (1989), written by Melinda M. Snodgrass.

'Klingons do not laugh': From 'Redemption' (1991), written by Ronald D. Moore.

'Klingons do not pursue relationships . . .': From 'In Theory' (1991), written by Joe Menosky and Ronald D. Moore.

'Klingons do not allow themselves to be . . . probed': From 'Violations' (1992), story by Shari Goodhartz, T. Michael Gray and Pamela Gray, teleplay by Pamela Gray and Jeri Taylor.

'If I didn't know you better . . .': From 'Liaisons' (1993), story by Roger Eschbacher and Jaq Greenspon, teleplay by Jeanne Carrigan-Fauci and Lisa Rich.

235 *'This is another example of a show . . .'*: Gross and Altman, *Captain's Logs*, p. 237.

'Rick Berman called me and said . . .': Ibid., pp. 235–6.

236*   'It just seemed to me . . .': *Star Trek: The Official Fan Club Magazine* (1994).

236–7   *'I have come on an urgent mission . . .'*: From 'Unification I' (1991), story by Rick Berman and Michael Piller, teleplay by Jeri Taylor.

238   *'Darmok and Jalad at Tanagra!'*: From 'Darmok' (1991), story by Philip LaZebnik and Joe Menosky, teleplay by Joe Menosky.
     'Shaka, when the walls fell': Ibid.

240   *'undergoing tremendous neurological activity'*: From 'The Inner Light' (1992), story by Morgan Gendel, teleplay by Morgan Gendel and Peter Allan Fields.

240–1   *'I always believed that I didn't need children . . .'*: Ibid.

241   *'I've always felt that the experience . . .'*: AOL chat, 1997, quoted in 'The Inner Light (episode)', <http://en.memory-alpha.wikia.com/wiki/The_Inner_Light_(episode)>.

243*   *'It was like I was touching a piece of my childhood . . .'*: Block and Erdmann, p. 274.

244   'There's just nothing better . . .': Nemecek, *The Star Trek: The Next Generation Companion*, p. 230.
     'It is not possible that there are five . . .': Ibid.

244*   *'It covered up my cleavage . . .'*: Block and Erdmann, p. 291.

246*   *'The last two years have found me . . .'*: Benjamin Svetkey, '"Star Trek: The Next Generation" readies for last episode', *Entertainment Weekly*, 6 May 1994.

CHAPTER 16: SPIN-OFFS, TAKE-OFFS AND TURN-OFFS

252   *'You say history considers me dead . . .'*: From *Star Trek Generations* (1994), story by Rick Berman, Ronald D. Moore and Brannon Braga, screenplay by Ronald D. Moore and Brannon Braga.
     'Did we do it? Did we . . .': Ibid.

253   'The Star Trek *saga has always . . .'*: Roger Ebert, 'Review: *Star Trek Generations'*, *Chicago Sun-Times*, 18 November 1994.

253*   *'Captain Kirk lived pretty much . . .'*: Schnakenberg, *The Encyclopedia Shatnerica*, p. 111.

256   *'Get them away from all the familiar . . .'*: Anna L. Kaplan, 'Ron D. Moore Q&A', for Fandom.com. Available at <http://www.lcarscom.net/rdm1000118.htm>.

257   *'Gene had very, very strong ideals . . .'*: Block and Erdmann, *Star Trek: The Next Generation 365*, p. 352.
     'He was always arguing for something . . .': Ibid.

257–8   *'Driven by violence and rage . . .'*: Robert Bianco, '"Galactica" back, better than ever', *USA Today*, 14 July 2005.

258 'The Borg were really liked by the fans . . .': Nemecek, *The Star Trek: The Next Generation Companion*, p. 322.

259 'I will not sacrifice the Enterprise . . .': From *Star Trek: First Contact* (1996), story by Rick Berman, Brannon Braga and Ronald D. Moore, screenplay by Brannon Braga and Ronald D. Moore.

260 'The one image I brought to the table . . .': Quoted in 'Star Trek: First Contact', <http://en.memory-alpha.wikia.com/wiki/Star_Trek:_First_Contact>.

'I'm a doctor, not a door-stop': From *Star Trek: First Contact*.

260* 'looks like no notion of sexy . . .': Roger Ebert, 'Review: *Star Trek: First Contact*', *Chicago Sun-Times*, 22 November 1996.

262 'By Grabthar's hammer . . .': From *Galaxy Quest* (1991), story by David Howard, screenplay by David Howard and Robert Gordon.

'They're not all "historical documents" . . .': Ibid.

263 'You're just going to have to figure out . . .': Ibid.

'All right, let's settle down . . .': Ibid.

'Let's get out of here . . .': Ibid.

264 'I had originally not wanted to see Galaxy Quest . . .': Patrick Stewart interviewed for the BBC. Available at <https://web.archive.org/web/20140113105956/http://www.bbc.co.uk/cult/st/interviews/stewart/page13.shtml>

'I think it's a chillingly realistic documentary . . .': 'George Takei Is Ready to Beam Up', SciFi.com. Available at <http://web.archive.org/web/20090325230032/http://www.scifi.com/startrek/takei/takei2.html>.

CHAPTER 16: REBOOT

267 'The only McGill graduate . . .': Leah Garchik, 'University students show no qualms about hailing "Star Trek" starship chief', *San Francisco Chronicle*, 12 July 1996.

268 'You need a reason to get off the island . . .': George Clooney on *Desert Island Discs*, 28 February 2003. Available at <http://www.bbc.co.uk/programmes/p00937r7>.

'fearing that the television series . . .': David Clarke, *How UFOs Conquered the World: The History of a Modern Myth* (London: Aurum Press, 2015).

'It's not really coming out . . .': Alexander Cho, 'Passion Play', *Frontiers*, October 2005.

268* 'yet another album of pop classics . . .': Schnakenberg, *The Encyclopedia Shatnerica*, p. 251.

269 'He was a man of principle and character . . .': 'Michael Piller Succumbs to Cancer, Age 57 (UPDATE)', StarTrek.com, 11 January 2005. Available

at <https://web.archive.org/web/20060628104408/http://www.star-trek.com/startrek/view/news/article/14414.html?page=1>.

'*I retain visitation rights*': Schnakenberg, *The Encyclopedia Shatnerica*, p. 106.

'*In these pictures . . .*': Quoted in Matthew Champion, 'These amazing photos were all taken by Leonard Nimoy', *Independent*, <http://i100.independent.co.uk/article/these-amazing-photos-were-all-taken-by-leonard-nimoy--ekYlBQcI6e>.

272   '*Damon [Lindelof, producer] and I . . .*': All quotes from the documentary *Star Trek: A New Vision* (2009).

273   '*Are you out of your Vulcan mind? . . .*': From *Star Trek* (2009), written by Roberto Orci and Alex Kurtzman.

'*Since my customary farewell . . .*': Ibid.

'*You have no idea what you're in for*': Zachary Quinto, as told to Rory Carroll, 'Zachary Quinto: Leonard Nimoy was like a father to me', *Guardian*, 3 March 2015.

274   '*He is intelligent, but not experienced . . .*': From *Star Trek II: The Wrath of Khan* (1982), story by Harve Bennett and Jack B. Sowards, screenplay by Jack B. Sowards.

275   '*There are those . . .*': David Hooks, '10 Ways Star Trek Just Isn't Star Trek Anymore', <http://whatculture.com/film/10-ways-star-trek-just-isnt-star-trek-anymore.php>, 24 February 2014.

'*He violates the Prime Directive . . .*': Ibid.

276   '*The primary thing as a science fiction writer . . .*': Quoted Ibid.

276–7   '*I think that Star Trek, in its DNA . . .*': David Wharton, 'Ron Moore On Why TV Star Trek Is Better Than Movie Star Trek', <http://www.giantfreakinrobot.com/scifi/ron-moore-tv-star-trek-movie-star-trek.html>, 4 April 2013.